Conceiving an Alternative

Conceiving an Alternative

Philosophical Resources for an Ecological Civilization

Demian Wheeler
David E. Conner
Editors

PROCESS
CENTURY
PRESS
ANOKA, MINNESOTA 2019

Conceiving an Alternative: Philosophical Resources for an Ecological Civilization

© 2019 Process Century Press

Process Century Press
RiverHouse LLC
802 River Lane
Anoka, MN 55303

Process Century Press books are published in association with the International Process Network.

Cover: Susanna Mennicke

VOLUME XIX: TOWARD ECOLOGICAL CIVILIZATION SERIES
JEANYNE B. SLETTOM, GENERAL EDITOR

ISBN 978-1-940447-40-7
Printed in the United States of America

DEDICATION

To that Great Cloud of Witnesses,
stretching back to Whitehead,
to the pioneers of the University of
Chicago Divinity School, and beyond,
who demonstrated that philosophy and
theology can be "empirical" and that
religion can be "of nature."

May they help us, even now, to
conceive healthier and more
holistic views of the world.

We live in the ending of an age. But the ending of the modern period differs from the ending of previous periods, such as the classical or the medieval. The amazing achievements of modernity make it possible, even likely, that its end will also be the end of civilization, of many species, or even of the human species. At the same time, we are living in an age of new beginnings that give promise of an ecological civilization. Its emergence is marked by a growing sense of urgency and deepening awareness that the changes must go to the roots of what has led to the current threat of catastrophe.

In June 2015, the 10th Whitehead International Conference was held in Claremont, CA. Called "Seizing an Alternative: Toward an Ecological Civilization," it claimed an organic, relational, integrated, nondual, and processive conceptuality is needed, and that Alfred North Whitehead provides this in a remarkably comprehensive and rigorous way. We proposed that he could be "the philosopher of ecological civilization." With the help of those who have come to an ecological vision in other ways, the conference explored this Whiteheadian alternative, showing how it can provide the shared vision so urgently needed.

The judgment underlying this effort is that contemporary research and scholarship is still enthralled by the 17th century view of nature articulated by Descartes and reinforced by Kant. Without freeing our minds of this objectifying and reductive understanding of the world, we are not likely to direct our actions wisely in response to the crisis to which this tradition has led us. Given the ambitious goal of replacing now dominant patterns of thought with one that would redirect us toward ecological civilization, clearly more is needed than a single conference. Fortunately, a larger platform is developing that includes the conference and looks beyond it. It is named Pando Populus (pandopopulous.com)in honor of the world's largest and oldest organism, an aspen grove.

As a continuation of the conference, and in support of the larger initiative of Pando Populus, we are publishing this series, appropriately named "Toward Ecological Civilization."

-John B. Cobb, Jr.

TABLE OF CONTENTS

INTRODUCTION

This book is comprised of essays that, in their original version, were presented at the Tenth International Whitehead Conference and Ninth International Forum on Ecological Civilization, which took place in Claremont, California, from June 4 through June 8, 2015. The announced topic of the Conference was "Seizing an Alternative: Toward an Ecological Civilization." One of the conference's primary sponsors was the Center for Process Studies in Claremont.

Readers who are not already familiar with the Center for Process Studies may find it helpful to know a little more about it. The center was founded by John B. Cobb, Jr. and David Ray Griffin in 1973. From its inception, the center has been associated with the Claremont School of Theology and Claremont Graduate University. Its purpose is to encourage exploration of the relevance of process philosophy to many areas of thought and action. In Claremont, process thought is understood mainly as an outgrowth of the work of philosophers Alfred North Whitehead (1861–1947) and Charles Hartshorne (1897–2000). For over 40 years the center has sponsored numerous meetings, publications (including a journal, *Process Studies*), internet resources, seminars, and course offerings. Partly because of the existence of the center, hundreds of students have come to Claremont to study process philosophy and process theology with Cobb, Griffin, Marjorie Suchocki, Philip Clayton, and other eminent scholars.

More recently, one important series of events has been the international Whitehead conferences. Currently ten conferences have been held. The meetings are truly international, having previously been located all over the world (the 2017 conference was held in the Azores), and almost always with some sessions being conducted in languages other than English. The conferences are well attended; the conferences at which the editors of this volume were present were attended by more than 2,000 registrants and guests. The large attendance means that a majority of the papers must be delivered in the context of smaller groups, which are organized by subject matter. For the group in which the papers in this book were presented, the stated theme was "Reimagining and Reinventing the Wisdom Traditions: Thinking Independently in the Tradition of Classical Greece." The sessions were convened under the very effective and gracious leadership of Donald Crosby, to whom, on behalf of our entire group, we now extend heartfelt thanks.

Though a few of the chapters closely mirror their content as originally presented, the majority have been revised by their authors, and a few rather extensively. Readers will notice that certain chapters are longer than others. This is because some writers knowingly chose topics that could not be addressed completely in one session, presenting at the conference only truncated versions of their material. Happily, the temporal limitations placed on oral discussions at conferences do not pertain to chapters in books, and we are pleased to provide uncut versions of each author's researches.

The aim of this anthology is to offer *philosophical* perspectives on global climate change, the endangerment of species, the over-population and exploitation of the Earth by humans, and other pressing ecological problems. The essays explore ways in which past and present philosophies, including the philosophies of Greece, Rome, Asia, and North America, and especially the philosophies of Alfred North Whitehead and other process thinkers, can help us conceive and, in turn, seize an alternative to the pervasive worldviews that have led our civilization to the brink of catastrophe.

The chapters, however, are not homogeneous in the ways in which they explore these themes. Though our contributors do display a general sensitivity to "the aliveness of nature," the chapters do not all deal directly with environmentalism, nor do they all address issues related to Whitehead's philosophy. Not every contributor is a card-carrying Whiteheadian. Even the chapters that do concentrate on process philosophy are not in complete agreement, and, in fact, there are instances of manifest divergence. We editors invite you, the reader, to join us in remaining firmly undiscouraged about these disagreements. The fact that scholarly opinions vary as to the meaning of Whitehead's ideas should not surprise us. There are differences of opinion pertaining to the interpretation of virtually all of the most groundbreaking philosophies. Indeed, a certain level of ambiguity or impreciseness may be regarded as a mark of the breadth and greatness of a system of ideas. We venture to say that this breadth and greatness pertain to the philosophy of Whitehead, too. In any case, all of the authors of this book do agree in appreciating the concern implicit in Whitehead's "Philosophy of Organism" for the well-being of the planet, and all endeavor to approximate Whitehead's intellectual acumen and innovative spirit in their own ecological philosophizing.

The underlying contention of this volume is that philosophy can help us respond imaginatively, constructively, and creatively to the ecological issues of our age. How? For one thing, our deep-seated and often unnoticed presuppositions about the nature of reality have direct bearing on our attitudes and actions, and philosophy can help us bring those presuppositions to light and think critically about them. What is more, philosophy can help us formulate and defend more adequate, plausible, and beneficial outlooks on the natural world and the place of human beings within the community of all earthly creatures.

Taken as a whole, these essays make no attempt to propose any uniform program or collective resolution. There is, however, an overwhelming consensus regarding the central—and disastrous—role that *anthropocentrism* plays in the current ecological crisis. A few of the essays examine alleged tendencies toward anthropocentrism in aspects of Whitehead's thought, while others insist that Whiteheadian and other iterations of process philosophy offer important safeguards against anthropocentric ways of thinking and acting. All of the authors do strongly agree that one of the primary tasks of philosophy in our time is to counter every form of humanocentrism, whether it stems from problematical views concerning the nature of God and the God-world relationship, from long-established assumptions that the human species is the apex of creation or the culmination of its evolutionary processes, or from misconceptions of nature itself.

We wish to thank each author for the painstaking labors that, we believe, are conspicuous throughout this volume. May the ideas and aspirations that are reflected in these pages wend their way into the attitudes of respect, awe, and reverence that are now so desperately needed among people everywhere towards planet Earth and all of its creatures.

Demian Wheeler
David E. Conner

PART ONE

ALFRED NORTH WHITEHEAD
AND THE WESTERN
PHILOSOPHIC TRADITION

$\rightsquigarrow 1 \rightsquigarrow$

REBALANCING WHAT IS USEFUL IN WESTERN
PHILOSOPHY FOR PRESENT PHILOSOPHY

Robert Cummings Neville

ABSTRACT: *This paper argues that Whitehead had an unusual read on the history of Western philosophy, for instance, regarding Descartes as the great empiricist and Locke as the great metaphysician. How would (or should) Whitehead revise his estimation of what is important in today's world? I claim that he would broaden his conception of "civilized experience" to include global cultures and that he would put environmental thinking among the highest priorities for philosophical analysis.*

WHITEHEAD WAS FAMOUS, or notorious, or amusing, for claiming that Descartes was the great empiricist, Locke the great metaphysician, and Kant the great dead-end, for the philosophical issues of Whitehead's time.[1] He had a rare generosity of mind and empathic understanding with regard to reading his tradition. But he recognized that for the philosophical issues dominating his own era, only some of that tradition is useful and figures might be useful in ways hitherto unexpected. I am to do a reading of our current philosophical situation that is interestingly different from Whitehead's situation, mainly because of its global nature and advances in cognitive psychology, which were undeveloped in his time. At stake is the identification of the best resources for wise guidance in the direction of interest, attention, inquiry, living, action, and communal life. Let me begin with a few brief comments on how Whitehead saw his own situation.

WHITEHEAD'S READING

As announced in *Science and the Modern World* and carried out in *Process and Reality,* a new set of philosophical categories is needed to account for the background of modern science, which we might call a metaphysics and he called a philosophical cosmology. The old Aristotelian metaphysics-turned-to-common-sense assumptions understood the world to consist of substances that bear properties. Modern philosophy exhibited great creativity in modifying the theme of substance. Think of Locke, Descartes, Leibniz, Spinoza, Hume, Kant, and Hegel, and their widely divergent theories of substance. For all their brilliance, those modern conceptions of substance simply cannot model a world defined by modern physics mainly in terms of mathematical relations.[2] The cosmological scheme Whitehead worked out in *Process and Reality* is unlike anything conceived by his modern predecessors, although Whitehead did liken his scheme to that of Leibniz in a certain respect: Whitehead's actual occasions are a little like Leibniz's world of monads except that the occasions have "windows" whereas the monads do not.[3]

What Whitehead liked from Locke, and the reason he called him the great metaphysician of modernity, is Locke's conception of a substance having force that can be felt. This registers in Whitehead's system throughout the doctrine of prehension and up to the doctrine of the vector force of feeling in nature and in human symbolic reference. Whitehead resisted Locke's so-called empirical theory of primary, secondary, and tertiary qualities of experience, which is what nearly everyone except Whitehead associated with empiricism.

What Whitehead liked from Descartes, and the reason he thought Descartes to be the great modern empiricist, was Descartes's appeal to experience. Negatively, this was Descartes's rejection of authority in church and philosophical antiquarianism. Positively, it was Descartes's insistence on inspecting the content of experience, either in the intuitive inspection of mathematical and purely logical relations, or in the experimental method of taking things apart to see what they really are. Whitehead's Descartes cautioned against imposing your ideas on what you think you know or experience without actually looking. Whitehead rejected Descartes's cosmological dualism of corporeality and mentality, though he strongly affirmed that what you find when you intuitively and experimentally look has to include everything that shows up in either side of the mind-body dualism. For Whitehead, the initial physical prehensions of an actual occasion are material, the process of concrescence is all mental insofar as the initial data are taken up in change, and its completed satisfaction is all physical again. Of course, Whitehead's cosmological conceptions of matter and mind are wholly unlike anything Descartes would have imagined.[4] Whitehead replaced Descartes's "looking" metaphors with "prehending" and "feeling" metaphors.

Another part of Whitehead's situation as he knew it was that it was largely bereft of any philosophical cosmology that might cope with the changes in assumptions demanded by 20th-century physics. This was Kant's fault in two ways. First, only the sciences can give us objective knowledge of the world, and philosophy is limited to critique and the construction of conceptions of human subjectivity according to which the sciences are possible. Philosophical cosmology, Kant thought, would necessarily breach the sharp divide between empirical reality, a construct of consciousness, and transcendental ideality, the misplaced attempt to talk about things apart from the self. Of Whitehead's great philosophical contemporaries, Wittgenstein, Heidegger, and Dewey, only the last made any extended attempt to talk about nature. And Whitehead thought Dewey's philosophy of nature did not take seriously the rigor needed for a new philosophical cosmology.[5] Kant's second fault, according to Whitehead, was his whole conception of transcendental subjectivity that limited scientific knowledge to knowledge of representations rather than knowledge of things represented. Whitehead thought Kant should have developed a naturalistic critique of pure feeling, elaborating the doctrine of the Aesthetic in the First Critique and skipping all the rest, that is, the transcendental logic and dialectic.[6] Whitehead would have wanted the analysis of feeling to follow a Lockean "historical plain method" and give a genetic, non-transcendental account. Kant himself noticed that the first version of the transcendental deduction of the categories was much too genetic and Locke-like, and completely rewrote that section for the second edition in a purely transcendental mode.

Yet a third element Whitehead noted about his situation was that much modern philosophy was far too reductive in scientific ways and therefore obscured the task of giving a philosophical account of what he called "the breadth of civilized experience." The main plot of *Science and the Modern World* is that science is the creative breakthrough of modern intellectual life but that the romantic poets and others called attention to what is left out. For Whitehead, the broad problem of value, specialized in poetry, the visual arts, music, architecture, the politics of high civilization, and religion, needed to be integrated with the world as reductively analyzed by the sciences. Whitehead was not big on morals as a part of high civilization.[7] This is where Whitehead appealed to Plato and counted himself a Platonist.[8] Plato had a strong grasp of the breadth of civilized experience and at the same time looked to mathematics as the conceptual key for holding much of this together. Whitehead appropriated this in many ways and places; for instance, in *The Function of Reason*, he argued for the cultivation of the *appreciation* of things, not just the ability to model them scientifically. This led Whitehead to thematize the necessary simplification of infinitely dense concrete reality, and to insist that one of philosophy's tasks is to be the critic of abstractions.[9] Beware the fallacy of misplaced concreteness!

SUPPLEMENTARY READINGS

The most important contemporary change from Whitehead's situation, that he would most certainly recognize based on his own position, is the transformation from a Western to a more nearly global public. He did discuss other religions than Christianity from time to time, especially in *Religion in the Making*, most especially Buddhism. But I doubt he ever thought he was writing for thinkers in those religions imbued with the motifs and texts of those diverse traditions. He was writing for the European/North American Anglophone world and encouraging them to broaden their horizons. In the century since Whitehead began to formulate his philosophy there has been a radical transformation of the intellectual background in which a philosopher such as he might write. For one thing, there has been a century of translations of the basic writings of the great intellectual and religious traditions other than the Euro/Christian. Although most American philosophy and theology departments do not train students in the background paideia of non-Western cultures, they could and should. Whitehead would certainly agree if he were alive today. Moreover, there has been a vast outpouring of secondary scholarly works interpreting these works in their historical and social contexts. That kind of historical and social contextualizing is only now becoming important in academic philosophy.

This globalization of the public within which philosophy is written should surely relativize the Western philosophic tradition in ways Whitehead would not have imagined. He would have thought it quaint if someone had said it is enough to relate to philosophy that is only German, or only French, or even only British, ignoring the rest. In our time the whole of the Western tradition is seen as one among many, and surely not the only tradition to define what the interesting philosophical problems and methods are. Perhaps David Hall and Roger Ames exaggerated, or epitomized and stylized, the difference between Western and East Asian cultures.[10] But their lesson was that the Western philosophic tradition is not only flanked by the

Chinese but turns out to be not as good in their view. The limitation of their reading is that things are even more complex. And then add the comparisons with the South Asian and Muslim traditions.

Here I should lift up the fact that most of the expanded global conversation has been in English. English, if not Chinese, is turning out to be the language of the global conversation. This too must be relativized. Whitehead would have welcomed all these correctives to the philosophical audience to which he spoke.

A second factor would cause Whitehead now to supplement his reading of the history of philosophy if he were with us today, namely, the increased recognition of the importance of semiotics, the theory of signs. I have two points to make about this.

First, Whitehead's own theory has a strange and ironic lacuna between his appeal to the breadth of civilized experience and his modeling of how actual occasions can give rise to consciousness. The former is detailed in its historical reference and eloquent in its evocation of civilized consciousness, as in *Science and the Modern World*, *Adventures of Ideas*, and *Modes of Thought*. The latter, in Parts 2 and 3 of *Process and Reality*, labors mightily to build up a model of consciousness as a complex of propositions that achieve an affirmation/negation contrast. Whew! And that's all. Part 4 presents the mathematics for analyses of parts and wholes in vectors of feeling but there is precious little there about conscious human feeling. In between the vast riches of civilized experience and the emergence of consciousness as an affirmation/negation contrast is the whole topic of interpretation, the use of signs, or hermeneutics. It is ironic that Whitehead says almost nothing about this except to extend his philosophical cosmology to what he called symbolic reference.[11]

Semiotics was the brain-child of Charles Sanders Peirce, who was eighteen years Whitehead's senior and who died about a decade before Whitehead moved to Cambridge. Whitehead surely knew about Peirce because Peirce was the director of the dissertations of Charles Hartshorne and Paul Weiss, who began editing Peirce's philosophical papers while they were graduate students. Like Whitehead, Peirce thought of himself as a mathematical logician who developed a naturalistic philosophy of everything that was so bizarre it was ignored by most of the philosophical establishment, at Harvard and elsewhere. Whitehead, I am sure, should have been fascinated by him, if Hartshorne and Weiss had clued him in. Volumes 2, 3, and 4 of their *Collected Papers of Charles Sanders Peirce* focus on semiotics, and Whitehead would have been one of the few philosophers who could read them with immediate understanding and delight. He seems not to have, for if he had he would have picked up on the emergence of semiotics in European thought from Ramon Lull to Saussure and thence to Peirce.

Peirce's chief advance on Saussure and other European semioticians was to insist that interpretation is triadic rather than dyadic.[12] The Europeans down to Derrida and Eco stress the relation between the signifier and signified. Peirce said there is no signifier except insofar as there is an interpreter who takes the sign to be a representation of its object in a certain respect. European semiotics lends itself to mapping signifier-signified relations within a semiotic system or within a field of consciousness. It is possible to say that nothing signified is anything except itself a conscious sign, with no real reference beyond the signs in interpretation. But for Peirce, a sign within its semiotic system can be used to engage something beyond the system. Perhaps some interpretations are interpretations of things within the semiotic system at hand, but most need not be. For the Europeans, the paradigm case of interpretation is the interpretation of texts. For Peirce and his pragmatic followers, the paradigm case is interpreting the wilderness of nature, with scientific experiments as the organized methodological way to go, not the intermingling of horizons of meaning in a hermeneutical circle. Interpretation for Peirce is not a play of consciousness alone but, more basically, a natural physical process, just as Whitehead would need. Like Whitehead, Peirce developed novel conceptions of physical nature. For Peirce, an effect is an interpretation of its cause by means of the general law or habit of nature which the interpreting effect takes to stand for the object-cause in a certain respect. Whitehead's cosmology in *Process and Reality* can be read as one exemplification of Peirce's theory: the satisfaction of an actual occasion is the interpretation of the initial data by means of the intermediate stages of prehension functioning as signs. None of this is to say that Whitehead would have accepted Peirce's philosophy of nature. He worked on a much more specific, non-metaphysical, level of generality than Peirce. But at least the opening is there to graft the whole enterprise of Peirce's semiotics onto Whitehead's theory of actual occasions, giving Whitehead the vast riches of the pragmatic theory of experience. (Much of my own philosophic work has been to do that grafting.)

The second point about what Whitehead might learn from the semiotic traditions he neglected has to do with the experiential issues of focusing attention, that is, of focusing on foreground objects interpreted against a background that is already part of the interpreting. Peirce was deeply concerned with issues of intellectual and emotional control, not thinking that it is sheer will, or that it is the identification of ready-made objects that really are objects adventitiously set within backgrounds. More and richer work has been done in the phenomenological tradition that carries on European semiotics but corrects it with a reading of experience through the body. Merleau-Ponty and Edward Casey are phenomenologists who carry this out with rigor, and because Whitehead should be able to incorporate their work, he should acknowledge their own antecedents in Hegel, Husserl, and Heidegger. The control of attention is a teleological move, something rejected by most scientists except when it comes to their work. Terrence Deacon has argued persuasively that cognitive science needs to develop models that acknowledge the openness and causal power of the future that is so obvious in intentionality. Deacon acknowledges that Whitehead recognized exactly this point, gives him credit, and then ignores him because Whitehead's cosmology it too technical to be of much help to cognitive science and its language is too far from that used in cognitive science.[13] Whitehead today would like to catch up to Deacon with respect to engaging cognitive science and thereby adopt the historical antecedents in evolutionary biology and neuroscience; in my view, Whitehead's treatment of the common problem is still more sophisticated than Deacon's.

An offshoot of this point gives yet another resource for Whitehead's potential antecedents. Beginning in the 1950s and 60s, the psychologist James Jerome Gibson developed a theory of what he called "affordances," namely the organized value structures in the environment that allow interpreting animals, particularly human beings, to grasp and appreciate largescale interpretations as a whole.[14] Instead of summing up zillions of little interpretations of natural causal antecedents, the natural environment offers affordances for human integrative interpretations in which the multitude of values of things can be grasped holistically. We can "read" situations, this ecological biology says, without a computer-like summing up of algorithms. Whitehead surely would reject computer analogies of mental activities and their mechanistic antecedents going back to Descartes and Hobbes, and this tradition of ecological psychology offers a way.

WHITEHEAD AND ECOLOGICAL THINKING

The various points I have made about Whitehead's unusual reading of the modern Western philosophical tradition and about what Whitehead today might adopt as supplementary resources lead me to some final observations about Whitehead and ecological thinking, the overall topic of this volume. Much of the Western philosophic and religious tradition, broadly speaking, has set a high contrast between the human and the rest of nature. Much of the Bible makes humankind the crowning achievement of creation and asserts that human beings should have dominion over the rest of nature, for instance in Genesis 1:26. The classical Greeks distinguished sharply between teleology in nature and human teleology that reflects human purpose. The early modern period in the West depicted nature as consisting of mechanical objects and human beings, at least in part, as subjects. Nineteenth-century evolutionary theory ran against the prevailing view that humanity is above nature when it claimed that humans descended from lower natural forms, and yet still supposed that humankind is the crowning achievement of natural evolution. As naturalists, Whitehead and the pragmatists were anomalous in the Western tradition and very carefully reconceived nature to show how the highest achievements of civilization are complexifications of natural processes.

A new resource that Whitehead could now read into his background is the metaphoric system of South Asia that emphasizes the community of all sentient beings united by processes of reincarnation. This is not the place to do more than acknowledge the many different versions of reincarnation in South Asian history, most notably Hindu and Buddhist ones, as well as Jain; in each of those traditions are multitudes of divergent and contradicting schools. Some involve karma, and some do not. Moreover, for many forms of Buddhism and Hinduism, the lives of reincarnation express a proximate truth that is superseded by a more nearly ultimate one. But all together create an enormous sense of community among all sentient things. Whitehead appreciated the metaphysics of Hinduism and Buddhism, especially the latter. But he did not attend much to the community aspects of the multiple lives of sentient beings. As we explore a Whiteheadian ecological sensibility, we can encourage a positive reading of those traditions fostering a community, with various appropriate responsibilities, of sentient beings. They remind us also that ecologies should not be thought of as static harmonies of elements but as constantly changing mixtures.

Nevertheless, the cultures of communities of all sentient beings still make a sharp division between such communities and non-animate or insensate elements of nature. It takes a stretch to get Buddhists or Hindus to have fellow-feeling for mountains and streams.

In light of this, we should note that the Chinese traditions, especially Confucianism, have, at least since the days of the Yijing, thought of the breadth of nature as including human societies and individuals within it. In those traditions there is no distinction except in the ways changes are put together among human life, sentient life, social institutions, rituals relating individuals and communities to mountains and stream, and natural things far removed from anything human. The Confucian traditions are more valuable here because the Daoist traditions sometimes cordon off much of human institutional life and pretenses at high civilization as "artificial" and un-Dao-like. At any rate, Whitehead today would be greatly strengthened to read the Chinese traditions as resources for his ecological philosophy. In principle, he already argued in the first half of the 20th century for a cosmological continuum between actual occasions, human individuals as societies of occasions, human groups as societies of societies and thence to the puff of existence in far-out space. He also had argued that any occasion anywhere and in any nexus of occasions is a bearer of value, a point about which the Chinese never doubted. Deference to the heavens, the mountains, and the seas, as well as to people in relation to oneself, is parsed on continua among all these things with exacting, if sometimes contradictory, attention to how differently to observe deference. China is a more natural cultural home for Whitehead's vision than the West, which he had to read so oddly.

Much American and European environmentalism and ecological thinking for the last century have argued for the protection of natural resources because they support human life, and their destruction will be bad for human life. This reflects the view that nature is for the sake of humankind. Perhaps some make this argument because they think that only by appealing to human selfishness could people be moved to care for the environment. Whitehead would read this as a great mistake. Rather, all of nature, including the human and our high civilizations but also the heavens, mountains, and seas as well, bears values of specific sorts determined by things' internal and external relations. The aesthetic sensitivity to appreciate a great breadth of nature as well as a great breadth of high civilization needs now to be cultivated upon the resources of all civilizations. Peirce said this in the 19ᵗʰ century in his claim that aesthetics is the master discipline and that the law of the universe is to extend and better integrate harmonies of all sorts. The Chinese have had major thinkers who have articulated this splendidly, for instance Xunzi. And Whitehead presents a worldview that at the cosmological level makes sense of this point about the aesthetics of being human. There is no reason to think that specifically human interests are the most valuable things to defer to and support, although most of our deliberations are about things in the human sphere. Whitehead would agree with Peirce that, although all human experience is guided in part by human purposes, the most important purpose is that of discovering the purpose most worth having. That might move far beyond what is good for human beings.

ENDNOTES

1   He made these points in various ways throughout Part 2 of *Process and Reality: An Essay in Cosmology,* Corrected Edition by David Ray Griffin and Donald W. Sherburne (New York: Free Press, [1929] 1978). See also the Preface to that book that begins on p. xi:

> These lectures are based upon a recurrence to that phase of philosophic thought which began with Descartes and ended with Hume. The philosophic scheme which they endeavor to explain is termed the 'Philosophy of Organism.' There is no doctrine put forward which cannot cite in its defense some explicit statement in one of this group of thinkers or of one of the two founders of all Western thought, Plato and Aristotle. But the philosophy of organism is apt to emphasize just those elements in the writings of these masters which subsequent systematizers have put aside. The writer who most fully anticipated the main positions of the philosophy of organism is John Locke in his *Essay,* especially in its later books.

Note that he ends the list of masters with Hume, not Kant.

2 See *Science and the Modern World* (New York: Macmillan, 1925), especially chapter 2.

3 See *Process and Reality*, 19, 48–50, 80. Whereas Whitehead noted that Leibniz's monads change, his own do not, they only emerge.

4 For my critical interpretation and engagement of Whitehead on this, see my *The Highroad around Modernism* (Albany: State University of New York Press, 1992), chapters 2–5. Jorge Luis Nobo's *Whitehead's Metaphysics of Extension and Solidarity* (Albany: State University of New York Press, 1986) is an excellent exploration of the issues of the continuity of the satisfied fixed past into an emergent concrescence.

5 See Whitehead's brief "John Dewey and His Influence," in *The Philosophy of John Dewey*, Paul Arthur Schilpp, ed. (Evanston and Chicago: Northwestern University Press, 1939), the Library of Living Philosophers, Vol. 1, 477–78. Compare this with John Dewey's "The Philosophy of Whitehead" in *The Philosophy of Alfred North Whitehead*, Paul Arthur Schilpp, ed. (New York: Tudor Publishing Co., 1941; Second Edition, 1951), the Library of Living Philosophers, Vol. 3, 643–61.

6 *Process and Reality*, 113.

7 This unusual claim is one of the main themes of David L. Hall's *The Civilization of Experience: A Whiteheadian Theory of Culture* (New York: Fordham University Press, 1973).

8 See, for instance, *Process and Reality*, 39, where Whitehead made the famous statement that

> The safest general characterization of the European philosophical tradition is that it consists of a series of footnotes to Plato. . . . Thus in one sense by stating my belief that the train of thought in these lectures is Platonic, I am doing no more than expressing the hope that it falls within the European tradition. But I do mean more: I mean that if we had to render Plato's general point of view with the least changes made necessary by the intervening two thousand years of human experience in social organization, in aesthetic attainments, in science, and in religion, we should

have to set about the construction of a philosophy of organism.

9   Perhaps Whitehead's most poignant expressions of the aesthetics involved in simplification are in his last two publications, "Mathematics and the Good" and "Immortality," both in Schilpp's *The Philosophy of Alfred North Whitehead*, beginning at p. 666. The claim that philosophy is the critic of abstractions is found throughout *Science and the Modern World*, as is the discussion of the fallacy of misplaced concreteness in chapter 3.

10 See David L. Hall and Roger T. Ames, *Thinking Through Confucius* (Albany: State University of New York Press, 1987), *Anticipating China: Thinking through the Narratives of Chinese and Western Culture* (Albany: State University of New York Press, 1995), and *Thinking from the Han: Self, Truth, and Transcendence in Chinese and Western Culture* (Albany: State University of New York Press, 1998). These three magnificent books set much of the agenda for comparative philosophy for the last generation. See also Robert W. Smid's *Methodologies of Comparative Philosophy: The Pragmatist and Process Traditions* (Albany: State University of New York, 2009), especially chapters 3 and 4 that compare their approach to mine.

11 Whitehead's *Symbolism: Its Meaning and Effect* (New York: Macmillan, 1927) is more a comment on the role of symbolism in civilization than a developed semiotic theory.

12 For a general introduction to Peirce's semiotics by someone well-versed in Whitehead, see Robert S. Corrington's *An Introduction to C. S. Peirce: Philosopher, Semiotician, and Ecstatic Naturalism* (Lanham, MD: Rowman & Littlefield, 1993). For my own defense of Peirce on this point see *The Highroad around Modernism*, chapter 1.

13 See Terrence W. Deacon's *Incomplete Nature: How Mind Emerged from Matter* (New York: Norton, 2012); the discussion of Whitehead is on pp. 77–79, and is rather elementary in its understanding of Whitehead's work, but unusual for a scientist in paying attention at all.

14 See J. J. Gibson, *The Ecological Approach to Visual Perception* (Classic Edition, New York: Psychology Press, [1979] 2015.)

❧ 2 ❧

ANOTHER FOOTNOTE TO PLATO

George Allan

ABSTRACT: *Whitehead uses Plato to argue that the form of real existence is teleonomic, the form of agency: to exist is to make a difference. Agency involves entertaining ideas (Psyche) along with an urge toward their actualization (Eros), plus an interconnection among such agencies, an order of things sufficient to assure continuity in what is actualized (Receptacle). Whitehead then reifies these categories, arguing for a primordial agency that originates this order and guides the efforts of finite agencies. I reject such reifications, turning to Langer's notion of the Act-Form (Eros) and its emergent expression as Mind (Psyche). The capacity of finite psyches collaboratively to create novel ideas with which to fashion and sustain a dynamically stable form of order, an open ambient (Receptacle), provides a metaphysically sufficient account of reality. The implication for current environmentalist initiatives is that neither tradition nor innovation are alone sufficient: planetary and cultural survival depend on fostering a constant interplay between the irreconcilable but fundamental values of stability and instability.*

I AM INTERESTED in the metaphysical hypothesis that reality is thoroughly contingent and in how that understanding is crucial to how we should live. Plato famously insists that what is most real is what is least contingent, and so it may seem odd that I should turn to Plato for support. But if Whitehead is right in claiming that Western philosophy is a series of footnotes to Plato, then even in writing a seemingly anti-Platonic footnote it makes sense that I should consult him. And this is true, especially and deliciously, if I take my lead from Whitehead's explicit appeal to the Plato of the later dialogues. My essay is thus a footnote to Whitehead's footnote to Plato.

In *Adventures of Ideas* Whitehead finds the key to Plato's mature thought in *Sophist* 247e—where, in Jowett's translation, the Eleatic Stranger says: "My suggestion would be, that anything which possesses any sort of power to affect another, or to be affected by another, . . . has real existence; and I hold that the definition of being is simply power."[1] Or as Whitehead paraphrases it: "The essence of being is to be implicated in causal action on other beings."[2]

Before making use of this key, however, I want to underscore two of its fundamental features. Firstly, note that the Eleatic Stranger's definition of power is a suggestion. He proposes it as a way to escape the dilemma posed by materialists who claim that only things we can see and touch have real existence, that ideas are either reducible to physical things or they are figments of our imagination. Figments they may be, says the Stranger, but that does not mean they do not have power to affect and be affected by other things. We cannot touch an idea but we can feel its impact on our lives, in the wild dream that leads to the demolition of an unjust law or the carefully hedged hypothesis that results in an important new medical therapy. And, indeed, insofar as we are persuaded by the Stranger's suggestion, its power will be manifest by its altering how we think and act, a power compelling not by its physical impact but by its allure.

Secondly, the Stranger goes on to say, *Sophist* 248e–249a, that "being as being known, is acted on by knowledge, and is therefore in motion, for that which is in a state of rest cannot be acted upon" but remains "in awful unmeaningness an everlasting fixture."[3] Whitehead's gloss on this is that "'action and reaction' belong to the essence of being: though the mediation of 'life and mind' is invoked to provide the medium of activity"[4] In other words, the power of affecting and being affected, which is the reality of being, is teleo-nomic. To really exist is to act, and to act is to be an actualizing process not an ever-lasting fixture. Or to put it another way, the form of real existence is the form of agency, which is to be persuaded by a possibility into fashioning something that makes a difference with respect both to what is given and to what is possible, and this is true whether the agency be material or immaterial.

With this key to power in hand, we can unlock the toolbox of seven Platonic notions that Whitehead says are needed for constructing any cosmology adequate to a civilized way of life: Physical Elements, Ideas, Psyche, Eros, Harmony, Mathematical Relationships, and The Receptacle.[5] I will focus on three of them: Psyche, Eros, and the Receptacle.

The Ideas, considered by themselves, are inert: "static, frozen, lifeless."[6] But when taken as possibilities for actualization, they are what make possible the creative advance: make possible the creating, perpetuating, and altering of realities, of what together comprise the temporal flow of things, including the origin and history of our planet, a history culminating for Whitehead in the emergence of civilized human existence. So the notion of Ideas immediately entails the notion of Physical Elements, the material facts that of themselves also would be static, frozen, and lifeless were they not infused with the Ideas that unfix them, that give them relevance beyond their momentary existence.

Psyche, says Whitehead, is the agency by which this dynamic process occurs, "the agency whereby ideas obtain efficiency in the creative advance."[7] 'Psyche' is an abstraction, a collective noun for "finite souls of varying grades, including human souls," which make "the determinations of compatibilities and incompatibilities" by which, from the motley of what at any moment is possible, a selection can be made "compatible for joint exemplification."[8] But Psyche's entertainment of Ideas, says Whitehead, is a matter of "mere knowledge, that is to say, of mere understanding."[9] Ideas can be efficacious tools in the creative advance only if the finite psyches that entertain them seek not simply their own "immediate enjoyment" but also have what Whitehead calls an "urge toward ideal perfection," an "appetition which melts into action."[10] Hence Psyche is not enough: Eros is also required, Eros understood as "the inward ferment" of the soul, "the soul stirring itself to life and motion . . . in the enjoyment of its creative function, arising from its entertainment of ideas."[11] We can say that Psyche is the power to think, Eros the power to feel. And if so, then I take Whitehead as suggesting that Eros is the more primordial, Psyche the more distinctively human. Yet they are both equally powers of the soul, for they are both inherently teleonomic. To entertain an idea, just as much as to feel an urge, is to sense a possibility and to be drawn toward it, lured by its potency into seeking its actualization. The difference is that Eros seeks to change the world for the better, Psyche to do this efficaciously.

Thus Eros and Psyche give the Ideas and Physical Elements life, and so make the creative advance of the world possible. But therefore still something else is required: The Receptacle, the notion of a "community of the world, which is the matrix of all begetting"—what Plato calls "the foster-mother of all becoming"—because its essence is "retention of connectedness." It is "the necessary community within which the course of history is set."[12] It makes possible the continuity of achievements, the enduring actualities that turn a flux of coming to be and perishing into a dynamically meaningful world. Whitehead notes that "the space-time of modern physics, conceived in abstraction from the particular mathematical formulae which applies to the happenings in it, is almost exactly Plato's Receptacle." It is an abstraction from "all particular historical facts" and from all "particular mathematical formulae," which is to say, says Plato according to Whitehead, the Receptacle is "bare of all forms."[13]

This move by means of abstraction to something bare of all forms but nonetheless real would seem to turn one of the tools in our toolbox into a monkey wrench, tossed into the cosmology to wreak havoc with its coherence. Whitehead is celebrating Plato's mature insight that real existence is power mediated by agency. But something bare of all forms is something devoid of power because it is without the form of agency. The Receptacle is an abstraction said to be real, but it's a reality that cannot be real because it can neither affect nor be affected by other things. It's ironic that Whitehead should so obviously succumb to the fallacy of misplaced concreteness, especially since he succumbs not once but thrice. For he also applauds Plato for taking the notion of Psyche not only as an abstract generalization referring to finite souls but also to a real existent, to Plato's Demiurge, to what Whitehead calls the "Supreme Craftsman, on whom depends that degree of orderliness which the world exhibits"—"a basic Psyche whose active grasp of ideas conditions impartially the whole process of the Universe."[14] Whitehead, but not Plato, makes this same move with Eros when he asserts the existence not merely of the urges of finite souls toward perfection but also the real existence of that abstract generalization, described as the "supreme Eros" which functions as "the determinant of the struggle" going on "within the past for objective existence beyond itself" by "incarnating itself as the first phase of the individual subjective aim in [every] new process of actuality."[15]

So a foundational reality, a super-agency, a combination of Psyche and Eros, is said to be needed as the condition for the effective use of a finite soul's teleonomic power. Not only is an abstract matrix required for whatever finite harmonies might be wrought, but Whitehead also thinks a cosmic primordial orderer of things is needed, an agency crafting a starter content for that matrix, a stable enduring structure within which finite psyches can function with reasonable effectiveness. And Whitehead thinks furthermore that a continuing erotic omnipresence is also required, shaping whatever finite harmonic ends might be attempted: an ongoing cosmic tinkerer, needed lest the finite agents wreck the creative advance, undoing whatever existing order there be, careening toward a chaos from which there could be no return.

Whitehead's three oxymoronic abstractions are not a propaedeutic against chaos but a source of metaphysical chaos. Abstractions cannot be agents; by treating them as though they were, Whitehead renders his metaphysics incoherent. So I suggest, first, that we jettison, as unneeded, the notion of a primordial finite order of finite things not made by finite things. Second, I suggest that we jettison, as intrusive meddling, the notion of an nonfinite omnipresent guide. And third, I suggest we interpret the Receptacle as concrete and dynamic instead of abstract and changeless, as a matrix of living powers rather than yet one more unmeaningful everlasting fixture.

In what follows, I will pursue the shift in focus which this amended account of the toolbox of metaphysical notions encourages. Whitehead's metaphysical concepts and the language in which they are expressed are based on microcosmic things, the momentary actual occasions from which all other things are composed. I will shift to concepts and language better suited to the world of mesocosmic things, to the emergent natural order of those biological organisms that Whitehead honors but that his metaphysics has trouble explicating. So I'm going to take us from Whitehead's Plato to Susanne Langer's Whitehead, and to the power of agency as the key to organic life, and thereby the metaphysical key to a cosmology of solely contingent realities.

In Whitehead's metaphysics, actual occasions satisfy the Eleatic Stranger's definition of a real thing: they have power, for they affect and are affected by other actual occasions. Creativity, an obvious Whiteheadian candidate for Eros, is a categoreal abstraction that identifies the dynamic form those real things all have: processes of concrescence that transform the manifold influences of prior occasions into uniquely new occasions, and thereby are among the manifold influences on their successors. In *Mind: An Essay on Human Freedom*,

Langer adapts Whitehead's characterization of this microcosmic structure so that it becomes a characterization of the mesocosmic structure of organic life. She does so by replacing concrescences with acts, which are life's fundamental units.

The Act Form, which is the form of every organic event, every element in the continuum of life, is Langer's substitute for Creativity as the meaning of Eros. The Act Form describes a four-phase drive: incipience, acceleration, consummation, and cadence.[16] The phases trace a process that begins with an impulse, which creates tension in the existing structure of things, building to a consummation which alters that structure in some manner, whether trivial or monumental, the tension thereby subsiding—until the changed character of things is in its turn shaken by a new impulse. Langer identifies this recurrent Act Form structure as the shape of any life, of the trajectory from origin to demise of any real organic existent. Indeed the Act Form is the distinctive feature of a thing that shows it to be organic: the presence of teleonomic behavior, of an impulse toward change, toward making a difference. Feelings for Langer are impulses of which the organism is aware, so Eros for her is more fundamental than feeling. This allows her to generalize the act-form downward into the inorganic, to link concrescences of occasions and impulses of organisms, to link Creativity and Life not metaphorically but metaphysically: as categoreally identical across kinds of orders of real existents.

We can then take the Receptacle as the ongoing totality of acts, as composed of the lives of organisms acting on or reacting to other organisms, fashioning a continuous ever-changing webwork of affecting and being affected. The Receptacle so interpreted is what Langer calls the Ambient. An ambient is an organism's situation, the relevant context within which it acts, its *Umvelt*. An organism's ambient induces its impulse toward change, threatening it by actions that press against its conditions for survival or opening it to opportunities for sustenance and shelter. Each creature has its own ambient, always thickly overlapping with the ambient of other nearby creatures. The conflict among each organism's own incipient impulses and between its consummatory efforts and those of other organisms is what comprises the matrix of all becoming. Organic agents are what make the matrix that makes them what they are. As Langer puts it: living organisms are each "an embodied drama of evolving acts, intricately prepared by the past, yet all improvising their moves to consummation."[17] The creative advance of life is thus a richly variegated interplay of particular and regional teleonomies, but no ultimate one, goals galore but no single overarching goal, no Omega Point.

With Eros understood as the form of the impulsive drives fundamental to organic life, Psyche can be used to refer to what Langer calls Mind. If feelings are an organism's sense of its actions, Psyche is the power to recognize the forms those actions take—to recognize not just the act but the act-form. It is the ability to apprehend what Langer calls "symbolic import"[18]: the power simple familiar things have to disclose profound realities. Thus Psyche is not just an awareness of forms as such but an awareness of them as having significance. A significant form, a form having symbolic import, is what Langer means by a symbol. A sign is an image, sound, or gesture that points to something, the smoke that points to the fire, the X on the treasure map that points to the treasure. In contrast, a symbol is an image, sound, or gesture that represents an idea of something, an idea that refers to a thing even though it may not be present.

The power of symbols is their ability to evoke intangibles, to evoke memories of things previously experienced, or to evoke imagined realities taken as having real referents, or to clothe immediate experiences with meanings transcending the immediate. By means of symbols that disclose significant realities, we finite psyches grasp the shape of what matters most to us. We grasp forms that show the horizons of the world we cherish, forms that tell the story of ourselves and our people, forms that bear the burden of our losses and tragedies, forms that promise our survival and flourishing. Symbols that are significant forms rich in symbolic import find their most distinctive expressions in art, in the creation of nondiscursive symbols, what Langer calls presentational symbols, by which we are shown what discursive language cannot show us: the intrinsic meaning of our acts and their ambient conditions.

Psyche, understood as what Langer means by Mind, is not the category of an ontologically different reality from Eros. Both are sequences of act-forms characteristic of organic life, but they are different phase-states of that form, as ice and steam are different phase states of water. Eros refers to the phase-state of basic drives, to impulses so coercive as to be all but predetermining powers. The alternatives they offer for consummation are narrow, and the push toward one rather than another is made without any awareness of the impulse itself much less of the alternatives it resolves. Eros in its less basic form, as the phase state of organisms aware of the impulses that drive them, organisms that feel their actions and so can direct the acceleration toward a chosen consummation, is an expression of what Langer calls animal consciousness. Mind is the breakthrough to the phase-state of actions governed by persuasive power. For a symbol is a thing an organism chooses to take as referring to an idea, an idea it then chooses to interpret as meaning some specific real existent or existents, or some abstraction from them. With the emergence of Mind, with Eros-become-Psyche, organic life acquires powers far beyond those of all other organisms. Because the power to symbolize is the power to imagine possibilities not limited to those directly apparent in the drive toward an immediate consummation, including even possibilities torn free from the organism's ambient constraints. Through the power Psyche has to effect the symbolic transformation of experience, Langer gives us a way to understand the power of the persuasive power of individual minds, the capacity of finite psyches to create the novel ideas needed to preserve stable forms of order by adaptive innovations, and to do so without the need for a Supreme Craftsman or Guide.

The apprehension of symbolic import can be socially divisive, of course, because different people can take the same symbol as referring to incompatibly different ideas. But the freedom persuasive powers unleash can be socially constructive instead, because symbolic forms can be created precisely for that purpose, as instruments of social cohesion. The purposeful construction of immediately visible or audible symbolic forms, which are about realities we experience as imbued with an aura of transcending significance, is how individuals come to feel themselves as participating with others in a reality that possesses a vital power and hence worth greater than any of their individual powers. The group is taken to be a superpower, an agency of which they are a part, an agency that existed long before they were born and that will continue its life, with them still a part of it, long after they have died.

In such ways, a society reconciles individual goods with the common good by developing shared normative traditions of acceptable behavior, of rights and wrongs, and of the public rituals that express them. This makes possible the emergence of civilization, a form of society in which individual creative departures from the norm are prized rather than stifled, resulting in enough flexibility in the society's established ways for it to adapt effectively to ambient changes, not merely to survive but to thrive amid the world's vicissitudes.

The central concern motivating the essays in this book is the threat to our planet's biological dynamics caused by the comparatively sudden changes resulting from the actions of civilized human beings. The Earth's climate is always changing, but in most cases slowly enough that biological systems can adapt to it, the natural diversity in the inheritable characteristics of organisms permitting the emergence of organisms better adapted than their predecessors to an altered climate. Where the changes come too quickly, however, the organisms are overwhelmed by an increasingly hostile environment and perish without having produced adaptive successors. Mass extinctions occur when it is the planet's whole ecosystem that is overwhelmed.

Environmental movements have taken on a new urgency in the 21ˢᵗ century because their members recognize that climate change is taking place with increasing rapidity, and is global in character. They fear that conditions are nearing a tipping point, that mass extinction is becoming a real possibility. These environmentalists argue for initiating a radical change in how humans live, a change sufficient to slow and, before too long, to reverse the human causes of climate change. Others argue contrarily that there is no problem, that the climate change is only regional and temporary, and not influenced except marginally by human activity. It is tempting for these opponents to reject each other as extremists. Those advocating fundamental alterations in our approach to nature are said to be tree-huggers favoring the survival of obscure species over the ability of workers to earn a decent living, shrill-voiced alarmists turning minor bumps in the road into chasms that can be bridged only by a revolutionary leap into the unknown. Similarly, environmentalists reject advocates of the status quo as head-in-the-sand ostriches unwilling to abandon their familiar beliefs and practices, stupidly confident that what has worked before will obviously work again.

Both kinds of criticism are themselves extremist: squint-eyed monocular views, when what is required is wide-eyed binocular vision. The only viable alternative to extremism is civilized behavior rooted in a commitment to effective compromise. For this to happen, environmental activists must be willing to accept defenders of the status quo as legitimate voices in a crucial conversation, and traditionalists must be willing to accept advocates of a departure from normal ways as legitimate voices in that same conversation. They must both recognize what they share in common: an interest in preserving and then enhancing the quality of their lives. This implies a concerted effort to find symbolic forms that can show them that this shared interest is fundamental, that their differences are valid expressions of a common heritage and a common hope. Constructing convincing symbols of this sort is especially difficult to do because it needs dissonance as the necessary pathway to harmony. It finds clashing goods to be the crucial resource from which a common good can be fashioned and embraced. This tension is what civilization depends on: a creative interplay of order and disorder, stability achieved by means of instability. If we are to be civilized people seeking in a civilized way the continued flourishing of civilization, we need to act in response to both the persuasive demands for repetition and the attractive possibilities for change that together comprise the treasure horde of past accomplishments. Without a vibrant tradition, we cannot imagine how to improve it, nor how effectively to fashion it. And without the unsettling dreams that question old ways and demand new ones, traditions lose their vibrancy. We need simultaneously to be loyal to the constraints of our Ambient, yet freed from those constraints by the persuasive power inherent in them, that we might undertake imaginative boundary transgressions that carry us into an altered Ambient. Civilized experience is an adventure into an open ambient where the best way forward is always a tentative compromise among obscurely grasped divergent goods. A compromise is needed now, this day, but then again in a new way tomorrow, and every day. For better or for worse.

ENDNOTES

1   Alfred North Whitehead, *Adventures of Ideas* (New York: Free Press, [1933] 1967), 119–20.

2   Whitehead, *Adventures,* 120.

3   Cited by Whitehead, *Adventures,* 120.

4   Whitehead, *Adventures,* 120.

5   Whitehead, *Adventures,* 147–50.

6   Whitehead, *Adventures,* 147.

7   Whitehead, *Adventures,* 147.

8   Whitehead, *Adventures,* 147.

9   Whitehead, *Adventures,* 148.

10 Whitehead, *Adventures,* 148.

11 Whitehead, *Adventures,* 148.

12 Whitehead, *Adventures,* 150.

13 Whitehead, *Adventures,* 150.

14 Whitehead, *Adventures,* 147.

15 Whitehead, *Adventures,* 198.

16 Susanne K. Langer, *Mind: An Essay on Human Freedom*, 3 vols. (Baltimore: The Johns Hopkins Press, 1967, 1972, 1982), 1:257–306.

17 Langer, *Mind,* 1:378.

18 Langer, *Mind,* ii:194.

❧ 3 ❧

LIVING FOR BEAUTY:
PATER, PLATO, AND WHITEHEAD

J. Thomas Howe

ABSTRACT: *This essay takes up questions having to do with the idea of beauty and the way in which it might be part of a meaningful human life; particularly, it examines Whitehead's claim that life should be lived "aesthetically." To come away with a better idea as to what this means, I put Whitehead in conversation with Walter Pater and Plato. All three share the fundamental idea that beauty is at the center of a meaningful human life, but they differ in terms of how a life lived for beauty plays out.*

WHAT WOULD IT MEAN to live for beauty? To pursue and create it, to direct one's self toward, always, its proximity? What if we took beauty to be our highest duty and derived our obligations towards others and our world from it? What would such a life look like? What sorts of contours and shapes would it have? Would it be a good life, one well-lived? Would it provide sufficient sustenance and be capable of carrying us along toward an affirmation of the fundamental worth of human life?

These larger questions are at the heart of this essay. To get at them, I will concentrate on some accompanying, but smaller, and

29

slightly more manageable, issues. In particular, I am interested in Whitehead's conception of beauty and his idea that life should be lived "aesthetically." In this essay, I put Whitehead in conversation with two other individuals, Walter Pater (1839–1894), a near contemporary who, as far as I can tell, shares an unrecognized sensibility with Whitehead on a number of themes, and Plato, who is a significant and acknowledged intellectual foundation to Whitehead's general way of thinking. All three are greatly interested in beauty, especially the ways in which it is an essential element in human life.

What might be gained by this conversation? Between Pater and Plato we see important differences amongst ideas of beauty when, as in the case of Pater, the pursuit of beauty is always in a reality of finitude. Pater's modern world is one forever on the move, and the pursuit of beauty is the way in which we might live on some seemingly "higher" plane. Pater's lover of beauty lives with great intensity. But while beauty elevates us, it does so only temporarily, and any transcendence that it provides is accompanied by a fall back down to more prosaic grounds. Plato's partygoers, too, perceive finite beauties, but their aesthetic education is one of climbing a ladder, ascending from the particular and contingent to more stable realms on up to the eternal. Beauty carries them aloft toward freedom and greater realities beyond the world. Whitehead stands, curiously, in between. Shared with Pater is an insistence on the fundamental finitude of experience, including, of course, aesthetic experience. But Whitehead's account includes aspects of transcendence that take us further than Pater's. While we don't go to the same heights as those reached on Plato's ladder, we can intuit a realm of permanence for our aesthetic achievements. I hope that bringing these three together, even if only on a point or two of what we can call the "aesthetic life," will lead to a better understanding of Whitehead's concerns and the context in which he is working.

WALTER PATER AND THE PURSUIT OF BEAUTY

For Walter Pater, life reaches its highest expression and finds its deepest value in aesthetic experience, in the experience of beauty.

In his most well-known book *The Renaissance*, Pater states his purpose partly as providing the means by which we, as readers, might become educated in the life of aesthetics. He has no interest in laying out a general theory of beauty but rather in teaching us to identify, each in our individual and varied moments of aesthetic pleasure, the factors and elements that create and make possible these special moments.

> The function of the aesthetic critic is to distinguish, to analyze, and separate from its adjuncts, the virtue by which a picture, a landscape, a fair personality in life or in a book, produces this special impression of beauty or pleasure, to indicate what the source of that impression is, and under what conditions it is experienced.[1]

When Pater, paraphrasing Hegel, praises Winckelman's writings for initiating "a new organ for the human spirit,"[2] we might assign this same goal to Pater. Growing into this new sensory device and this knowledge about beauty, we should, he suggests, be able to increase our susceptibility to these moments of beauty, finding ourselves more and more in their midst with ever increasing depth and variety. Pater, quite simply, lives for beauty and thinks we should too.

For Pater, then, there is a sense in which the ideal culture is an aesthetic one that can be defined by applying his own description of the Renaissance.

> *The Renaissance is the name* of a many-sided but yet united movement, in which the love of the things of the intellect and the imagination for their own sake, the desire for a more liberal and comely way of conceiving life, make themselves felt, urging those who experience this desire to search out first one and then another means of intellectual or imaginative enjoyment, and directing them not only to the discovery of old and forgotten sources of this enjoyment, but to the divination of fresh sources thereof—new experiences, new subjects of poetry, new forms of art.[3]

The need for beauty becomes more important when we realize that we are lodged within a view of reality that finds it is a realm of incessant change. For Pater, human experience, constituted by impressions, is a "perpetual flight" of fleeting moments, leading to movements of passage and dissolution: a "continual vanishing away, that strange, perpetual, weaving and unweaving of ourselves."[4] Life is but the "concurrence, renewed from moment to moment, of forces parting sooner or later on their ways."[5]

While he praises the Renaissance as the prime example of an aesthetic culture, Pater constantly draws attention to the differences between their worldview and that of the mid-19th century. "How different from this childish dream," Pater writes of Pico Della Mirandolla's sense of the world as a bounded, limited place with crystal walls, "like a painted toy" held in the hands of "the creative *Logos*," is "our own conception of nature, with its unlimited space, its innumerable suns, and the earth but a mote in the beam."[6] Everything in Pater's world is in motion and uncentered in a space that is wildly vast and thoroughly impersonal.

We can cope with the radical fluidity of our experiences by seeking, always, within our lives, the beautiful. "While all melts under our feet, we may well grasp at any exquisite passion, or any contribution to knowledge that seems lifted by a horizon to set the spirit free for a moment, or any stirring of the senses, strange dyes, strange colours, and curious odours, or work of the artist's hands, or the face of one's friend."[7] Thus these incessantly passing moments can be impressed by beauty.

Without the ability to discern the presence of beauty, life is simply the passing of time. "A counted number of pulses only is given to us of a variegated, dramatic life. How may we see in them all that is to be seen in them by the finest senses?" Our task is to seek intensity, to make the "most" of every moment. In one of the best known passages in Pater's work, he defines what counts as success in life: "To burn always with this hard, gem-like flame, to maintain this ecstasy."

Everything, he continues, "is melting under our feet," and, though we too will melt, we can, for a moment, burn with ecstatic intensity. "Not to discriminate in every moment some passionate attitude . . . is, on this short day of frost and sun, to sleep before evening."[8] In sum, for Pater, beauty can ennoble our finite lives and provide us a reprieve from the brute forces of nature.

Whitehead, like Pater (and I think it is important to keep in mind that both are responding to the same or near-same cultural situation), calls for a renewed sense of aesthetic appreciation, for a renewed ability at discerning and caring for aesthetic value. It is crucial to emphasize that Whitehead's is not a call for the cultivation of specialized or esoteric pursuits or some kind of aesthetic elitism that is focused on finery. Rather than being some hobby (like winetasting?), it involves nothing less than the practice of everyday life, for the creation, enjoyment, and pursuit of beauty is the very nature of life. "What we want is to draw out habits of aesthetic apprehension," Whitehead writes in the final chapter of *Science and the Modern World*. He continues: "According to the metaphysical doctrine which I have been developing, to do so is to increase the depth of individuality.'

To say that habits of aesthetic appreciation increase the depths of individuality is to say something more than simply that the enjoyment of beauty *adds* meaning to our lives. It means that the addition of value is not simply the accrual of pleasant experiences, the sort we might put on a list (beautiful places I've been, the best music, the most beautiful flowers I've seen, etc.) but rather that these values become part of us, that they get woven into our very identities. To be open to beauty, to experience and to make it, for Whitehead, is to add layers of depth and complexity to our very beings. We become more capacious beings as our souls become richer and more thickly layered with complexity. And by doing so we increase the aesthetic value of reality. With more time we could easily expand the exploration of common ground between the efforts of Pater and Whitehead to restore aesthetic value to a prominent place in the world of English modernity.

But how might Pater's sense of the aesthetic life play itself out? What might it look like? These are questions about sustainability, about the ability of the aesthetic to keep one going, engaged with life and propelled forward. On one hand, there is certainly much that is attractive about this description. Pater's aesthetic individual is ever interested in life, is attuned to value and seeking to make the most of things, deeply engaged with the life of human culture. "The aim of our culture should be to attain not only as intense but as complete a life as possible." [10] Pater is interested in fullness and the life toward beauty is the way.

On the other hand, there are problematic aspects to all this, with two issues coming to mind. The first has to do with the incessant call to pursue, always, intensity. Realizing that time is limited, there will be the felt need to make the most of it, to experience life to the fullest. With this kind of urgency there is, arguably, an accompanying feeling of frenetic restlessness. To live this life seriously is to always be on the move, grabbing, seeking, looking to maximize. Unsatisfied with the banal and pedestrian we will often, I think, be in search of more and more. And perhaps to be preoccupied with intensity entails that in every moment there is also a feeling of lack, the sense that around the corner is something better, that we are "missing out." It is a life that is always moving between desire and what can only be penultimate satisfaction, for which there is no end. Thus one wonders if such a life can lead to a feeling of being a "complete life."

This leads me to a second issue, the question that has to do with what, for Pater, we are actually experiencing when we experience beauty, and where, so to speak, it takes us. Consider the following: "The basis of all artistic genius lies in the power of conceiving humanity in a new and striking way, of putting a happy world of its own creation in place of the meaner world of our common days." [11] And again: "In its primary aspect, a great picture has no more definite message for us than an accidental play of sunlight and shadow for a few moments on the wall or floor: is itself, in truth, a space of such fallen light." [12]

Thus the beauty produced by art is a gloss, an unreal apparition of chance. It does not reflect the actual reality in which we exist. While everyone would claim that art involves some gap between appearance and reality, for Pater there seems to be no bridge between the two. To be sure, the experience of art and beauty involves transcendence, but not to some higher reality; only, rather, to a momentary and unreal reprieve from the meanness of everyday life. It is a moment of forgetting, blissful and intense though it may be. Thus perhaps, in the end, the aesthetic life is, for Pater, one of evasion, of coping, of always seeking diversions by means of aesthetic pleasure.

To be sure, there is a high moral seriousness to Pater's proposal. And Oscar Wilde's Dorian Gray and Evelyn Waugh's Anthony Blanche are definitively overblown caricatures of Pater's aesthetic individual. But when we consider Whitehead's remark that "apart from some transcendent aim human life either wallows in pleasure or relapses slowly into a barren repetition," [13] the distance between these literary caricatures and Pater's lover of beauty seems not altogether great. We come away with the sense that in the aesthetic experience, even with its intensity and poignancy, one is only staving off the perpetual perishing of time.

Whitehead's conception of the aesthetic life has many interesting and unexplored similarities with Pater's (and there's much more that could be said here) but Whitehead's conception has the ability to evade the restlessness and emptiness of Pater's. Before directly spelling this out, I will turn to some ideas of Plato and what might be said about his own conception of the "aesthetic life." This will help us better understand some of the important features of Whitehead's conception.

PLATO AND THE RISE TOWARD BEAUTY

Beauty is fundamentally important in the philosophy of Plato; it makes life worthwhile and puts us in touch with what is ultimately important. The genuine lover of beauty is a philosopher and in pursuit of wisdom. Socrates's famous speech in *The Symposium* about the love of beauty begins in a place of common ground with Pater and Whitehead: there is an abundance of beauty all around, and so much in our world is worthy of our attention by virtue of its ability to catch our eye, to dazzle us, and to draw us toward it. Plato, like Pater and Whitehead, is thoroughly interested in providing us with an aesthetic education, and the pursuit of beauty is at the center of it.

In the beginning of this endeavor, it will be one particular beautiful body that grabs our attention and compels us to want to be in its presence. And after some time, we will soon realize that other bodies, too, are beautiful, thus bringing us to the conclusion that they must all have something in common. Coming into this awareness is sure to incite a great deal of activity on our part, and it could, potentially, lead us to the kind of restless pursuits we attributed to Pater: with so much beauty all around how could we not be in an excited hurry? But rather than causing a state of frenetic desire for more, Socrates sees this realization as leading to a place of greater calm. To see that beauty abounds in a multiplicity of particulars is to realize that what we are drawn to is not definitively tied to its particular housing. Rather, beauty must transcend each particular instance of it (for how else could we identify some common feature?) As such, we can realize that beauty's nature is not one of contingency and finitude and, thus, not subject to decay. We can be spared the disappointment that necessarily comes from the love of finite creatures. "By scanning beauty's wide horizon, he will be saved from a slavish and illiberal devotion to the individual loveliness of a single boy, a single man."[14] Our experience of beauty, our sustaining relationship to it is not dependent on the status of the particular within which it only seems to be contained. We needn't be in any kind of hurry here. What was restlessness and urgency for Pater is now a calm, patient confidence.

Of course, the ascent does not stop at this point. We continue up the ladder toward better beauties, whose qualities grow by means of their dissolving particularity, until finally we reach beauty itself.

There bursts upon him that wondrous vision which is the very soul of the beauty he has toiled so long for. It is an ever-lasting loveliness which neither comes nor goes, which neither flowers nor fades, for such beauty is the same on every hand, the same then as now, here as there, this way as that way, the same to every worshiper as it is to every other.[15]

With such a vision, a "man's life is ever worth the living."[16]

One of the reasons why the discovery of beauty itself makes life worthy is that we are now accessing something eternal. Beauty saves us; it takes us up out of a hurried life, subject to the vagaries and vicissitudes of a devotion to finite realities, and brings us to a place of peace. "And once you have seen [beauty itself], you will never be seduced again by the charm of gold, of dress, of comely boys, or lads just ripening to manhood; you will care nothing for the beauties that used to take your breath away and kindle such a longing in you."[17] The relevant part for our discussion of the aesthetic life is that both the restlessness and emptiness associated with Pater's proposal are absent. The love of beauty is calming, and it is an authentically transcendent affair.

Certainly this, too, has something attractive about it. To live for beauty is to find an ultimate place of satisfaction, calm and serene, fulfilled and at the proper end of desire. It is to be free of restlessness and from the pettiness and avarice that might come with the love of particular creatures. And yet when we imagine one who lives with the contemplation of eternal beauty, questions about its sustainability arise. In living for beauty, does one really want to accomplish this freedom and transcendence at the cost of going beyond the world of finite particulars? While there is more subtlety and nuance to Plato's account of what is involved with all of this, I am persuaded by Martha Nussbaum's claim that a person who really makes this ascent presents us with a question mark and a challenge: "Is this the life we want for ourselves?. . . . We feel, as we look at him, both awestruck and queasy, timidly homesick for ourselves."[18] Nussbaum's point is that in grasping Beauty itself we can become self-sufficient and protected from the genuine risks of love for particular creatures, becoming something other than recognizably human.

To sum up: I have set forth two different conceptions of the aesthetic life, each with important aspects and associated problems. Pater's account, while attentive to the transience of life and the quickening, energizing power of beauty, is weakened by the inducement of a fatiguing restlessness. Plato's conception, at least as contained in Socrates' account of the ladder of love in *The Symposium*, shows a life in search of beauty as one that is calming and peaceful, elevating us out of the muddle of finite life. Yet all of this comes with a price, something analogous to a feeling of uncanniness, of living beyond our means.

This brings us to Whitehead, who stands curiously in between Pater and Plato. In the space that remains, I will focus on the issues of restlessness and peace as they appear in Whitehead's thought.

WHITEHEAD AND THE AESTHETIC LIFE

Living for Beauty is at the very heart of Whitehead's philosophy. It is an element of both his ethics (a good life is one that is lived for beauty) and his metaphysics (the creation of beauty is, quite simply, what is going on in the universe). "The teleology of the Universe is directed to the production of Beauty."[19] But while "telos" indicates a goal and a purpose, there is, in Whitehead's use of the term, no suggestion of a final, static goal of accomplishment by which all will come to a finish as there is in Plato's scheme.[20] Whitehead's account of reality shares Pater's emerging modernist sensibility regarding the constant flux and fluidity of the world. The cosmos itself, with loose resemblance to Pater's lover of beauty, is imbued with a kind of restlessness in that it is forever and always seeking, attaining, but desiring again new occasions of beauty. Also, for Whitehead, to live for Beauty is to be thoroughly embedded in the finite world of particulars. Beauty is always contained and embodied; it never exists in some eternal, spotless form. Thus all that can be called beautiful comes and goes.

If, as Whitehead claims, human beings flourish when they align their actions and sense of purpose with the ways of the cosmos, it stands to reason that living for beauty—seeking, creating, and enjoying it—should shape the contours and drives of our lives. But in living for beauty we open ourselves to the sort of restlessness that we saw in Pater. The pursuit of beauty is a never-ending journey, and whatever satisfactions and values it produces can always be surpassed. We feel, perhaps, hurried to do so and find that feelings of lasting accomplishment are beyond our reach.

Whitehead was well aware of these risks within his outlook. In *Adventures of Ideas*, he admits that the pursuit of beauty can potentially be "ruthless, hard, cruel" and bring about a "restless egotism" and "destructive turbulence."[21] A life devoted to beauty has the power to uproot us, both in the sense of disconnecting us from the communities in which we live, and from a sense of meaningful and constructive purpose. To live for beauty is to love that which does not last.

Yet while this is indeed a possibility, Whitehead promotes the inclusion of another factor that mitigates these risks, which he calls the experience of Peace. There's a great deal to say about Peace and its importance in Whitehead's philosophy. Right now, I'm interested in the way that the experience of Peace alleviates the problem of restlessness.

In our discussion of Plato, we saw how restlessness was eased by going up the ladder, transcending particular beauties. Peace, for Whitehead, has a similar effect of enabling us to accept (affirm even) that all particular beautiful entities are subject to perishing by means of the attainment of a deeper and wider vision of reality, specifically with an element of understanding that while perpetual perishing is a metaphysical fact, one can grasp a sense of the "infinite."[22] Thus, one glimpses, dimly perhaps, the possibility of transcendence, the possibility that all instances of finite beauty achieve some form of everlastingness.

Peace can be defined, says Whitehead, as "primarily a trust in the efficacy of Beauty."[23] "Efficacy of Beauty" refers, I think, to the claim that beauty matters, that it is worth pursuing. One needs to "trust" because the claim about its worth is not necessarily persuasive. While beauty is something intrinsically valuable, the pursuit of finite beauty (which is, for Whitehead, the only kind there is) can still be disappointing, can still lead one to the conclusion that living for beauty does not make life ultimately meaningful. This, arguably, is the result of Pater's vision of the aesthetic life. Living for beauty makes our "pulses" count, but in the end they don't add up to anything beyond their immediate experience. To "trust in the efficacy of beauty" is to abide by the faith that the value of beauty extends beyond the present moment. Without this trust, an ongoing devotion and commitment to a life of beauty is likely to be derailed. "The zest of human adventure presupposes for its material a scheme of things with a worth beyond any single occasion."[24]

One of the issues I identified with Pater's proposal is that while one can seek the experience of beauty in an ongoing fashion from one moment to the next, there is nothing that harmonizes these experiences or holds them together. In fact, one can't even assume that the world outside of our experiences is actually beautiful. One would realize, sooner or later, that every occasion of beauty is relentlessly transient, like a bubble popping out of existence just as quickly as it popped into it. For Whitehead, occasions of beauty, too, are finite; yet in our experiences of them there is possibly an intuition of their permanence—not as an actual, eternally existing entity, but as an accomplished fact. "As soon as high consciousness is reached, the enjoyment of existence is entwined with pain, frustration, loss, tragedy. Amid the passing of so much beauty, so much heroism, so much daring, Peace is then the intuition of permanence."[25]

In this experience of Peace one finds relief from the hurried sense of restlessness, of the feeling that life is limited. As such, its "emotional effect is the subsidence of turbulence which inhibits.[26]

Plato's climb up the ladder has a similar emotional effect, showing us (from the heights) that our commitment to beauty, our desire to be in its midst is not tied to any one occasion of it. It does so by inviting us to consider that all occasions of beauty in this world are possible only because of Beauty itself, which has no limitations or defects. In the case of Whitehead we don't find perfect, eternal beauty. Rather we find a way to remain committed to the pursuit of finite beauty. The experience of Peace is an experience of transcendence. We realize that although aesthetic value is finite, our fidelity to the high ideal of beauty is not some delusion. "High aims are worthwhile," says Whitehead near the very end of *Adventure of Ideas.* Yet—and here it is difficult but important to get this right and clear—the question is what sort of permanence beyond the passing of temporal existence do we intuit in the experience of Peace if it is not the same as that which one finds in Plato's form of Beauty. Whitehead is not very precise about these matters. It does, though, have something to do with the consequent nature of God and the continued influence and efficacy of the past on the present. Achieved values exert influence. "A realized fact is conceived as an abiding perfection in the nature of things, a treasure for all ages . . . to perish is to assume a new function in the process of generation."[27] Created occasions of beauty happened and are established moments of accomplished fact. As such, they continue to exert influence in each new present moment.

But it is also clear that in the transcendental experience of Peace we still find ourselves with feelings associated with the loss involved in the facts of finitude. Peace is not a numbing agent. "It keeps vivid the sensitiveness to the tragedy."[28] Peace is, Whitehead famously says, "the union of Youth and Tragedy"[29]: "Youth" in the sense that Peace is an invitation into a life in pursuit of Beauty, of high ideals; "Tragedy" because such commitments embroil one, necessarily, in a life of loss. The quality of Youth helps mitigate the restlessness found in Pater's sense of the aesthetic life, and the Tragic element keeps us in the world, lower than the dizzying heights of Plato.

ENDNOTES

1 Walter Pater, *The Renaissance: Studies in Art and Poetry*, ed. Adam Phillips (Oxford: Oxford University Press, 1996), xxx.

2 Pater, 114.

3 Pater, 1.

4 Pater,, 152.

5 Pater, 150.

6 Pater, 27.

7 Pater, 152.

8 Pater, 152.

9 Alfred North Whitehead, *Science and the Modern World* (New York: Free Press, 1967), 199.

10 Pater, 121.

11 Pater, 137.

12 Pater, 84.

13 Whitehead, *Adventures of Ideas* (New York: Free Press, 1967), 85.

14 Plato, *The Symposium* in *The Collected Dialogues*, eds. Edith Hamilton and Huntington Cairns (Princeton: Princeton University Press, 1961), section 210c.

15 Plato, section 210e-211a.

16 Plato, section 211d.

17 Plato, section 211d.

18 Martha Nussbaum, *Fragility without Goodness: Luck and Ethics in Greek Tragedy and Philosophy* (Cambridge: Cambridge University Press, 1986), 184.

19 Whitehead, *Adventures*, 265.

20 See Whitehead, *Process and Reality*, Corrected Edition, edited by David Ray Griffin and Donald W. Sherburne (New York: Free Press, 1978), 111.

21 Whitehead, *Adventures*, 284 and 285.

22 Whitehead, *Adventures*, 285.

23 Whitehead, *Adventures*. 285.

24 Whitehead, *Adventures*, 288.

25 Whitehead, *Adventures*, 286.

26 Whitehead, *Adventures*, 285.

27 Whitehead, *Adventures*, 291.

28 Whitehead, *Adventures*, 286.

29 Whitehead, *Adventures*, 296.

❧ 4 ❧

BERGSON AND WHITEHEAD:
DUELING PLATONISTS

Pete A. Y. Gunter

ABSTRACT: *This article deals with a common source of Bergson's and Whitehead's thought, namely, the dependence of both on "Platonism"— for Whitehead, Plato himself; for Bergson, Plato's intellectual descendant, Plotinus. Whitehead's visionary treatment of Plato's world of forms (for him, eternal objects) and Bergson's transformation of Plotinus' emanations into the* élan vital *disclose both thinkers as joined to a common source but disagreeing as to how to treat it. Whitehead's reliance on eternal objects obliges him to conceive possibilities (potentiality) as preceding actual events in the world. Bergson, by contrast, regards possibilities as emerging in the world but not existing before their emergence. The author treats these two philosophies as constituting a dilemma or antinomy.*

BERGSON AND PLOTINUS

T HE SHORTEST ROUTE to Plotinus is through his concept of God. In the *Republic,* Plato argues that there is a highest form of existence, the Form of the Good. This ultimate being is for Plato timeless and perfect, summing up in itself all positive attributes. By contrast

45

the world, temporal and imperfect, participates only in part in this ultimate reality. This same entity appears, somewhat transformed, in Aristotle's world-system, where it is variously formed as the Unmoved Mover or, with great historical import, God.

The Platonic-Aristotelian ultimate Being was to be transformed again by Plotinus, in ways that his two great predecessors would have found strange. Plotinus felt that Plato and Aristotle had, in spite of having isolated and defined it, underestimated their ultimate Being. For Plotinus this Being must not merely sum up all positive attributes: it must both sum them up and transcend them. Such overfullness of being, such overcompleteness, cannot remain within itself. It must overflow, creating the world: the sun, the galaxies, ultimately creatures like ourselves.

This creative outflow, or emanation, is for Plotinus twofold: a process proceeding from God (protasis) and another, logically subsequent, process (apodosis) returning to God. Plotinus does not see this outward expression of God as structurally formless. It occurs in stages[1]: the result is a structured, cohesive universe, ontologically imperfect but not chaotic. Its constant process of formation, its cosmic homeostasis, is informed by the *logoi spermatikoi*: the timeless forms which, part of and fundamental to the cosmic emanation, account for the order of the world. But where for Plato the world participates in the forms, for Plotinus the forms are projected into the world. They "become" and give order to "becoming."

One final point. If for Plotinus God is not merely real but (for lack of a better word) super-real, so our knowledge of that God, in order to be adequate to its object, must be not merely rational but supraintellectual. To those who will argue that such a theory of knowledge leads us to irrationalism, Plotinus would have replied that his critics have confused such ultimate knowing with an *infra*intellectual or *sub*intellectual noesis. He would have added that a supraintellectual insight can engender valid cognition (it is adequate to its object), while infraintellectual awareness can lead only to darkness (it is not adequate to its object). I make this point not only because it helps us to understand Plotinus but because it will be essential to the understanding of Bergson's theory of knowledge: i.e., to his concept of intuition (understood as *supra*intellectual).

This bare sketch of Plotinus' philosophy is structured (I think, obviously) so as to shed light on Bergson's philosophy, both in itself and, later, in comparison with that of Alfred North Whitehead. If the shortest route to a grasp of the general import of Plotinus's thought is through his concept of God, I will argue similarly that the shortest route to finding Bergson's debt to Plotinus is through Bergson's concept of God. This debt (though I will argue that it shows itself in one of his earlier works, *Matter and Memory,* for example) is made clear only in his *Creative Evolution* (1907) where he speaks of God as:

> a center from which worlds shoot out like rockets in a fireworks display—provided, however, that I do not present this center as a *thing*, but as a continuity of shooting out. God, thus defined, has nothing of the already made. He is unceasing life, action, freedom.[2]

This deity contrasts vividly with the God of Aristotle: "necessarily immovable and apart from the world."[3] If Bergson is right, God is a source of emanations which are in themselves capable of further creativity. This picture does not appear *de novo* in *Creative Evolution.* It is preceded by the following text in *An Introduction to Metaphysics* (1903): "the intuition of duration, far from leaving us suspended in a void as pure analysis would do, brings us into contact with a whole continuity of durations which we must try to follow, whether downwards or upwards."[4] In one direction, moving toward physical matter, we find "a much more attenuated duration,"[5] that is, durations of extremely brief extent. In the other, "we approach a duration which strains, contracts and intensifies itself more and more; at the limit would be eternity."[6] This would be an "eternity of life," a "living and still moving eternity," in which our own particular durations are included as the vibrations are in light.

An Introduction to Metaphysics is an introduction to the metaphysics of *Creative Evolution*. Here, the temporal hierarchy of *An Introduction to Metaphysics*[7] is transformed into dynamic becoming: the emergence of matter and of life. That is, for Bergson, God's emanations, his creation of worlds, is twofold. As matter, it gives rise to the various material "particles" (which he treats as vanishingly brief durations) and to stars, planets, galaxies (some of which, he notes, are even now in the process of formation). As life, it gives rise (once the planetary situation makes it possible) to the multiple divergences and consequent extraordinary diversity exhibited in biological evolution.

Let us return briefly to God, who after all, as the creator of such a vast dynamic universe, certainly deserves special attention. Bergson's deity—clearly indebted to that of Plotinus—is far removed from the Engineer-and-Architect God of the Enlightenment, and from much popular theology. This engineering God, possessing the correct mathematics and a sufficient computer, designs the world as a machine so flawless that, once created, never needs attending to. Bergson's deity is equally far removed from Aristotle's timeless deity, separate from the world and entirely self-sufficient.

The deity proposed by Bergson contrasts vividly with these two alternatives. If it creates the world, it is not different in kind from that world, which bears within it a continuing creative impulse derived from God.

The difficulty lies in coming to grips with this deity in itself. The Bergsonian deity may give rise to distinct quarks, protons, planets, and living cells. But it is not itself divided into parts; the most that can be said is that it contains diverse aspects. Similarly, the profound self of Bergson's first work, *Time and Free Will*, is also an undivided one. But also like this self, the complexity of Bergson's deity involves parts which "mutually penetrate,"[8] or constitute a "multiplicity of fusion."[9] The analogy here would be a plasma, or a photon created by a particle-antiparticle interaction ("annihilation"): indivisible and not yet divided. Bergson terms this being "infinite,"[10] meaning at least that it cannot be exhausted by any finite enumeration.

The result of an emanation is understood by him not as a simple unpacking of previously existing entities. The new entities or terms will be *created in the process of separating out.* That is, looked at in the broadest sense, creativity involves not the singling out of pre-existing possibles, but the sheer *creation of possibility.*[11]

I must make short work here of what would otherwise be an extremely involved and extended discussion. The analogy between the Bergsonian suprarational deity, its emanations, and their end products (like specific organisms), and the Bergsonian intuition with its gradual expression in discrete, discursive concepts (involving specific symbolism) is, I will insist, accurate and essential. The starting point of both is in itself beyond language and beyond "reason" as we usually understand it. But the end result is structured, intelligible. It is composed of parts whose relations can be studied and correlated: this whether they are biological organisms (the product, again, of evolution) or scientific theories or models (the products of novel intuition). In both cases the original and originating datum sets the conditions for what follows, without containing its specificity. The real here creates the possible. If one likes, its existence precedes essences.

Having discussed Bergson, Plotinus, and their relations, it may be helpful to present their comparative characters in a table. (*See Table 4.1.*) A similar table (*4.2*), relating Bergson and Whitehead, will follow.

BERGSON AND WHITEHEAD

It is clear that Bergson takes the concept of emanation from Plotinus. It is also clear that Bergson transforms this concept in at least three ways. It is: (1) not a simple loss of fullness or being; rather, it exhibits a continual gain in fullness; (2) not a simple recapitulation of "possibles" contained in God but a creation of possibilities; and (3) a radical increase in freedom, not a mere recursion to a prior mode of existence.

Plotinus	Bergson
1. The Plotinian-Alexandrian (henceforth P/A) procession and convergence both operate at the same time. It is like a pulley or an escalator.	1. The Bergsonian universe has a beginning at T_0. It has a cumulative history and any return to the source is problematic.
2. The P/A procession creates nothing new; its characteristics or forms were already present in God.	2. The Bergsonian procession (emanation) endlessly creates novel entities whose characteristics do not preexist their emergence.
3. The P/A procession embodies a gradual diminution of being: from the fullness of God towards virtual nonbeing.	3. Bergson's universe involves not a diminution but an enrichment and increase of being: e.g., through the emergence of new, more complex organisms.
4. In the P/A procession freedom is defined as a return to the original Being: a reuniting with the fundamental prior given.	4. The Bergsonian universe portrays freedom as a going-beyond any prior "given." This viewpoint is not sacrificed, but is rendered complex in his later theology.

Table 4.1

Bergson's position here appears entirely different from Whitehead's. For the English mathematician, all the essences (the "eternal objects") exist from all eternity in the primordial nature of God. For Bergson the essences (the discrete conceptual content) do not exist in God, but are produced both by God's creativity and that of the world God creates. But as stated immediately above, the originating *datum* (God or human conceptual creativity, for example) does contain the conditions for what follows: negatively, for what can *not* follow; positively, for what *can*.

The reader may wonder why any mention of Whitehead has been delayed to this point, and whether anything relevant may be said about Whitehead in the future. I can only ask readers to be patient. One more point must be explained before it is possible to compare Whitehead and the French intuitionist. The point will be epistemological.

In his *The Logic of Scientific Discovery*, Karl Popper makes the following interesting remark: "My view can be expressed by saying that every discovery contains an 'irrational element' or a 'creative intuition' in Bergson's sense."[12] Popper's remark is interesting for two reasons. First, because it backs Bergson's claim that the really great achievements in the sciences and the arts are due to and involve intuition, but second, because of Popper's misguided claim that creative intuition is irrational. If an insight can be developed into a structure which is intelligible, expressible in symbolism (whether scientific or artistic), consistent, applicable to the world, and hence potentially useful, such an insight must be called rational. Asylums and coffee houses are full of self-proclaimed geniuses proclaiming great insights. But somehow nothing comes of it; no insight is developed and embodied and tried out. Must we not term the other real insights, which are or can be expressed, formulated, and tested, rational? This would include *proto*rational and obviously-rational under the general reading of *rationality*.

Many would find this very broad, inclusive concept of rationality unacceptable. But for the present context it is extremely useful. That is, in using it we find it very hard to type Bergson's philosophy as anti-scientific, anti-intellectual, or irrationalist. Such terms, if they are to be used at all in classifying Bergson's thought, must be seriously qualified and then qualified again until they risk dying the well-known death of a thousand distinctions. But this broad notion of rationality is extremely helpful both in making sense of Bergson's philosophy and, especially in the context of Whitehead, of showing the extent to which their philosophies are close kin—neither being "anti-intellectual," both being concerned with the "future of the sciences," both being "unashamed metaphysicians," both being "Platonists": Whitehead a fascinating Platonist *à la* Plato, Bergson an unexpected Neoplatonist following Plotinus.

What follows is intended as an outline only: a checkerboard comparison spelled out in successive sections. Its major vice will be abstractness and even, I admit, some superficiality. Its virtues are clarity (even if abstract) and brevity.[13]

Bergson	Whitehead
1. God is necessary to explain the universe.	1. God is necessary to explain the universe.
2. God is the "source" of nature.	2. God is a "principle of concretion": necessary to explain how the universal can be found in the particular.
3. God contains what is required for the universe to exist as we find it.	3. God contains what is required for the universe to exist as we find it.
4. The primordial nature of God contains that which will become definite and distinct after a process of creative division.	4. All eternal objects exist in the primordial nature of God.
5. Creativity in God, nature, and people involves the creation of the possible.	5. Creativity involves the reassembling of possibles inherent in God's primordial nature.
6. Freedom involves the creation of possibility.	6. Freedom is the choice between preexisting possibles.

Table 4.2

SOME DISCUSSION

CATEGORIES VS. MYTHS

Up to this point the discussion has been based on this analogy: Whitehead: Plato = Bergson: Plotinus. I would like here to present a second analogy, namely, Bergson: Plato = Whitehead: Aristotle. The point of this second analogy is straightforward: Whitehead, in developing his metaphysics, painstakingly puts together a "categorical scheme," the backbone of *Process and Reality*. In his *magnum opus*, *Creative Evolution*, however, Bergson, instead of producing a carefully worked-out set of interlocking categories, caps his argument with images: the fireworks display,[14] the vital impetus,[15] the cavalry charge,[16] and the "current" of life.[17] It might be objected that these are little more than literary ornaments. In fact, I will argue, these images have the function of Platonic myths. In presenting his myths, Plato hopes to sketch fundamental features, but without spelling out their precise contours, their detailed structure. Why Plato chose to present his philosophy in this way, is interesting to speculate. The polar opposite of this approach is, of course, that of Aristotle, who develops categories (as does Whitehead) in great detail, painstakingly relating them to particulars.

Why *not* develop a set of categories? Perhaps, because of doubts about the capacity of the human mind to do so successfully. But there is another reason, involving such doubts in certain respects but pointing in a very different direction. Bergson's imagery is based on an unwillingness to prejudge the exact contours of future science, or art, or ethics, given current knowledge. Imagery, for all its literary value, has the virtue of suggesting alternative theories and modes of conceptualization involving new approaches. That is, it can suggest directions of research without dictating their exact dimensions ahead of time. Their vice is vagueness—arguably an inescapable vice; their virtue is openness—a considerable virtue. Who today proceeds to do physics, or even biology, using Aristotle's scheme, or, for that matter, Kant's architectonic functioning, as a purely epistemological set of categories? So with any set of categories based (to use Thomas Kuhn's terminology) on a prevailing paradigm.[18] Paradigms can shift. Imagery remains pregnant with the development of future possibilities.

POSSIBLES VS. "RAW BECOMING"

I have noted briefly Bergson's and Whitehead's differences over the concept of the "possible." For Whitehead the notion of the possible is grounded in the primordial nature of God, which contains all (note the universal qualifier) the eternal objects (that can ever "ingress" into the world). If this is so, as I argue, creativity consists in the embodiment of alternative combinations of eternal objects which preexist their embodiment, and freedom is a choice between preexisting alternatives: preexistent in all their details. On Bergson's view, this—as I hope I have already established—is not true. For him, possibles are literally, and not figuratively, *created* and do not preexist their creation. This is as true of his God as of any finite creator: a poet, for example. There is for Bergson no one division or fragmenting of the divine being. Hence, there is no one set of conceptual contents or, more broadly, characteristics, which God will express. The sheer superabundance of God forbids that any finite set of possibles can be derived from the divine fecundity. The characteristics of our universe might have been different, *ad infinitum*.

What disturbs me about Whitehead's system is the following. My friend Gerald Morgan tells me that Dylan Thomas would struggle through as many as two hundred versions of a poem before finally settling down on the final version.[19] So far as I can see, on Whitehead's terms, every version of Thomas' poem is already present in the primordial nature of God: of that and of every other poem ever written or, for that matter, not written. If this is so, it is not clear on his terms just what creativity and its correlative, novelty, mean.

I cannot forbear pointing out here the close similarity between the absolute inclusiveness of the external objects in God's primordial nature and the completeness of Whitehead's categorical scheme to generate or at least to deal satisfactorily with all future possible developments in the sciences or elsewhere.

One might argue, in response, that the primordial nature of God is deficient. Or that, perhaps there are possibilities for the combination of eternal objects not contained in the objects themselves. Or that there might be new eternal objects. The former, however, is ruled out by Whitehead's contention that all relations are themselves eternal objects. No new relations are thus possible for whatever terms one might deduce. The latter is interesting. But Whitehead explicitly rules it out. To bring in the possibility of novel eternal objects would be, I believe, to have to significantly transform the categorical scheme.

CLEAR AND DISTINCT PERCEPTS VS. INTERPENETRATIVE DATA

Another difference between the two philosophers involves the character of the "given." For Whitehead, as for David Hume, if an object (of thought or of perception) is distinguishable, it is "separable": that is, it can be exhibited independently without loss of fundamental character. White is white, period. Its presence on a round or square object doesn't matter, nor does its relationship to a red or blue patch or background.

This is, of course, an atomism. The contrary view is found in Bergson's notion (presented above) of interpenetration. If interpenetration is possible, qualities are to some degree internally related, so that red next to blue is to some degree different from red next to brown. Or, a note heard as part of a melody is different from the same note heard independently. Or, to take William James's example, thunder after thunder is different from thunder after silence.

Bergson believed he had found the paradigm case of the interpenetration in the depths of human consciousness. There, in the true inner self, fundamental factors are not separated out; they share in each other's characters. This self, in a state of perpetual becoming, cannot twice repeat itself: it is unique and can give rise to acts which are unique.

Exactly this—removing ourselves from Bergson's psychology to his theology—is what we find in Bergson's God, whose richness of content does not contain divisions. Henry James once remarked that in a good novel every part is contained in every other part. The same is true for Bergson's God, whose components or characteristics are not yet divided and whose divisions-to-come cannot be specified a priori.[20]

Put another way: for Whitehead, "interpenetration" is logically impossible. If this were so, shades of white, to recur in the example above, could not be atoms of experience: each would be in some degree different due to its context.

A BRIEF CONCLUSION

I hope that this essay has established two things.

First, the major differences between Bergson and Whitehead are not those of a rational thinker versus an irrationalist, or a proscientific versus an antiscientific philosopher. Rather, they are both Platonists, though of different stripes: Whitehead is a Platonist owing much to the *Timaeus.*; Bergson is a Neoplatonist indebted to the *Enneads.* In important respects, thus, they exhibit profound similarities. And yet they are different. No restating or reorganizing of their basic ideas can result in definite agreement.

Second, the textbook tradition that makes Bergson's intuition an essay in Dadaism or, as in Bertrand Russell's interpretation, a primitive, opaque instinct, must be done away with. Bergson is if anything an ultra- or suprarationalist. His intuition gives rise to intelligible thought—intelligible in terms we would all agree are intelligible. It is *proto*intelligent, *proto*intellectual. By no stretch of the imagination can we term it *anti*-intellectual.

I conclude by cautioning that what has been said here neither puts down Whitehead nor puts up Bergson. The two philosophies for me constitute a dilemma or antinomy: between which I have not yet been able to find a satisfactory alternative.

Since the present book concerns the world environment and the pressing need to understand and protect it, it will not be out of place to say a few words here about Bergson, Whitehead, and the implications of their philosophies for "ecology": scientific and political. Metaphysics today is often assumed to have no serious implications for the real world. But the metaphysical views of Bergson and of Whitehead, however abstract, general, and subtle, are intended to outline the vision of a world in which all parts are interrelated, and relations are, by degree, internal. Each thing thus contributes to the character of the things with which it interacts and helps to sustain them in existence. This is precisely (if very broadly) the ecological point of view. It is no accident that in the first half of the 20th century Bergson and Whitehead were the only two major philosophers to take the environment and its problems seriously.[21] The theories of emanation and ingression developed by these philosophers were intended to demonstrate how a real life system could come into existence, and flourish.

ENDNOTES

1   For a step-by-step description of the stages of order found in Plotinus' emanation, see Edouard Zeller, *Outlines of the History of Greek Philosophy,* 13th ed., trans. L. R. Palmer (New York: World Publishing Company, 1964), 316–18.

2   Henri Bergson, *Creative Evolution,* trans. L. R. Palmer, with an introudction by Keith Ansel Pearson (Houndmills, Blasingstoke: Palgrave Macmillan, 2007), 160–61.

3   Bergson, 205.

4   Henri Bergson, *An Introduction to Metaphysics,* trans. T. E. Hulme, with an introduction bu John Mullarkey (Houndmills, Blasingstoke: Palgrave Macmillan, 2007), 37.

5   Bergson, *An Introduction to Metaphysics,* 37.

6   Bergson, *An Introduction,* 3.

7   Pete A. Y. Gunter, "Temporal Hierarchy in Bergson and Whitehead," *Interchange* 36, no. 1-2 (2005), 139–57.

8   Henri Bergson, *Time and Free Will,* trans. F. L. Pogson (London: George Allan and Unwin Ltd., 1950), 101.

9   Bergson, *Time,* 162.

10   Bergson, *Time,* 4–5.

11   Pete A.Y. Gunter, "Bergson's Creation of the Possible," *Substance* 36, no. 3, Issue 114 (2007), 1-9.

12   Karl R. Popper. *The Logic of Scientific Discovery* (New York: Harper Torchbooks, 1968), 32.

13   Alfred North Whitehead. *Process and Reality,* Corrected Edition, eds. David Ray Griffin and Donald W. Sherburne (New York: The Free Press, 1978), 444. For Whitehead's denial that there can be new eternal objects, see pp. 32, 257. God's primordial nature consists in "the complete envisagement of eternal objects" (4).

14   Bergson, *Creative Evolution,* 161.

15   Bergson, *Creative,* 163.

16   Bergson, *Creative,* 173.

17   Bergson, *Creative*, 172.

18   Thomas Kuhn, *The Structure of Scientific Revolutions*, 3rd Edition (Chicago: University of Chicago Press, 1996), 212.

19   Gerald Morgan, *This World of Wales: An Anthology of Anglo-Welsh Poetry* (Cardiff: University of Wales Press, 1969), 160.

20   Rose-Marie Mossé-Bastide, *Bergson et Plotin* (Paris: Presses Universitaires de France, 1959), 422. The present brief essay makes no pretense of going deeply into Plotinus' philosophy or Bergson's reception and transformation of it. This has been done very ably by Mossé-Bastide, who cites, for example: a) Bergson's lectures in his first year at the Collège de France on Plotinus' concept of the world-soul (1) and b) his remark to A. D. Sertillanges that of all the ancient philosophers his views are closest to those of Plotinus (2).

21   Pete A. Y. Gunter, "Bergson and the War Against Nature," in *The New Bergson* (New York: Manchester University Press, 1999), 168–82; "Whitehead's Contribution to Ecological Thought: Some Unrealized Possibilities," *Interchange* 31, no. 2-3 (2000), 211–23; "A Whiteheadian Aesthetics of Nature and the Forest" *Process Studies* 32, no. 2 (2004), 315–22. See also Pete A. Y. Gunter and Max F. Oelschlaeger, *Texas Land Ethics* (Austin: University of Texas Press, 1997), 156.

❧ 5 ❧

BEYOND HUMAN VIRTUE

Patrick Shade

ABSTRACT: *Environmental thinking looks beyond apparently self-contained objects to their connecting relations and acknowledges dependencies and interdependencies. Thinking environmentally enables us to see beyond ourselves, beyond our social communities, and even beyond our human community to natural communities with which we are interdependent. A significant resource in cultivating environmental thinking is being more attentive to the role that wonder, funded by discipline and curiosity, plays in our intellectual life. Wonder offers us an appreciation of the "beyond" that lies at the heart of environmental thinking, helping us to transcend the boundaries of our perspectives, our purposes, and our welfare. This "beyond" is both spatial and temporal, including not only creatures and systems that lie outside of our bodies but also things personal and interior, such as the creatures within us and the way each of us functions as an ecosystem for myriad cells and bacteria. To examine the "beyond" more concretely, I argue that the tradition of virtue ethics—with critical revisions—offers resources for crafting a more environmentally informed vision of ourselves and our welfare. I draw on neo-Aristotelians as well as botanists, evolutionary biologists, microbiologists, and geologists to*

59

characterize notable modes of dependence and interdependence, the recognition of which moves us beyond traditional conceptions of human welfare. I consider the world both within us and without us to stress that our relations to nonhumans are significant to who we are and to how we can better think of ourselves to ensure our continued sustenance and that of others.

W E HUMANS often exaggerate our capacity or need for independence and self-sufficiency. This tendency is particularly troubling in the context of our current environmental challenges, since many of them are exacerbated by our failure to reflect on the wide-ranging consequences our acts have for ourselves and for nonhuman life. Especially relevant here is what Alfred North Whitehead calls "the fallacy of simple location," a fallacy that results when we presuppose the independence of individuals, obscuring or neglecting their relations to one another.[1]

Too frequently, assumptions of simple location are apparent in our self-conceptions. We often characterize ourselves by our capacity to move freely from context to context, making modifications here and there—especially with respect to protective shelters, clothing, and technologies—while remaining largely the same selves regardless of context. This emphasis on resiliency has multiple sources. One is the fact that much of our ordinary experience is framed in terms of macroscopic objects that endure. The tradition of substance metaphysics is long-lived and closely tied to how we think of ordinary experience. Moreover, each passing year adds new examples of our ability to change environments to suit our needs, suggesting a contrast between ourselves as creative agents and other entities as largely passive and plastic. We celebrate our independence in choices, many of which are augmented by the wonders of technology, so much that we often overlook our interdependence with other humans or with nonhumans.

A contributing factor to this self-understanding is the blindness that William James attributes to our practical nature. James argues that

[w]e are practical beings, each of us with limited functions
and duties to perform. Each is bound to feel intensely the
importance of his own duties and the significance of the
situations that call these forth. But this feeling is in each of
us a vital secret, for sympathy with which we vainly look to
others. The others are too much absorbed in their own vital
secrets to take an interest in ours. Hence the stupidity and
injustice of our opinions, so far as they deal with the significance of alien lives.[2]

Pursuing our unique projects requires not only energy but also focus,
the intensity of which comes at the exclusion of factors deemed irrelevant to our preferred purposes. This makes it easy to take for granted
what lies beyond ourselves, especially when it is sufficiently stable
to require no special attention. The "beyond" is there nonetheless.
As a response, James advises us to refrain from interfering with the
projects of others.

While his analysis is penetrating, James's advice is too simplistic,
even within the exclusively human context. Our lives are interwoven
with those of others so that maintaining distance is at best an ideal.
James himself is mindful of this problem in his metaphysical rumina-
tions where he notes that the word "and" attaches to our descriptions
of reality and prescriptions for action:

Things are "with" one another in many ways, but nothing
includes everything, or dominates over everything. The word
"and" trails along after every sentence. Something always
escapes. "Ever not quite" has to be said of the best attempts
made anywhere in the universe at attaining all-inclusiveness.
The pluralistic world is thus more like a federal republic than
like an empire or a kingdom.[3]

To meet the challenges posed by simple location, we need
to cultivate environmental thinking. Environmental thinking is
contextual by nature. It acknowledges Whitehead's insight that simple
location is an abstraction from the concreteness of reality and, when

taken as absolute, presents a fallacious view of reality, shorn of relations that constitute entities and systems. To think environmentally is to think beyond a simple subject by attending to what is omitted by our selective attention, especially insofar as factors beyond that subject impact its reality or nature, activity, and well-being, as well as how we perceive and understand it. Environmental thinking looks beyond apparently self-contained objects to their connecting relations and acknowledges dependencies and interdependencies.

Many of us struggle to look beyond ourselves to the social and political structures that make possible our unique way of being. Culture studies can expand our understanding so that we can recognize the blinding force of privilege. The natural sciences also provide new knowledge and perspectives that help us acknowledge our interdependence with nonhuman creatures and systems, especially in two ways. First, we now know a good deal more than our ancestors knew about the biological realities that underscore our dependence on nonhuman beings. From the general atmosphere in which we breathe and move to the microbes that help us maintain the healthy operation of our bodies, scientifically informed environmental thinking enables us to escape the narrow bounds of simple location and become more contextual and systematic in our worldview. We live in ecosystems, but each of us is also in an important sense a mobile ecosystem whose integrity is more complex than we often assume, relying on social and political but also biological processes that we neglect at a cost to our health. Second, careful attention to life reveals great diversity and variety. Nonhuman creatures have modes of flourishing that are both distinctive from and continuous with our own. Appreciating them leads to respect for the delicate balance of life and also enhances our understanding of our own nature. There is much evidence that life forms exhibit complex modes of behavior that we have simplistically overlooked or neglected, largely because of our presupposition that our own capacities for flourishing are unique. Thinking environmentally enables us to see beyond our selves, beyond our social communities, and even beyond our human community to natural communities with which we are interdependent.

A significant resource in cultivating environmental thinking is being more attentive to the role wonder plays in our intellectual life. Recall Aristotle's contention in the *Metaphysics* that "it is owing to their wonder that men both now begin and at first began to philosophize."[4] Aristotle links wonder with the desire to know in order to overcome ignorance. We can augment his account by identifying two dominant factors that fuel wonder, curiosity, and discipline. The questions of young children—those prototypes of philosophical thinking—are animated by an unquenchable curiosity about the world that extends from the details of insects to the breadth of the sky and the unity of the universe. Adults and the constraints of daily life often limit curiosity's expression; consequently, if we are to nurture wonder, we also need to promote a complementary form of discipline to ensure that after each tentative answer to the question "why" another question of comparable intensity follows. Funded by discipline and curiosity, wonder expresses an appreciation for both the intimacy of varied details and the broader contexts or horizons within which they can be found. Wonder is a "both/and" proposition concerning both individual and whole, both dynamism and stability.[5]

Wonder is an important intellectual instrument we do well to cultivate—wonder in the natural sciences and in metaphysical speculation—since it is attends at once to the whole and the details of the parts that constitute and compete with the whole for our attention. Wonder at its best captures the tension between the whole and the part and beckons us to expand our vision, thereby correcting for at least some of our blindness. The comprehensiveness of vision it promises moves us *beyond*. "Beyond" is a preposition that repeatedly appears in Whitehead's works. He uses it to refer to mentality and novelty, for each proves a vital component in the forward movement of Creativity, one in his Category of the Ultimate. As Whitehead notes in *The Function of Reason*, "[m]ental experience is the organ of novelty, the urge beyond."[6] This is not the "beyond" of mere externality and disconnection, but the "beyond" of conditions of mutual immanence that often go unnoticed until they are threatened, overwhelmed, or severed.

My aim in the following is to show how an appreciation of the "beyond" lies at the heart of environmental thinking, helping us to transcend the apparently self-contained boundaries of our perspectives, our purposes, and our welfare. This "beyond" is both spatial and temporal, pointing not only to creatures and systems that lie outside of our bodies but also to things personal and interior, including the creatures within us and the way each of us functions as an ecosystem for myriad cells and bacteria. The title of this essay, "Beyond Human Virtue," points to what lies outside and inside of what is human, acknowledging factors on which we depend as well as which have import beyond the human scope.

To challenge our propensity to see and value ourselves as independent, and perhaps exemplary beings, two complementary moves are needed. The first is recognizing that the world beyond us is far more complicated than we often assume, buzzing with vitality and action. Nonhuman animals and nonanimal life exhibit considerable complexity that merits and rewards attention to details. The second move acknowledges our dependencies and so our proximity to the earth and its creatures. These dependencies implicate social modes of interaction that are human but also nonhuman. The sciences, especially the genetic and biologic, reveal a world not only of great variety but also of continuities and interdependencies.

To develop the "beyond" more concretely, I argue that the tradition of virtue ethics has resources we can tease out to craft a more environmentally informed vision of ourselves and our welfare. This tradition celebrates themes sufficiently close to our ordinary experiences of growth and development to have intuitive appeal, but we need to critique its conventional concepts in light of new scientific insights. Aristotle was attentive to complexity and dependencies; his

philosophy at once acknowledges our continuity with other animals—
we are rational *animals* after all—as well as the distinctively social
dimensions of our excellences. Nevertheless, his substance metaphysics
and his ideal of static self-sufficient completeness require critical
scrutiny, since each threatens to obscure what lies beyond the human.
It is here that Whitehead's metaphysics, with its characterization of
the inherently relational actual entity, offers us tools well-suited for
highlighting interconnections more fully than Aristotle. Moreover, I
draw on neo-Aristotelians as well as a number of botanists, evolutionary
biologists, microbiologists, and geologists to characterize notable modes
of dependence and interdependence that move us beyond traditional
conceptions of human welfare. I consider the world both within us
and without us to stress that our relations to nonhumans are significant
to who we are and to how we can better think of ourselves to ensure
our continued sustenance and that of others.

GREEK ENVIRONMENTAL STRAINS

In this section I explore facets of the virtue tradition that are conducive to environmental thinking. Understanding Aristotle's treatment
of the virtues and human flourishing requires attention to his characterization of life, and here we find not only themes that emphasize
our continuities with nonhumans but also those that stress the form
of self-sufficiency that is purportedly distinctive of humans. The
tradition is thus not without its limitations and so requires revision.

Aristotle's treatment of human nature gives due attention to both
the details and the connections between different parts of that nature,
especially our animality. His overall philosophy suggests that life's
different processes can be distinguished by the degree of directness
or intimacy required. Reproduction and nutrition occur through
direct contact with other organisms. When we eat, we draw an entire
organism within our bodies and break it down so that its matter—its
stuff—is reorganized according to the reigning form of the eating
organism—in this case, ourselves. Sense-perception occurs more

indirectly and less destructively. When we see a frog, we receive sensible form of the frog in abstraction from its composite with matter, doing no damage to the frog thus seen. Intellectual life is even more indirect, for thinking involves abstracting intellectual form from the congeries of sensible forms previously experienced. The "higher" life processes are at once less direct and destructive and more abstract and independent of the objects and activities of the immediate environment. Dependence on the physical presence of an entity is a restriction from which higher life forms thus enjoy some liberation. Activity becomes more self-contained and more complete as a consequence.

This move towards greater independence is apparent in our moral life as well. The moral virtues perfect the animal self, albeit under the guidance of our superior rational principle. Even so, their development and expression implicates a broader social world. As children, we habituate our behavior by modeling that of our parents. Whether the resultant habits are good or not is best judged by a person of practical wisdom, the φρόνιμος, who functions as a moral coach capable of discerning the mean relative to each of us that constitutes excellence. Ideally, our interactions with this person cultivate the same wisdom in ourselves so that we choose actions according to the mean for their own sake.

Cultivating and expressing the moral virtues requires a rich social context. Indeed, in his *Politics* Aristotle follows Plato in stressing the specific education and laws needed to create an environment in which virtuous behavior can dominate. Nevertheless, remembering that his original definition of human flourishing allows for the identification of a hierarchy of virtues, Aristotle turns to the intellectual virtues. Using a set of key criteria including self-sufficiency to determine which mode of life is indeed best, he methodically compares moral activity with that of the intellect, concluding that the latter is more excellent and so a more suitable form of human flourishing. Our dependence on others for the development and expression of the moral virtues weakens the status of these virtues overall.

Close attention to Aristotle's treatment of self-sufficiency in Books I and X of the *Nicomachean Ethics* suggests a tension in his position. In Book I, he stresses our social nature, explaining that "[w]e do not mean by self-sufficiency what suffices for someone by himself, living a solitary life, but what is sufficient also with respect to parents, off-spring, a wife, and, in general, one's friends and fellow citizens, since by nature a human being is political."[7] Nevertheless, in answering the question of whether the political or the contemplative life is best, Aristotle concludes that "the wise person, by contrast [with persons characterized by the moral virtues], is capable of contemplating even when by himself, and the wiser he is, the more capable of doing so he will be. And though it is perhaps better to have those with whom he may work, nonetheless he is the most self-sufficient."[8] Self-sufficiency is never complete but always a matter of degree, yet at the end of the *Ethics* Aristotle presses us towards independence as much as possible. While he attends to the complex dependencies and interdependencies we have as rational animals, his ultimate ideal celebrates the independence achieved by thought.

Despite a tendency to celebrate independence, Aristotle recognizes the importance of the broader environment that affects the development and activities of individuals in at least five ways that illustrate his appreciation for the kind of relation and interrelation that lie at the heart of environmental thinking. *First*, as we have already noted, the virtues are acquired excellences and so require human influence for their development. The intellectual virtues require training in formal education. The moral virtues are acquired through habituating the behavior of role models who themselves possess the virtues. Furthermore, the person of practical wisdom is vital in determining the mean relative to individuals, much as Milo the wrestler requires a wise coach to determine his proper nutritional and exercise regime. *Second*, many of the moral virtues are inherently social, representing excellent ways of treating and interacting with others. Justice is the chief exemplar of this, but generosity and friendliness also require a social environment for their exercise. *Third*, Aristotle considers a life without the presence of friends to be incomplete. While there are diverse forms of friendship based on the different kinds of goods possible, the most significant is that rooted in shared good character, thus interweaving friendship with moral virtue.

The *fourth* manner in which the environment bears on virtues concerns the broader patterns of communal life. These are represented in both government and in city construction. Proper cultivation of the virtues requires good role models who can exemplify and teach the different virtues. Government must be conducive to promoting the virtues as well. These are rather apparent, though sometimes neglected, contextual factors that indicate the extent to which the virtues are social and as such implicate human contexts indicative of the need for environmental thinking. We can reinforce the relevance environmental thinking plays in Aristotle by noting parallels with Hippocrates. While Aristotle's references to this great physician (or, more accurately, school of physicians) tend to be brief, his indebtedness to Hippocrates is apparent in two ways. First, Aristotle grants that health is an external good required for flourishing. His doctrine of the mean shares with the Hippocratic conception of health an emphasis on balance, on what is precisely right.[9] For Hippocrates, this balance concerns the four humors internal to the human body, and, importantly, he recognizes the temporal and spatial factors that affect these as well. Persons born during different seasons have distinct humors that dominate. Character and health cannot be understood in abstraction from broader environment factors. Additionally, Hippocrates attends to the geographical location of cities, especially their comportment relative to the winds and the ways this affects the health of its citizens.[10] Aristotle echoes this concern in *Politics* Book VII Chapter 11 when he notes that the location and position of a city—hence its general natural environment—affect matters of public health, political convenience, and military and economic strategy. He argues that the ideal position of a city is facing either the East or the South, for these areas are most optimally affected by the winds.

Fifth, while virtues can be celebrated in their own right as excellent or admirable character traits—Aristotle argues that we prize them for themselves—virtues are importantly constitutive of human flourishing or the good life. Strictly speaking, Aristotle is better identified as a eudaemonist than a virtue ethicist. Linking virtues to the larger canvass of a human life characterized by flourishing is environmentally reasonable, for as Aristotle notes, we more readily cultivate and exercise the virtues when there are social structures—ranging from specific forms of education to specific laws—deliberately chosen for their effect on our character. Additionally, appealing to human flourishing provides us a broader context and set of criteria for determining whether virtues are sufficiently good. Without such an appeal, courage becomes a trait that is exhibited virtuously as readily by thieves as by saints.[11] The case that courage is a moral virtue is bolstered by its connection with human flourishing.

While human flourishing provides a larger context for considering the virtues, Aristotle's teleology may give some pause, especially to the extent that it stands in tension with both evolutionary thinking and socio-political theories that stress pluralism in an environmentally conscious manner. The chief challenge posed in moving from virtues to flourishing is Aristotle's requirement that we specify *the* human good. Typically, this has been achieved by identifying the telos or essence of humans. Contemporary discourse has sensitized us to not only the variability in accounts of our nature but also the moral and political privileges that are often illicitly and uncritically codified or simply restated by such a move. Aristotle's celebration of the life of a philosopher, predicated on leisure made possible by the labor of an underclass, illustrates the limits of the essentialist move. Failure to recognize the context taken for granted thus proves a problem at this point in Aristotle's thinking. The denial of essentialism does not, however, leave us without recourse to more nuanced and flexible ends. Since essentialism problematically identifies a single, and usually overdetermined, end that insufficiently represents the goods and modes of flourishing appropriate to a range of people, contemporary thinkers like Alasdair MacIntyre and Julia Annas have broadened our conception of the appropriate candidates for ends indicative of human flourishing. In *After Virtue*, MacIntyre identifies the quest for the good, embedded in ongoing traditions, as the kind of good that can legitimately countenance various forms of human flourishing. He contends that "the good life for man is the life spent in seeking the good life for man, and the virtues necessary for the seeking are those which will enable us to understand what more and what else the good life for man is."[12] MacIntyre still appeals to distinctive human traits, but in a more pluralistic mode that allows for variable expression. In *Intelligent Virtue*, Julia Annas offers a comparable view. Annas contends that while we all aim to live the good life, we each clothe this admittedly abstract aim as we live, reflectively seeking a to realize and coherently organize our various goods and activities in an ongoing manner. She argues that "[t]he final end, then, is the indeterminate notion of what I am aiming at in my life as a whole. And the role ethical thinking is to get is to think more determinately about it, to do a better and more intelligently ordered job of what we are already doing anyway."[13] In MacIntyre and Annas's accounts, flourishing still provides the key criterion relative to which the virtues are justified but without the restrictions of a controversial and perhaps arbitrarily selected essential feature that privileges some humans over others.

One final component of the Aristotelian mindset relevant to contemporary environmental thinking is his recognition of the teleological nature of *all* creatures. Nonhuman living beings—whether animals or plants—all have unique patterns of flourishing that are appropriate to their kind. MacIntyre embraces this Aristotelian position but further highlights the continuities between different kinds of creatures. In *Dependent Rational Animals*, he follows Aristotle in attributing practical wisdom to nonhumans, especially dolphins, arguing that our neglect of continuities with nonhumans blinds us not only to their welfare but also to our own vulnerabilities.

As a consequence, MacIntyre both attends to the flourishing of others and remedies the traditional emphasis on self-sufficiency by articulating virtues of dependence that regulate obligations of giving and receiving. More specifically, he argues that it is impossible to become an independent rational thinker without cultivating virtues of dependence which make possible our moral and intellectual development and which generate obligations to give to others that complement the ways we have received from others. We will return to MacIntye below. For now, it suffices to emphasize his status as a philosopher who acknowledges, revises, and expands upon resources in Aristotle, many of which I have argued are conducive to environmental thinking that moves *beyond*.

WHITEHEADIAN ENVIRONMENTS

Whitehead's metaphysics is a rich system that emphasizes contextual embeddedness in a manner that gives us resources for thinking more fully beyond the simple boundaries of the typical substantialist view of the human self. Environments are prominent in Whitehead's philosophy in a variety of ways. The first concerns his general tendency to promote environmental thinking. In speaking of systems, for instance, he offers a paradigmatic claim: "There is always a vague 'beyond,' waiting for penetration in respect to its details."[14] Similarly, Whitehead characterizes the act of expression, which he interprets broadly, as representing "the immanence of the finite in the multitude of its fellows beyond itself."[15] Most generally, Whitehead gives primacy to relations, thereby indicating that individuality is a function of relations and context. Environmental thinking is fundamentally the process of going beyond, especially going beyond the notion of independent individuals that can both be and be understood apart from their relations to other things. Whitehead's rejection of the fallacy of simple location lies at the heart of his philosophy.

Environment is also central to Whitehead's fundamental unit, the actual entity, which is inherently relational. Each entity inherits from its past and contributes to its future; it is both subject and superject. As such, the actual entity provides the basis for more complex social forms of being whose constituent members share common features by virtue of which they influence and are influenced by one another. As such, interdependence is a given; independence is a myth generated by abstraction from or neglect of these relations and the conditions they provide to any entity. Every actual entity has an environment from which it arises and which it objectifies; in turn, it affects subsequent entities in its superjective nature and so constitutes part of their environment. Whitehead's actual entity is a social entity; it is inherently bound up with a world beyond itself.

Beyond actual entities are societies that endure; Whitehead considers these, and not actual entities, the proper analogue for traditional substances.[16] A society is a nexus that exhibits social order. It is a group of mutually immanent entities whose members share a common form by virtue of their prehensions of one another; the members share in genetic derivation from one another, imposing on one another the conditions that bind them together as a society. Whitehead stresses that societies constitute environments, explaining that "a set of entities is a society (i) in virtue of a 'defining characteristic' shared by its members, and (ii) in virtue of the presence of the defining characteristic being due to the environment provided by the society itself."[17] Even that which endures is thoroughly relational.

Societies are best considered contexts which are themselves embedded within contexts. Whitehead argues that "there is no society in isolation. Every society must be considered with its background of a wider environment of actual entities, which also contribute their objectifications to which the members of the society must conform."[18] We find this kind of embeddedness throughout nature. In living societies, amid nonliving societies there are subordinate societies that are living, i.e., that are characterized by mental spontaneities that "do not thwart each other, but are directed to a common objective amid varying circumstances."[19] This common objective represents the teleological introduction of novelty, a steady purpose of an organism made possible by the larger complex coordination of societies that constitute, for instance, a human. In humans, the animal body is a society of occasions that are spatially and temporally coordinated, but that body is dominated by a subordinate personal society whose members enjoy serial succession. As Whitehead explains, "the living body is permeated by living societies of low-grade occasions so far as mentality is concerned. But the whole is coordinated so as to support a personal living society of high-grade occasions. This personal society is the man defined as a person."[20] Persons are not simply located, however. Whitehead argues that "the world beyond is so intimately entwined in our own natures that unconsciously we identify our more vivid perspectives of it with ourselves. For example, our bodies lie beyond our own existence. And yet they are part of it. . . . But the body is part of the external world, continuous with it . . . if we are fussily exact, we cannot define where a body begins and where external nature ends."[21]

In living organisms, then, we have enduring objects that are themselves an environment or, as Whitehead calls it, "a subordinate universe [that] includes subordinate enduring objects."[22] Some environments constitute the complex structured societies which constitute living bodies. As societies, each member shares a definite character qua member of that society. In its complexity, though, the environment introduces sufficient novelty that the stability provided by the society itself is matched with the intensity of satisfaction of some of its members. (This novelty can be either abstracted from, in the case of inorganic bodies, or added to and intensified, in the case of living bodies.) These members with their intensified novelty arise by virtue of, and depend upon, the more stable structures provided by their larger environment. Without such stability, there would be insufficient resources from which to draw novelty.

Life constitutes the dominant character of a highly specialized form of society. That character requires a heightened degree of novelty.

For such novelty to arise and be efficacious in sustaining itself, it must occur against a larger background of stable order. Life, whether human or not, is dependent on the special organization of ordering of the living body that makes it a possibility. Without such order, there can be no heightened inheritance indicative of life. Moreover, the living body is itself made possible by its relation to the larger order of its environment, and so forth.

Translated into more familiar terms, living creatures require an environment that is rich in sustaining resources. By itself, that environment occasions the possibility of life; living creatures adapt to the environment and also modify it to suit their needs. But the important point is that the relationship of dependence is fundamental. Even among those structured societies that make up organisms that can move from physical environment to physical environment, thereby demonstrating some degree of independence, complete independence is impossible. Change the stabilities too fully and the novelties derived from it collapse. Rid our environment of oxygen or change the ground to lava and humans can no longer survive.

Drawing on Whitehead's philosophy, then, we have grounds for arguing that self-sufficiency is thus always contextual and a matter of degree. We *are* capable of abstracting from virtually everything in our environment, thinking on thinking, as it were. But abstraction is always abstraction *from*, and to the extent that we act without due recognition of this fact—thereby treating contextual independence as absolute—we potentially (and today increasingly) undercut the conditions of stability that make possible our unique but dependent and fragile form of life.

MacIntyre, then, is very right to characterize us as dependent rational animals, though the dependence goes beyond that of a body or a social group of humans to an ecology that includes other living things as well as inorganic chemical and physical conditions. Our embeddedness, however, is a double-edged sword. On the one hand, we cannot survive without our environment. On the other hand, what we do also affects the environment. Whereas in the past only a limited range of human action modified these larger societies in any measurable manner, today many of them do so both quickly and on a large scale. This is the key source of the dangers we face.

BEYOND HUMAN VIRTUE

If this Whiteheadian interpretation of individuals as environmentally conditioned and situated is correct, we should expect to find plenty of evidence in our world of factors of dependence and interdependence. We should expect that beyond human virtue lie environments that constitute conditions necessary for our survival and flourishing but that are also replete with other, nonanthropocentric values. In this section, I argue that the sciences, with their attention to and curiosity about nonhuman life forms, offer this kind of evidence, helping us better understand other creatures' unique modes of flourishing and the ways in which these affect us. I here consider new insights and theories generated by the sciences that help us look beyond human virtue in two general ways. The first moves *outward* to nonhuman creatures—including nonhuman animals and also plants—with whom we interact and share environments. The second looks *within* to the microbiota that affect our health and impact the exercise of our virtues.

Looking outward, our most pervasive environment includes conditions pertinent to the survival and flourishing of the life forms we know. While there may be public debate about the outer limits, no one seriously contends that we can live without the rather specialized environment that our planet provides, replete with carbon and oxygen, within a fairly narrow but stable temperature range. Also uncontroversial is the fact that animal life depends upon plant life and that, while some of our actions at times belie the fact, what happens in one group of creatures tends to affect another. We typically ignore these basic conditions precisely because they are stable. Nevertheless, one lesson from our increased knowledge of the natural world—whether concerning physical and chemical laws governing its processes or the dynamic balances created between living creatures and systems—is that we should not take these conditions for granted or think them infinitely plastic. Astro- and geobiologists Peter Ward and Joe Kirschvink argue that our aerobic environment developed gradually over Earth's history.[23] Aerobic environments are perhaps the chief environmental conditions we take for granted, but our increased knowledge of the Earth's history and its occupants demonstrates that this is not a given but a contingent consequence of nonhuman life processes. Distinct phases of extinction indicate that life in its present form is but one of many different possibilities concerning, for example, the types of specific species that occupy the planet or their size and nutritional needs. Our technological advances, coupled with practices of farming exercised on increasingly wider scales, have shown that our capacity to modify the environment can be dramatic and quick. Responsible attention to the effects of such modifications and how they impact our survival is a minimal requirement of prudence.

Our broader environments support a diversity of life forms to which we are infrequently attentive and whose discontinuities with our own characteristics we tend to exaggerate. Too often we consider our own welfare independent of that of others and consider ourselves wholly unique among the creatures of the Earth. As we have noted, MacIntyre argues in *Dependent Rational Animals* that we should attend to the welfare of nonhuman creatures because they do in fact flourish in complex ways that are often aided by social modes of interaction not unlike our own. While we might think that perception of environmental resources and changes, intelligent adaptation and modification of the environment, and complex social modes of interaction that can be learned to make possible more complex or efficient action are the exclusive property of human animals, evidence suggests otherwise. Dolphins, for instance, demonstrate learned social behavior that contributes to their distinctive mode of flourishing;

MacIntyre notes that they "flourish only because they have learned how to achieve their goals" such as hunting or playing "through strategies concerted with other members of the different groups to which they belong or which they encounter."[24] Like humans, they communicate via sound to coordinate group behavior, and adults engage in direct tutoring of the young. While not human, their perceptual and communicative activities can be characterized as prelinguistic rather than nonlinguistic, finding expression in ways that parallel the prelinguistic abilities of human children.[25]

One benefit of attending to nonhuman flourishing is better understanding the ways animal vulnerability affects our own flourishing. More precisely, a deeper understanding of human flourishing arises from considering analogues of human behavior in nonhuman creatures, especially the social dynamics of educating the young and caring for the vulnerable. In a manner reminiscent of Whitehead, MacIntyre notes that "[h]uman identity is primarily, even if not only, bodily and therefore animal identity and it is by reference to that identity that the continuities of our relationships to others are partly defined." Considering these continuities reveals the fascinating complexities we too often assume to typify only our own species. It also chips away at our propensity to celebrate self-sufficiency in our moral life. By contrast, MacIntyre argues that "the virtues of *independent* rational agency need for their adequate exercise to be accompanied by . . . the virtues of acknowledged *dependence* and that a failure to understand this is apt to obscure some features of rational agency."[26]

Even as we aspire to realize degrees of independence in our rational life, we remain dependent animals. MacIntyre argues that "adult human activity and beliefs are best understood as developing out of, and as still in part dependent upon, modes of belief and activity that we share with other species of intelligent animal."[27] Failure to attend to these is problematic since "without the virtues we cannot adequately protect ourselves and each other against neglect, defective sympathies, stupidity, acquisitiveness, and malice."[28] Our dependence—a condition we all share but that is especially apparent in children and those beset by illness, disease, or loss of ability—gives rise to what MacIntyre describes as *virtues of acknowledged dependence*, e.g., generosity, compassion, attentiveness, and care. These virtues perform the important role of ensuring that the young learn how to function in social contexts. They also find vital expression in caring for the vulnerable and maintaining healthy relationships, constituting a supportive social environment. MacIntyre argues that there is a reciprocal relationship between the norms of giving and receiving; "like virtues of giving, those of receiving are needed in order to sustain just those types of communal relationship through which the exercise of these virtues first has to be learned."[29] Even when we mature and flourish, the relative independence we achieve is a consequence of our dependence as animals on the complex modes of attention and expression we develop through interaction with other humans. MacIntyre's full position is that the key to becoming an independent practical reasoner is developing and acknowledging virtues of dependence which concern the reciprocal relations of receiving and giving.

Of course, studying primates reveals that their flourishing, too, grows out of the social dynamics that condition and constitute non-human welfare. Orangutans have the longest primate childhood, at eight years. During that time, the mother teaches her single offspring food selection, determining what is edible and when it is ripe or safe to eat, as well as how to gauge the strength of branches needed for traveling amongst the trees. Tocque macaques live in a rigid hierarchy with specific social conventions. When the dominant male looks his subordinates in the eye, they must show submission by chattering their teeth or suffer the consequences; this applies to the very young and must be learned quite early to ensure group membership. Frans de Waal has done extensive research on primates that further testifies to the continuities between humans and nonhumans, especially concerning the norms that impact their behavior. In *Primates and*

Philosophers, he offers data suggesting that bonobos and chimpanzees are capable of cognitive empathy—i.e., empathy coupled with an appraisal of the situation and needs of others—as well as targeted helping.[30] De Waal provides evidence of gratitude and consolation behavior among members of the same group. Additionally, he recounts an instance in which Kuni, the bonobo, when prompted to release a bird she captured, unfolded its wings and threw it. De Waal argues that this cross-species interaction demonstrates Kuni's recognition of flight as what is good for a bird (though surely not for a bonobo) and acted to help the bird. The lives of nonhuman creatures are not as thin as we sometimes suppose.

Both MacIntyre and de Waal identify important analogues that suggest continuities between human morality and the nonhuman behavior. They help shrink the perceived gap between humans and nonhumans by acknowledging both that animals are more complex than we sometimes assume and that humans share significant modes of behavior with our nonhuman kin. Some animals—human and nonhuman—are capable of developing and applying modes of intelligence and social interaction that contribute to their flourishing. We creatures share evolutionary pasts and so occupy worlds that are less distinct than we often assume. Our blindness to these facts obscures possible alternatives within human life—shortchanging virtues of receptivity, as MacIntyre argues—but beyond, giving us the dubious sense that we are evolution's finest and highest product. That we need to overcome such biases—seeking larger connections and continuities in the kind of expansive vision that wonder generates—is further reinforced by Barbara Natterson-Horowitz's argument in *Zoobiquity* that we need to join the cultures of human and animal medicine to discover whether humans and animals might suffer comparable conditions.[31] Her proposal is not that we should do research on nonhuman animals given their likeness to us, but that what we know of illness, disease, and healing in the animal kingdom often translates to humans as well. Too frequently, physicians neglect what veterinarians have already discovered, even when the latter know more about a disease that affects both humans and animals. Physicians and veterinarians let the fact that their patients belong to different species prevent them from sharing the results of one another's practices. Natterson-Horowitz's draws evidence from comparative oncology to show that risk of breast cancer is reduced in animals who lactate and that viruses sometimes play a causative role. Zoobiquity, she argues, can also enhance our understanding sexual health. For instance, erectile dysfunction isn't all (though it can be partly) in one's head; animals get a version of it too. (Natterson-Horowitz suggests that "failed copulations across species are connected through ancient neural feedback loops that protect mating males;"[32] it is a response to danger in the environment that impedes the relaxation needed for an erection.) Moreover, understanding the ways animal feeding varies with seasonal access to food and the overall life cycle facilitates increased understanding of obesity as a disease of the environment. Refusing to consider or share information with other doctors because patients belong to different species impedes understanding of the operative mechanism and the preventive measures we can take. Vets, for instance, understood the relevance of the microbiome in affecting animal metabolic function sooner than physicians and have used fecal therapy to normalize patients' digestive tracts after the administration of antibiotics.[33]

It is easy to forget that while many of us today accept claims about the continuities of human and nonhuman animal behavior, such a move was viewed as unproductive and unacceptable not so long ago. But while we might go beyond human virtue to acknowledge modes of flourishing that perhaps implicate virtue analogues among nonhuman animals, is there any reason to go beyond even *that*? There are two such reasons. First, the more we learn about the development of cells and the varied functions that occur within them, the more justification we have for considering nature to be replete with dynamic interactivity. The specific nature a cell assumes is a function of its relation to surrounding cells, thereby illustrating

Whitehead's account of the social nature of certain nexūs of actual occasions. Second, while plants are in many respects significantly different from animals in lacking mobility and sense organs, they respond to their environments in patterned ways that enable them to flourish. Evolutionary theory suggests that all of life is responsive to interactive pressures, and we now have reason to think there are analogues to sensual and communal life among plants, suggesting greater degrees of complexity that close the gap between humans and nonhumans.

Botanist James Cayhill argues that there is evidence that plants exhibit behavior. They perceive and actively interact with their environments in more complex ways than we often acknowledge. Plants have environments, i.e., interact with things beyond them in a manner that affects their functioning and flourishing, from the soil and air to predators and compatible creatures of the same or different species. They register and respond to facts about their environment, from where to find nutritive resources above or below ground to whether there are predators in the environment against which they should take defensive measures. Cayhill explains that plants engage in foraging, finding food in a manner not wholly disconnected from that of animals. Time lapse videos reveal plant behavior more nuanced and complex than what we glean from our everyday observations. Their roots grow directionally and at different paces, speeding up as they grow towards patches of nutrients and effectively slowing down once they arrive to feast on the banquet. The current hypothesis is that plant foraging results from homing in on chemical language. While plants cannot move, they can alter their chemical composition to communicate with neighboring plants and insects. For instance, Ian Baldwin argues that the wild tobacco plant when faced with predation can change quite dramatically by switching pollinators in less than eight days. It typically flowers at night when it attracts moths as its chief pollinators. These moths tend to lay their eggs on the leaves of the plants, though, which emerge as caterpillars that can decimate their host's foliage. In response, the tobacco plant can shift its blooming period from night to dawn, change the composition of its nectar and so the smell that attracts insects, and even change the shape of its flowers to accommodate new pollinators, becoming more elongated for instance to favor hummingbirds. The plant's perception is chemical based rather than sensory or nerve based, but it is interactive and purposive all the same. Some botanists suggest that plants share and integrate information, indicating that they have a system akin to our nervous systems. Botanist Daniel Chamovitz, for instance, contends that plants perceive factors of light, odors, and sound in their environment by virtue of having analogues to animal sensory systems. He argues that plants respond and adapt in patterned ways that promote their well-being. They convey and respond to information both internally and externally, especially concerning light, and they do this partly in virtue of the same genes that function comparably in us.[34] Hence, capacities like sensing and processing information that we identify as integral features of our human experience have deep biological roots in nonhuman and nonanimal life.

Some plants also appear to engage in discriminating social behavior that involves not only members of their own species but also those of others. Forest ecologist Suzanne Simard's research on Douglas fir forests, for instance, indicates that they develop complex symbiotic relationship with networks of mycorrhizal fungi that connect them to other Douglas firs.[35] This is most advantageous to young saplings whose vulnerability is heightened by their limited access to resources both above and underground. Mycorrhizal fungi grow at the tips of the roots of the firs. They not only receive nutrients from the trees but also provide the firs access to nutrients from spaces too small for the tree's roots. Importantly, nutrients (typically carbon and nitrogen) also seem to be shuttled from "mother" firs to saplings by means of these networks. While plants certainly compete with other living organisms for resources, the firs also engage in facilitative relationships, creating social networks in forests that exist above but mostly below ground. Human practices such as clear-cutting may seem well-intentioned—we think that by removing larger trees we give younger trees more access to the sun—but risk failing to recognize the complex relationships that have evolved but remain undetected in ordinary human perception. (Fir saplings do just fine without us, requiring fungi rather than clear-cutting.) Again, our new technology, from time-lapse photography to the use of radioactive carbon to trace pathways of nutrient sharing, offers evidence of greater complexity in nonhuman life. The relevant data suggest that humans are not alone in cultivating social modes of interaction that facilitate distinct modes of flourishing.

Thus far, our consideration of what lies beyond human virtue has concerned beings and processes occurring *outside* the human body. *Within* that body, however, we have learned that there is much complex activity that implicates more than simply the human being. Complicating even further our tendency to prioritize ourselves is evidence that we individual humans are in important ways unique ecosystems that include not only what we traditionally identify as "human" cells but also bacteria and perhaps some parasites. On this account, there is an environment within us whose welfare is inseparable from our own. Each of us houses in our guts a complex microbiota that is at once sustained by us and sustains us as well. As biologist Alanna Collen argues in her book, *10% Human*, "At their microscopic size, the body of another organism, particularly a macro-scale backboned creature like a human, represents not just a single niche, but an entire world of habitats, ecosystems and opportunities . . . for microbes, this is Eden."[36] These bacteria process portions of our food we cannot digest; they also aid in the processing and sharing of nutrients we lack the mechanisms to break down. Without these bacteria, then, human nutritional processes would not be possible. We feed the bacteria, and they feed us, generating a symbiotic relationship. Moreover, we have evolved together. In a sense our bodies represent the environment not only for the personal threads of conscious life (to recall Whitehead's position) but also the billions of bacterial cells that outnumber the strictly human cells. Each of us is a mobile ecosystem.[37] Any pretense that the bacteria reside in our guts exclusively for our sake is quickly dashed when we realize how readily they can make us ill. Maintaining a proper balance of bacteria is crucial to our health, in a manner akin to but more complex than what Hippocrates envisioned. We could not survive without at least some of these bacteria, and our health is impacted by an improper balance of them.

Much like Collen, biologist Rob Dunn argues that our inattention to the complex (ecological) interactions between humans and the parasites that live within us is harming us. A variety of converging factors have created something of a perfect storm. The first is our discovery that antibiotics can kill germs that cause illness and disease. This discovery has brought much relief and saved many lives. Unfortunately, however, we have and continue to apply this discovery indiscriminately, killing widely. Sometimes we aim to kill some germs but inadvertently kill many, upsetting the balances that have evolved between human and parasite or microbe to the mutual benefit of each and leaving a vacancy in our systems for new germs to invade. At other times, we simply aim to kill all germs, hoping to promote our own welfare through the wholesale destruction of different albeit microscopic species. Dunn views this as an extension of our capacity to control what lives around us,[38] driven to such an extreme that we destroy species and ecosystems, usually without considering what effect their absence might have on our welfare. Collen notes that we suffer the delusion that anything that appears to be "non-self" is dangerous and needs to be attacked.[39] We not only neglect the environment beyond or without us, but we also do the same for the environment within. We forget that our parasites and microbes co-evolved with us. Often they perform functions which we cannot, such as providing enzymes we lack that are nevertheless needed to digest our preferred diets. (This fact is true for termite-microbe as well as for human-microbe relations.) Our immunity system similarly evolved interacting with these creatures. Eradicating them without understanding the consequences of our typically wholesale efforts may contribute to contemporary ailments, from Crohn's disease and autism to preponderance of allergies and obesity. Mental health and development may also be affected, as depression has some links to the welfare of our microbiota.

If dysbiosis, or imbalances of our microbiota, contributes to developmental problems and disease, it is likely because disturbing our microbiome (with antibiotics, for instance) typically reduces its diversity in a manner that affects how the different microbes interact. As Collen argues, "Diversity will drop. Sensitive species will die out. Invaders will flourish."[40] Research on rats, especially of the germ-free variety, provides preliminary support for the hypothesis that an array of relatively new human diseases, including autism and epidemic obesity, may result from the microbiotic imbalances that our germophobic practices are creating. It is believed there may be a gut-brain connection such that imbalances in the gut of developing children affects the genes activated in brain development. A contributing factor to obesity may be dysbiosis that causes fat cells to extend through inflammation, changing the ways they store energy.[41] Obesity is not a matter of simply creating more fat cells. The rise in cases of allergies and irritable bowel syndrome may similarly be rooted in dysbiosis.

If these diagnoses are accurate, it is simplistic to conclude that obese people are merely intemperate, or that socially and mentally challenged children simply lack self-control. A poor diet and excessive eating may be contributing factors to obesity, but biological factors concerning the species that live within us appear to be as well. The conclusion to draw is not that virtues are thereby not matters of personal achievement but rather that environmental factors play some role in their development and maintenance. Happily, we can monitor and, perhaps, modify these factors. Our current behavior, prompted by a false image of human autonomy and independence from environmental factors, is something we can change with knowledge of the delicate balances that exist between us and what we tend to think of as "not-us." Socrates may have been right after all that a good measure of virtue is knowledge, albeit knowledge of the conditions that make optimal health and activity possible.

Some hope that probiotics and even fecal transplants may provide remedies to some of our current ailments. Fecal transplants are rather unpleasant, and so it is no surprise that, as Collen notes, some researchers hope to develop a pill form as a more palatable alternative to existing measures of repopulating the gut. Such a response, however, risks being simplistic and masking the important insights the growing knowledge of our microbiota offers us of ourselves as complex ecosystems. While we are right to consider solutions to existing problems, we should be mindful of relevant complications, especially those that result from failing to think environmentally about the complex dependencies and interdependencies of humans and their nonhuman partners.

A key challenge some persons suffering from a disturbed microbiome face is that responsive measures may come too late and offer too little to restore the needed balance. Most studies Collen discusses indicate that it is not merely our microbes but their interaction that is pertinent to our welfare. As dandelions are quick to harvest freshly plowed fields, so too can one strain of microbe that is harmless when balanced with others proliferate and cause damage when presented with a gut cleansed of many microbes via antibiotics. If we suppose that our ailments are the result of a single species of bacteria, we fall prey to a version of the fallacy of simple location. We need to think holistically about our microbiota. Just as we should be critical of conceptions of the self that render it a simply located individual rather than a complex system, so too should we view gut microbiota in an ecological manner.

Collen and Dunn's discussions offer us lessons about ourselves that counterbalance tendencies to exaggerate our independence and self-sufficiency. As just noted, we need to think of and treat our microbes in relation to one another. Achieving maximal health is not a simple matter of eradicating the "bad" microbes, for what counts as bad is a function of the balance between diverse microbial populations. Additionally, since humans have co-evolved with microbes, thinking of evolution as a linear process that simplistically culminates in the genesis of higher beings is dubious. The so-called higher beings live in active ongoing relationships with the so-called simple or lower life forms. The evidence Dunn and Collen offer us suggests we may best view the human self as an ecosystem whose health requires a balance of self and non-self. Of course, one distinguishing mark of humans—even when understood as ecosystems—is that we have the capacity to move about and adjust to different environments. For example, we can tolerate a range of climates. Nevertheless, this range is not infinite, and its limits are not negligible. We are socially dependent and interdependent creatures, and this calls for an increased appreciation of our vulnerability as well as our kinship with the vital integrity of other creatures.

The danger of our tendency to seek control of our environment without thinking environmentally is exacerbated by the blindness created by the specialization of knowledge. In addition to Natterson-Horowitz's call for greater exchange of knowledge between experts of human and nonhuman animals, the other authors we have here considered show the need for more sensitive attention to nonmammalian life. What is known about the ecological balance between ants and certain fungi that promotes their mutual welfare, for instance, tends to remain relatively unknown to those who study the human body, even though there may be parallels with humans and our microbes. Too often the presupposition of human distinctness and superiority—the belief that our nature and our achievements arise in notable independence from anything beyond us—impedes both broader and deeper understanding. Dunn argues that what we lack in our efforts to understand ourselves and our welfare is an "ideal distance," namely one "far enough away (figuratively) to see both termite bodies and human bodies, but also the big sweep of the ecological world. From such a distance it is hard to avoid looking at ants."[42] Wonder and generalist perspectives are needed, whether in philosophers, scientists, or journalists. These wider perspectives are among the key virtues of informed environmental thinking.

The diverse data and perspectives we have considered in this section indicate relevant features of the environments that lie beyond the narrow scope of human virtue and even human flourishing. They highlight factors that suggest greater continuity between human and nonhuman forms of life, especially relative to those who would suggest our uniqueness and independence from the rest of nature. Critics will likely object to two components of the position we have developed. The first is the admittedly tentative nature of some of the scientific positions here presented. Most concern research from the past two decades, and in the scope of scientific investigations, this is a narrow window. We can only acknowledge this limitation, but it marks an important shift away from the all-too-frequent refusal to consider or take seriously continuities that evolutionary theory makes all the more likely.

A second concern is that, especially in operating from the perspective of human virtue, the goods we have espoused are too anthropocentric and the values attributed to nonhumans are largely instrumental. Whitehead is a resource here, for his philosophy indicates that just as every entity is both self and other-functioning, so too does each entity have intrinsic as well as extrinsic or instrumental value. Indeed, the instrumental value of an entity expresses its other-functioning side in its superjective nature, and this is in turn a function of its self-functioning. Acknowledging this Whiteheadian insight presents us with the challenge of overcoming our tendency to either neglect the intrinsic value of nonhuman beings and life forms or to unduly prioritize human lives and systems over nonhuman. This tendency is formidable, but one resource we have and can augment, especially as teachers, is the virtue of wonder. Wonder-fueled education is not a silver bullet; complex problems impacted by so many diverse contexts—biological, economic, political, even religious—admit of no easy solutions. Nevertheless, we are prudent to make ample use of our existing resources, especially those like wonder, even as we seek new means of understanding and better orienting ourselves towards the environment. In the next and final section, I offer general points about how wonder might function more fully.

CONCLUSION

This returns us to our theme of environmental thinking, especially as it is funded by wonder. In my experience of wonder, curiosity has always been a dominant component. When in a state of wonder, I do not simply stand in awe of something beyond my grasp; I reach out towards it. Aristotle notes that ignorance is a key condition that inclines us to wonder. He is no doubt right about that, but there is more. Wonder prompts me to investigate, and what I usually find is complexity that prompts even further consideration. Overcoming ignorance is not the only factor involved: being fascinated with what is before me is operative as well. Recall the opening line of Aristotle's *Metaphysics*: "All humans by nature desire understanding."[43] This is a respectable translation, but it is worthwhile to consider alternatives to "desire," so shopworn has the term become. The Greek term is ὀρέγονται, and one of its meanings is to reach or stretch out towards. In wonder we reach out towards the world in a continuous manner. We learn more, and this generates more questions that prompt us to continue reaching out. Fascination with the new may threaten to overwhelm us; this is why discipline must complement curiosity. Wonder possesses a dynamic tension between novelty and order, between attention to details and consideration of networks of relation that span ever outward in the experience.

We need more thinkers like Aristotle, driven by an unquenchable thirst to investigate the world around him. The way his philosophy exemplifies this drive is probably more important than his final conclusions, though examining his positions helps us appreciate the need to critically question our presuppositions on a regular basis. Similarly, we need more thinkers like Whitehead, people who have facility with the burgeoning bodies of new knowledge arising in scientific contexts and also capable of engaging in sophisticated speculation that seeks connections to articulate a "big picture." Dunn argues for something comparable, and though he does not seem to have in mind creating generations of philosophical scientists or scientific philosophers, his position is very compatible with such a goal. Dunn and most of the other thinkers whose works we have considered represent the kind of environmentally minded intellectual we need to cultivate in our classrooms. While many of the crises we face are urgent, requiring those who think environmentally to successfully engage contemporary adults who make decisions with long-range consequences, generations arise quickly. We should also reflect carefully on the ways in which we can imbue the minds and characters of our youth with an enhanced sense of wonder, preserving and augmenting their natural curiosity with a sustaining discipline.

The first steps in achieving this goal are fairly straightforward. One is to promote and hold ourselves accountable to environmental thinking in our professional lives. One of the enduring strengths of the virtue tradition is its emphasis on mentoring and modeling preferred behavior. When speaking of the natural world, too many teachers espouse a view one student recently expressed to me: "I don't know any science, but here's what I would say . . ." Instead of faux humility that gives rise to an unsupported or ill-informed interpretation, we need genuine efforts to inquire and investigate. We should not and do not need to merely speculate, especially about our fellow creatures, when we have the rich resources the sciences provide us. Of course, we need to remain critical of scientific investigations, including the reigning presuppositions and values, but such criticism requires scientific literacy. MacIntyre's appeal to Aristotle as the philosopher to which we should turn when it comes to thinking about the activities and flourishing of nonhuman creatures should be a striking wake-up call. Is our only resource really a philosopher who lived some 2500 years ago? We have many contemporary colleagues who investigate the natural world with sharper tools and offer more nuanced insights. They should be our regular conversation-partners. So should their students. Philosophy classes are enriched not only by attracting students in the sciences but also by encouraging them to share their knowledge, their insights, and their questions. Comparably, we should recommend that philosophy majors take classes that provide them with a broad range of knowledge relevant to the moral, metaphysical, and epistemological questions they hold dear.

Of course, this educational mission is best realized when it begins early on, taking advantage of the natural resources of youth. Young children are known for their wonder, often expressed in an unending series of questions. We can build on this propensity by connecting it to modes of scientific and philosophic investigation that are appropriate to each stage of the educational process, so that wonder and discipline develop together. We should give special care to the modes of thinking we promote, especially environmental thinking, and not simply bodies of information that are memorized and then tested. From this perspective, a key educational goal is to cultivate in our children growing attention to our dependencies and interdependencies as well as an appreciation of the complexities of other life forms and systems. Our educational endeavors can then help create more environmentally sensitive thinkers.

The recommendation to cultivate wonder can be a rather generic and meaningless gesture. To avoid such banality, let us return to the twin features of wonder, curiosity and discipline. A child's wonder is typically incited and expanded by encountering a new context or environment in which things become apparent in both their splendid particularity and in their relation to other things. The chief spurs to curiosity are the diversity, complexity, and irreducible particularity of new objects, coupled with the suggestion of rich relatedness that warrants further attention. In this digital age, there is no want of access to new information—much of it diverse and complex, but it frequently comes in a glut without any means for exploring the rewarding, meaningful connectedness of new data. The natural world with its colorful, often slimy and unusual creatures still remains unique in bringing together part and whole in organic tension and unity. Living beings relate to their environment directly, implicating varied spatial, temporal, and developmental relationships that draw our attention from one creature to its fellows, its tools, and its supportive as well as challenging environs. Whether scampering bugs, or wafting leaves and limbs, nature rarely lets our attention settle on one thing.

The second component of wonder, discipline, is all the more important in training young minds to sense and pursue the hint of deeper new connections, and so again, an adult's role as a model of inquisitive investigation provides one of the most valuable spurs to sustained exploration that generates new, deeper questions. Wonder requires available resources to prompt investigation, but it grows most readily in a community of inquirers who share new knowledge, insights, and questions. A good family physician and a thoughtful filmmaker or storyteller can be just as effective as a school teacher in cultivating a wonder-enriching context in which wonder can come to fruition.

These final comments on curiosity and the kind of environmental thinking that takes us beyond—what can aptly be called the love of learning—indicate some of the specific measures we can take as inquirers and educators. My hope is that we can cultivate generations of thinkers and writers who appreciate and ably articulate the multifarious and often complex details needed to convey a vision of the world "beyond," a vision that offers insight and guidance for our ongoing interaction with each other and with our environments.

ENDNOTES

1   Alfred North Whitehead, *Process and Reality,* Corrected Edition, ed. David Ray Griffin and Donald W. Sherburne (New York: Free Press, 1978), 55. More formally, Whitehead explains that "[t]o say that a bit of matter has simple location means that, in expressing its spatio-temporal relations, it is adequate to state that it is where it is, in a definite region of space, and throughout a definite duration of time, apart from any essential reference of the relations of that bit of matter to other regions of space and to other durations of time" (*Science and the Modern World* [New York: The Free Press, 1967], 58).

2   William James, "On a Certain Blindness in Human Beings," in *Talks to Teachers on Psychology: And To Students on Some of Life's Ideals* (New York: W.W. Norton & Co., Inc., 1958), 149–69.

3   William James, *A Pluralistic Universe* (New York: Longmans, Green and Co., 1909), 321–22.

4   Aristotle, *Metaphysics,* Book I, Chapter 1, W. D. Ross translation, available at http://classics.mit.edu/Aristotle/metaphysics.1.i.html.

5   While Whitehead does not stress the term wonder, it bears important similarities with what he calls the romantic stage of education with its emphasis on immediacy and enthusiasm. The second and third stages, precision and generalization, are needed as well in any educational enterprise, but wonder is too frequently relegated to early childhood years. My contention is that we need to attend to the ways to sustain and revitalize it. For Whitehead's account of the three stages, see "The Rhythm of Education," in *The Aims of Education* (New York: The Free Press, 1929), 15–28.

6   Alfred North Whitehead, *The Function of Reason* (New York: Beacon Press, 1971), 33.

7   *Aristotle's Nicomachean Ethics*, trans. R. Bartlett & S. Collins (Chicago: University of Chicago Press, 2011), 11 (I.7 1097b7-10).

8   *Nicomachean Ethics*, 224 (X.7 1177a32-35).

9   See *Nicomachean Ethics*, 28 (II.2 1104a12-25): "Such things [as the virtues] are naturally destroyed through deficiency and excess, just as we see in the case of strength and health." Compare to Hippocrates'

"Nature of Man" (in *Hippocrates*, Vol. 1, trans. W. H. S. Jones [New York: G. P. Putnam's Sons, 1923], 2–41): "Now he enjoys the most perfect health when these elements [blood, phlegm, yellow bile, and black bile] are duly proportioned to one another in respect of compounding, power, and bulk, and when they are perfectly mingled" (11).

10   See "Airs, Waters, and Places," in *Hippocrates*, vol. 1, trans. W. H. S. Jones (New York: G. P. Putnam's Sons, 1923), 65–137.

11   For more on this point, see my "The Ends of Courage," in *The Handbook of Virtue Ethics*, ed. Stan van Hooft (Durham: Acumen Publishing, 2014), 210–19.

12   Alasdair MacIntyre, *After Virtue,* Second Edition (Notre Dame: University of Notre Dame Press, 1984), 219.

13   Julia Annas, *Intelligent Virtue* (Oxford: Oxford University Press, 2011), 124.

14   Alfred North Whitehead, *Modes of Thought* (New York: Macmillan Co., 1938), 8.

15   Whitehead, *Modes*, 28.

16   Whitehead, *Process and Reality*, 56.

17   Whitehead, *Process*, 200.

18   Whitehead, *Process*, 201.

19   Alfred North Whitehead, *Adventures of Ideas* (New York: Free Press, 1961), 207.

20   Whitehead, *Process and Reality*, 208.

21   Whitehead, *Modes of Thought*, 29–30.

22   Whitehead, *Adventures of Ideas*, 206.

23   Peter Ward and Joe Kirschvink, *A New History of Life: The Radical New Discoveries about the Origins and Evolution of Life on Earth* (New York: Bloomsbury Press, 2015).

24   Alasdair MacIntyre, *Dependent Rational Animals: Why Human Beings Need the Virtues* (Chicago: Open Court, 1999), 22.

25   MacIntyre, *Dependent*, 37.

26   MacIntyre, *Dependent*, 8. Emphasis added.

27 MacIntyre, *Dependent*, 41.

28 MacIntyre, *Dependent*, 98.

29 MacIntyre, *Dependent* 127.

30 Frans de Waal, *Primates and Philosophers: How Morality Evolved* (Princeton: Princeton University Press, 2009), especially 41.

31 Barbara Natterson-Horowitz and Kathryn Bowers, *Zoobiquity: The Astonishing Connection Between Human and Animal Health* (New York: Alfred A. Knopf, 2012), 17.

32 Natterson-Horowitz and Bowers, *Zoobiquity, Zoobiquity*, 71.

33 Natterson-Horowitz and Bowers, *Zoobiquity*, 150.

34 Daniel Chamovitz, *What a Plant Knows: A Field Guide to the Senses* (New York: Scientific American/Farrar, Straus and Giroux, 2012). Chamovitz's conclusions should come as no surprise to students of evolution. After discussing how plants translate visual signals into physiologically recognizable instruction affecting their growth in a changing environment, Chamovitz concludes that "[t]he evolution of light perception continued from this one common photoreceptor in all organisms and diverged into the two distinct visual systems that distinguish plants from animals" (26).

35 For Simard's position, see Amanda L. Schoonmaker, Francois P. Teste, Suzanne W. Simard, and Robert D. Guy's "Tree proximity, soil pathways and common mycorrhizal networks: their influence on the utilization of redistributed water by understory seedlings," *Oecologia* 154 (2007), 455–66; François P. Teste, Suzanne W. Simard, Daniel M. Durall, Robert D. Guy, Melanie D. Jones and Amanda L. Schoonmaker's "Access to Mycorrhizal Networks and Roots of Trees: Importance for Seedling Survival and Resource Transfer," *Ecology* 90, no. 10 (2009), 2808–822; and Francois P. Teste, Suzanne W. Simard, Daniel M. Durall's "Role of mycorrhizal networks and tree proximity in ectomycorrhizal colonization of planted seedlings," *Fungal Ecology* 2 (2009), 21–30.

36 Alanna Collen, *10% Human: How Your Body's Microbes Hold the Key to Health and Happiness* (New York: Harper Collins, 2015), 11.

37 In *The Human Superorganism: How the Microboime is Revolutionizing the Pursuit of a Healthy Life* (New York: Dutton, 2016), professor of

immunotoxicology Rodney Dietert recommends that our human selves are superorganisms, each the functional equivalent of an ecosystem. Like tropical rain forests and coral reefs, the human ecosystem includes numerous diverse species (including bacteria, fungi, and viruses) living together (along with our "human" cells) in a "powerful network of ecological interactions" (31). See especially chapter 2.

38   See Rob Dunn, *The Wildlife of our Bodies: Predators, Parasites, and Partners That Shape Who We Are Today* (New York: Harper Perennial, 2011), 12.

39   Collen, *10% Human*, 120.

40   Collen, *10% Human*, 60.

41   Collen, *10% Human*, 72.

42   Dunn, *The Wildlife of our Bodies*, 87.

43   Aristotle, *Metaphysics*, Book I, Chapter 1.

PART TWO

VARIETIES OF
PROCESS THOUGHT

✺ 6 ✺

COMING DOWN TO EARTH:

A PROCESS-PANENTHEIST REORIENTATION TO NATURE

Anna Case-Winters

ABSTRACT: *The interaction of Christian theology with process thought has helped us toward a more ecologically promising theology. Process thought challenges habits of desacralizing the natural world. Through its elements of panentheism, dual transcendence, and shared creativity it reinvests nature with a sense of divine presence and interactivity. Anthropocentric approaches in Christian tradition that have tended to subjectify the human being and objectify nature are also challenged by process approaches. Process-relational ontology rejects the substance metaphysics that is at the base of this kind of thinking, and the philosophy of organism invites us to think of the natural world as a world of subjects rather than objects.*

THE PRESENT ECO-CRISIS makes it imperative that we find ways of living with and within the natural world that are more just, participatory, and sustainable. I take our primary challenge to be *theological*. Our ideas of who God is, how God is related to the world, how the world works, and who we are as human beings all shape how we interact with the natural world. Those engaged in ecojustice work often observe that drawing out the statistics on global warming

or species extinction or habitat destruction—the data of despair—
does not seem to motivate the needed changes. The problem is not a
matter of information but rather orientation. We need a fundamental
reorientation—a "conversion to the earth," as Rosemary Radford
Ruether put it. Our callous disregard and rapacious ways may be a
symptom of not knowing our place within the wider natural world.
Perhaps we need a more *down-to-earth* sense of ourselves.

Here I will try to show how the interaction of Christian theology
with the philosophy of Alfred North Whitehead has proven transfor-
mative in areas where a reorientation is needed. Two common habits
of thought that I take to be theologically and ecologically problematic
are the desacralization of nature and the objectification of nature.
Process thought offers a helpful corrective here and points the way
forward to a better alternative.

THE DESACRALIZATION OF NATURE: RECONNECTING GOD AND THE WORLD

Classical theism has taken trouble to define divine attributes *over against*
the attributes of the world of nature. God is not the world or anything
in the world. Intended as a proper apophatic reserve, this has hardened
into binary opposition between God and the world: the eternal vs.
the temporal, the changing vs. the unchanging, and so on. God has,
in effect, been *structured out* of the natural world—a desacralization.
This way of proceeding finds an alternative in Whitehead's "dipolar
theism" (or, in Hartshorne, "dual transcendence"). Rather than setting
up these metaphysical polarities—eternal vs. temporal, changing vs.
unchanging—and assigning one metaphysical pole to God and
the other to the world, divine perfection is conceived as embracing
both poles, manifesting each attribute in the way in which it is most
excellent to do so. God need not be defined right out of relation to
the natural world.

Another element of Whitehead's system that may move us toward
a needed resacralization is the proposal that God's relation to the

world is internal rather than external. In classical theism, it was assumed that while the world was internally related to God (and therefore could be affected by God) this relation was not reciprocal. God was only *externally* related to the world and was unaffected by the world (impassible). Embracing *internal relations* opens the prospect of mutual influence and mutual indwelling. Every reality is, in a sense, co-constituted with the divine. Thus divine reality includes and does not exclude material reality. God is genuinely "all in all"—and is so even now. This is not something deferred to the eschaton.[1]

In another promising reconsideration process thought refuses the traditional absolute divide between Creator and created—the "infinite qualitative distinction." In its place, Whitehead introduces the category of *creativity.* God may be thought of as the "chief exemplification" of creativity, even as the leader of the creative advance, but God does not have a monopoly on creativity. Creativity characterizes all actual entities. As the Ground of Order and the Ground of Novelty, God, in a sense, makes creativity possible, but the stark separation between Creator and created no longer applies. As Whitehead proposes, "It is as true to say that God creates the World as that the World creates God."[2]

Perhaps the most decisive step toward resacralization is process panentheism. God is in the world and the world is in God[3] yet God is more than the world. Whitehead put it this way, "It is as true to say that the World is immanent in God, as that God is immanent in the World."[4] The whole philosophy of organism, he said, "is mainly devoted to the task of making clear the notion of being present in another entity."[5] With this step all else falls into place. The world is resacralized.

For Christian theology, this view unveils—among other things—the deeper meaning of incarnational theology. Whitehead offered that, "The world lives by its incarnation of God in itself."[6] Rather than incarnation being an exception to God's ordinary way of being and acting, it turns out to be the "chief exemplification" of it. What happens in Jesus of Nazareth, for example, is emblematic of what is already the case about the whole of creation. Just a couple of footnotes here: Classical theism's treatment of the incarnation as "exceptional" has been accompanied by two difficulties (at least two). One is the problem of exclusivism. Is God's self-revelation *only* in Jesus of Nazareth and not in other times and places? Might there not be what Laurel Schneider has called, "promiscuous incarnations?" If God is genuinely indwelling all things, as in panentheism, then there is always already a kind of "*pan*-carnation."[7] A second difficulty with Western classical theism's exceptionalism is its anthropocentrism.[8] It sees incarnation primarily as a response to human sinfulness—it really is all about us. In this, we fail to see that it is the whole creation that God loves and is making new. Panentheism helps us see this.

This process-panentheist[9] alternative with its elements of dual transcendence, internal relations, shared creativity, and divine incarnation in all things creates a space for resacralization of the natural world. At the heart of the natural world is an openness to the God who "enfolds and unfolds"[10] it—the God who is "all in all" (I Cor. 15:28). If taken seriously, this view implies a "real presence" of the divine in the natural world. What is made visible in incarnation and reiterated in sacrament is the cosmic incarnation—the whole world is "a place of grace," as Joseph Sittler used to say. The human being is decentered. Instead of being *incurvatus in se* ("curved in" on ourselves) we are reoriented, turned outward to care for the wider world that God pervasively indwells. This changes the way we understand and treat the natural world.

THE OBJECTIFICATION OF NATURE: SEEING THE NATURAL WORLD IN ITS INTEGRITY AND AS COMPOSED OF SUBJECTS

The objectification of the natural world that has attended classical theism has made exploitation and abuse more allowable. This is a world of mere *objects*—not subjects. This way of thinking has also further reinforced the anthropocentrism as human beings are cast as subjects in this world of objects. Elements in Whitehead's system that are particularly helpful toward refuting the objectification of nature include his rejection of substance metaphysics and his introduction of the philosophy of organism. Through these steps he effectively restores the integrity of nature and extends to it subject status. Next I will tease out these two contributions and their implications.

THE INTEGRITY OF NATURE

An essential ingredient that process thought brings to the work of ecojustice is a conviction of the *integrity of nature*. The sense that all things are held together as a connected whole is an essential insight for ecological thinking. As it happens, it is an insight well supported by the science of our day. Quantum mechanics, with its discovery of non-separability[11] or entanglement at the quantum level, reveals that our assumptions of independence and separation are a false report on reality. Though Whitehead would not have been working with a knowledge of quantum mechanics, he did believe that individuation is an abstraction from the deeper reality—an instance of what Whitehead would term "misplaced concreteness." Theologically, of course, there is a longstanding tradition that holds the view that in the divine life, we are utterly connected. Ecologically, it is clear that connection is the way of nature. Process thought, then, conspires with science, theology, and ecology to remind us that human being is part of an interconnected/interdependent web of life. Whitehead articulates this profound non-separability, as he says, "every actual entity is present in every other actual entity."[12] This insight was beautifully reflected in an address by Vaclav Havel when he proposed, "We are mysteriously connected to the entire universe, we are mirrored in it, just as the entire universe is mirrored on us."[13]

Process thought contests substantialist thinking, which has assumed that the final real things are substances, things that, according to Descartes, "need nothing but themselves to exist." Substantialist thinking tends to yield materialistic, reductionistic, and mechanistic models that have proven unhelpful for ecological considerations. The problem is in assuming things exist as independent entities (or substances) that are only externally (accidentally, incidentally) related to one another. In a machine, the parts themselves are truly independent; they do not need relations with other parts for their own existence. A machine can be disassembled without damage to the parts and then reassembled with the function restored; not so with organisms, where the parts are fundamentally interdependent. We are learning that the earth is more like an organism than a mechanism.

Whitehead's insistence that reality is composed rather of "events" or "droplets of experience" resists substance metaphysics with its mechanistic/materialistic worldview and associated dualisms (matter vs. spirit, for example). By giving priority to process and developing a relational ontology, Whitehead provides an alternative orientation to reality. All things are understood to be co-constituted by their relations. This is a much better framework for understanding our ecological reality and encourages a much-needed sensibility of inter-dependence in us. With this framework, we may perceive the web of relations and avoid the old bifurcations—mind-body, spirit-matter, nature-culture—so common and so distorting in Western classical tradition. We may begin to ask distinctly relational questions. When any particular course of action is advocated as good, we ask, Good *in relation to what*? Good *in relation to whom*? We are pushed to consider the effects of our actions upon all those others to whom know we are internally and utterly connected. Pursuing purely selfish interest is revealed to be an irrational habit of thought and action—living *as if* we were autonomous individuals and not co-constituted by our relations. Living life *incurvatus en se* (curved in on ourselves), as Augustine put it, is a disorientation and an alienation.

If we are reoriented, we may begin to see things *whole*—in the complex patterns of relationality. A corollary to the habit of seeing things whole is the ethical orientation toward *making things whole* in the sense of healing—healing the damage that has been done and reversing the *dis*-integration of ecosystems and social systems. The whole ecojustice project is an insistence that we affirm the integrity of nature and therefore make the connections.

In the North-South global conversation, for example, people from the northern hemisphere are accused of not making the connections between ecology and economics when they insist on preserving the rainforest without acknowledging the economic needs that impinge upon persons living in and near the rainforests, needs that motivate them to turn rainforests into pastures and farmlands. To think in this way is to *disintegrate* ecosystems from social systems and economic systems. Economics has to enter the picture; it is the other half of the *eco*-crisis. Whitehead's relational ontology is suggestive for conceptualizing and interpreting in ways that *integrate*. We may be helped by this alternative to rediscover the integrity of nature—to see things whole and to make things whole.

THE NATURAL WORLD AS COMPOSED OF SUBJECTS

We may also be helped by the Whiteheadian alternative to embrace the natural world as composed of subjects. Jürgen Moltmann makes the point that theology has contributed to the present ecological crisis through the "subjectification of the human being" and the "objectification of nature."[14] We declare a human monopoly on spirit. Among other things, anthropocentrism places the human being in a transcendent—even God-like—relation to nature, thereby lifting the human being right out of the natural world as a spiritual creature in a material world. Such a view assigns only instrumental value and not intrinsic value to nature and thereby permits and may even promote its exploitation. Nature becomes (to borrow Frances Wood's phrase) "a permissible victim."[15]

A non-anthropocentric ecojustice ethic will base the call to preserve and protect the natural world in its *intrinsic* value, not in its value to us. When we seek to motivate care by remarking upon how dependent *human beings* are on "*our* natural environment" and "*our* natural resources," those are anthropocentric, instrumentalist valuations and motivations. It would be far better for us to come to insist upon the *intrinsic value* of species, ecosystems, the biosphere, etc.

Whitehead affirms that, "Value is inherent in actuality itself."[16] Whitehead's philosophy of organism takes an interesting step of proposing that all entities have both physical and mental poles (in varying degrees). Whitehead is working with a meaning for "mentality" that is not anthropocentrically defined and does not require consciousness or sentience; it is simply the "capacity for experience." Griffin's suggestion of "panexperientialism" conveys the meaning better than "panpsychism," a misleading term sometimes employed. Each actual entity in its own coming to be is a subject and has intrinsic value. Process thought admits of degrees of intrinsic value relative to capacities for sentience, but this represents a continuity with no absolute divide.

Another interesting consideration that Griffin introduces is extrinsic value, that is, something's value beyond value to itself, value to others and/or to the ecosystem—"ecological value."[17] He offers an interesting observation that suggests a greater equalizing of value among species. He notes that if we take into account "ecological value," some creatures (like plankton, worms, bacteria, etc.) that may not be capable of the richest experience may in fact have great value in ecosystems. Human beings, on the other hand, who are capable of the richest experience, may have little ecological value. "In fact most of the other forms of life would be better off and the ecosystem as a whole would not be threatened, if we did not exist."[18] The Gaia hypothesis goes so far as to suggest that we are like harmful bacteria to the organism that is Earth, and it needs to eliminate us! We are a danger to ourselves and others.

As Whitehead follows through on the insights of his panexperientialism, the old spiritual-material dichotomy dissolves. There are no pure spirits, and there is no "dead" matter. There are only material beings (sentient and non-sentient) with varying capacities for experience. The important point is that in Whitehead's philosophy of organism, interiority extends all the way down to the submicroscopic. "Wherever there is actuality of any sort, it has a spontaneity and capacity for prehending its environment, albeit in a non-conscious way."[19] "By virtue of their capacities for inwardness or subjectivity . . . all deserve respect and care on their own terms and for their own sakes, not simply for their usefulness to human beings."[20] Earth community is, as Thomas Berry has said, "a communion of subjects."[21] The human being, in this way of thinking, does not have a monopoly on spirit. As John Cobb often says, "process theology does not commit monopoly."

This reorientation to nature that we are receiving from Whitehead promotes its integrity and its subject status. It might be said that this alternative "gives face" to nature. Here I will shift to some more contemporary sources to draw out the theological and ethical implications of what Whitehead has proposed in his philosophy. In my appeal for the alterity and integrity of nature and its subject status, I am helped by the thought-provoking work of Immanuel Levinas and Edward Farley. What they have so helpfully done in their work on interhuman relations, I want to see taken and applied in terms of human relations with the rest of nature.

As Farley puts it, the other is a subject, an "I" which is "not I."[22] The existence of such an "other" disputes any claim I have to be the one "I, the only perspective, the autonomous actor."[23] The uninterchangeability and irreducibility of the other makes clear the alterity of the other. This primordial structure of alterity at the heart of the inter-human is a most helpful analogy for thinking through human relations with the rest of nature. The recognition that I am not the only I and that I am not the center of the universe has a destabilizing and decentering effect which could reorient our relation to the other—in this case, the wider natural world. For Martin Buber, it is the turning to the other in the "I—Thou" (as opposed to "I—it") encounter and becoming aware of the other in a way that breaks the order of mere observing or onlooking. Gabriel Marcel thinks the move outward from egocentricity to experience the "summons" or "invocation" of the other requires a kind of "reflective break," *a kind of redemption.*[24]

Levinas[25] has proposed that when we encounter the "face" of another we experience a claim, a call to commitment and responsibility. Farley expands this in the direction of *compassionate obligation*, a concept I find rich with meaning in the human encounter with the rest of nature. Compassionate obligation characterizes the face-to-face encounter because in being together we become for one another "mutual interlocutors." We experience ourselves as vulnerable before the interpretations and actions of the other, and we experience the other as vulnerable to our interpretations and actions. Thus what is disclosed in the encounter is our "*mutual fragility.*" A response of compassion is called forth from us. Then, once summoned by the face, we become alert to the objective predicament of the other and our obligation to "join with the other in her or his fragile struggles against whatever threatens and violates."[26] Through the suffering face of the other we are awakened to an ethic of love. The "suffering-with" (of compassion) flows into a "suffering-for" (of obligation). One cannot respond to the face of the other as if it were a mere externality, a thing, or an artifact.[27] This is a subject, an "I."[28] What a difference "giving face" to nature might make!

Acknowledging the integrity of nature and seeing the world as composed of subjects could have the potential of steering us toward a new understanding of the natural world and the place of the human being in it. The recognition of "mutual fragility" and the response of compassionate obligation are surely essential to the work of ecojustice.[29]

CONCLUSION

In conclusion, at this stage in our history, we human beings are called to live in ways that are "socially just, ecologically wise and spiritually satisfying, not only for the sake of human life but for the sake of the well-being of the planet."[30] I am convinced that our challenge in doing this is primarily theological. The ways we have been thinking about God and the world and the human being are deeply problematic. Process thought offers a genuine alternative that might aid the needed reorientation. Classical theism contributed to the desacralization of nature. By contrast, Whitehead's concept of God's relation to the world, with its elements of panentheism, dual transcendence, and shared creativity, reinvests the natural world with divine presence and inter-activity. Transcendence is maintained, but it is *relational* transcendence that gives place to a genuine other. The problem of anthropocentrism embedded in the tradition—with its subjectification of the human and objectification of nature—is also challenged by Whitehead's system. When his process-relational ontology replaces substance metaphysics it restores integrity to nature. His philosophy of organism provides a way of granting subject status to the natural world.

Whitehead once said that, "it is a disease of philosophy when it is neither bold nor humble, but merely a reflection of the temperamental presuppositions of exceptional personalities."[31] Whitehead is surely an exceptional personality and one we might be tempted to emulate. I think he would not call us to be Whiteheadians (!) but rather to progress in this work, using our own constructive imaginations to address the challenges of our own context. Those challenges are as grave as they are urgent; we are hearing a compelling call to action. I have tried to speak to the matter of some reorientations that might take us to an altogether new place, one that is further down the road to an "ecological civilization" and closer to a "just and sustainable conviviality," as Catherine Keller has called it.[32] My hope is that we may indeed be humble—coming out of our anthropocentrism to a more down-to-earth sense of ourselves. Presented with an alternative that chooses life and supports the flourishing of all, may we also be bold and seize it.

ENDNOTES

1   Catherine Keller, *Cloud of the Impossible: Negative Theology and Planetary Entanglement* (New York: Columbia University Press, 2015), 52. One may speak even now of the "indwelling presence" (*shekinah*) of God in the world of God's "glory" (*kavod*) appearing in our midst. Mayra Rivera puts it this way: "glory is the trace of the divine relationship woven through creaturely life and its relationships. It is the cloudy radiance of the ungraspable excess that inheres in ordinary things—something that manifests itself, that gives itself." Mayra Rivera, "Glory: The First Passion of Theology," in *Polydoxy: Theology of Multiplicity and Relation*, ed. Catherine Keller and Laurel C. Schneider (London: Routledge, 2011), 177.

2   Alfred North Whitehead, *Process and Reality: An Essay in Cosmology*, Corrected Edition, David Ray Griffin and Donald W. Sherburne, ed. (New York: The Free Press, 1978 [1929]), 21.

3   Following Nicolas of Cusa, it is best to think of this as an enfolding rather than an enclosure. His panentheism "destabilizes any picture of a container-God." Keller, *Cloud of the Impossible*, 113.

4   Whitehead, *Process and Reality*, 348.

5   Alfred North Whitehead, *Process and Reality*, 50.

6   Whitehead, *Science in the Modern World*, 149.

7   Keller, *Cloud of the Impossible*, 118.

8   Another set of insights which helps with addressing anthropocentrism comes from Niels Gregersen's work, "Deep Incarnation: Why Evolutionary Continuity Matters in Christology," *Toronto Journal of Theology* 26, no. 2 (2010), 173–88. He proposes that incarnation "reaches into the depths of material existence" (174). "The eternal Logos embraces the uniqueness of the human but also the continuity of humanity with other animals, and with the natural world at large." The choice of the Greek term *sarx* (for "flesh") in John 1:14 ("the word became flesh and dwelt among us") conveys a much broader concept than "the word became human" might have done. *Sarx* is the Greek term that would be used to translate the Hebrew (*kol-bashar*, "all flesh") and would imply the whole reality of the material world. For contemporary readers, it would include everything "from quarks

to atoms to molecules, in their combinations and transformations throughout chemical and biological evolution" (177).

9 Among the panentheisms on the horizon, I think there is greater promise in the process approach. It does not so easily fall into pantheism, on the one hand, or pancosmism, on the other. It has a relational rather than an emanational shape. Thus it maintains the transcendence of God, on the one hand, and the alterity of the natural world, on the other. God's transcendence is redefined. It does not lie in being separate from all else, but in what Hartshorne has termed its "surrelativity." (Charles Hartshorne, *The Divine Relativity: A Social Conception of God* [New Haven: Yale University, 1948], 88). That is, God is supremely relative, internally related to all that is and therefore "all in all." So this is a transcendence that includes rather than excludes relation. The alterity of the natural world is also preserved in this approach. I think this is important to the present project. Unless we preserve this alterity, it will be difficult to speak meaningfully of human ecological responsibility; for whatever human beings do is really God's action and not their own. Relationality as such would be in jeopardy since there would no longer be an "other" with whom to relate.

10 Nicolas of Cusa, *On Learned Ignorance,* Book II.3.

11 This comes from the observation that two particles that are members of the same quantum system continue to influence one another no matter how far they are subsequently separated. Even measuring one affects the other. This happens instantaneously and thus is not thought to be a matter of one "comunicating" with the other.

12 Whitehead, *Process and Reality,* 50.

13 Quoted by Larry Rasmussen in *Earth Community: Earth Ethics* (Maryknoll: Orbis, 2001), 10.

14 Jürgen Moltmann, *Creating a Just Future* (Philadelphia: Trinity, 1989), 25.

15 Frances E. Wood, "'Take My Yoke upon You,'" in *A Troubling in My Soul,* ed. Emilie M. Townes (Maryknoll: Orbis Books, 1993), 40.]

16 Whitehead, *Process and Reality,* 100.

17 David Griffin, "Whitehead's Deeply Ecological Worldview," in

Worldviews and Ecology: Religion, Philosophy, and the Environment, ed. Mary Evelyn Tucker and John A. Grim (Maryknoll: Orbis, 1994), 192 ff.

18 Griffin, "Whitehead's Deeply Ecological Worldview," 203.

19 Jay McDaniel, "Process Thought and the Epic of Evolution Tradition: Complementary Approaches to a Sustainable Future," *Process Studies* 35, no.1 (Spring/Summer 2006), 78.

20 McDaniel, "Process Thought and the Epic of Evolution Tradition," 70.

21 Thomas Berry, *Evening Thoughts: Reflecting on Earth as Sacred Community* (San Francisco: Sierra Club, 2006), 149.

22 Edward Farley, *Good and Evil* (Minneapolis: Fortress, 1990), 35.

23 Farley, *Good and Evil*, 36.

24 Farley, *Good and Evil*, 38.

25 Emmanuel Levinas, "Ethics as First Philosophy," in *The Levinas Reader*, ed. Sean Hand (Oxford: Blackwell, 1989).

26 Farley, *Good and Evil*, 43.

27 Farley, *Good and Evil*, 42.

28 The face as referenced here need not be a human face. Keller, drawing out insights of Nicolas of Cusa, in *De vision Dei*, notes that the human face should not be privileged for "the icon of God has radically distributed itself across the face of the universe, across the surface of all materialities" (Keller, *Cloud of the Impossible*, 109).

29 There are at least some hints of this wider frame into which I am urging the discussion in Farley's own analysis. What he is presenting here is his theological anthropology, and the work is directed toward the sphere of the interhuman. Nevertheless, Farley does speak of a *"universal face"* that is "attested to through and mediated by communities of the face" (Robert Williams, *Recognition: Fichte and Hegel on the Other* [Albany: State University of New York Press, 1992], 292). "In the Christian paradigm of redemption, the transregional face is experienced in connection with the experience of the sacred" (Williams, 289). It is the presence of the sacred that draws situated peoples to transcend though not to repudiate their

self-reference. "It is the sacred manifested through the face that lures regional (familial, national, tribal) experiences of the face *toward compassionate obligation to any and all life-forms*" (Farley, *Good and Evil*, 289). I think the connections and applications I am making are at least arguably consistent with Farley's direction here.

30 McDaniel, "Process Thought and the Epic of Evolution Tradition," 80.

31 Whitehead, *Process and Reality*, 17.

32 Keller, *Cloud of the Impossible*, 52.

⇜ 7 ⇝

SEIZING A WHITEHEADIAN ALTERNATIVE:
A RETRIEVAL OF THE EMPIRICAL
OPTION IN PROCESS THOUGHT

Demian Wheeler

ABSTRACT: *According to philosopher Robert Corrington, Whiteheadianism is bedeviled by a number of anthropocentric, even quasi-naturalistic, tendencies—for example, a panpsychist ontology, a panentheistic concept of God, and a "cosmology of optimism." However, there is another trajectory of process thought that is thoroughly naturalistic and non-anthropocentric. I am referring to the empirical school of process philosophy and theology, a tradition that stretches from the mid-20th-century Chicago schoolers Henry Nelson Wieman, Bernard Meland, and Bernard Loomer, to a handful of contemporary theologians and philosophers, most notably, William Dean, David Conner, Nancy Frankenberry, and Donald Crosby. The present essay seizes this important but often overlooked Whiteheadian alternative, calling for a retrieval of process empiricism. The process empiricists, I argue, remove, or at least reduce, many of the lingering traces of anthropocentrism and anthropomorphism within Whiteheadianism, presenting a process philosophy and theology truly befitting of an ecological civilization.*

ROADBLOCKS TO AN ECOLOGICAL CIVILIZATION?
ANTHROPOCENTRIC AND QUASI-NATURALISTIC TENDENCIES
IN PROCESS PHILOSOPHY AND THEOLOGY

JOHN COBB BOLDLY and passionately proclaims that Whitehead's vision of reality offers the most promising alternative to the modern ideas and practices leading the planet to the brink of catastrophe.[1] Whitehead's realization that entities are dependent on their environments and constituted by their relationships; his emphasis on the deep interconnectedness of things; his rejection of a reductive materialism and a substance metaphysics in favor of a philosophy of organism and an ontology of events; his conviction that feeling, subjectivity, mind, purpose, and value exist in the natural world; his suspicion of supernatural interventions; his insistence on the inseparability of the physical and the mental in experience; and, most importantly, his overcoming of anthropocentrism and the pernicious dualisms that alienate humans from the rest of nature make Whitehead, on Cobb's reading, "the philosopher, par excellence, of [an] ecological civilization."[2]

But Whitehead could also be a roadblock to an ecological civilization, because neither he nor much of the process philosophy and theology he helped inspire manages to *completely* overcome anthropocentrism. As a process-relational thinker myself, I strongly agree with Cobb that Whiteheadianism carries enormous promise as *a* rigorous and compelling worldview for our ecologically imperiled age. Nevertheless, I also agree with the American philosopher and founder of "ecstatic naturalism," Robert Corrington, that Whiteheadian thought is bedeviled by a number of anthropomorphic, even quasi-naturalistic, tendencies. I will mention three, in particular.[3]

First, Corrington accuses process philosophers of violating Justus Bucher's principle of "ontological parity." Radically anti-essentialist and non-foundationalist, parity-based ontologies are receptive to "whatever is in whatever way it is," honoring the spectacular diversity of natural complexes and stipulating that no single order or characteristic is more or less fundamental or real than any other. The history of philosophy, on the other hand, has been characterized by the more imperialistic habit of "ontological priority," the imposition of some provincial (and usually anthropomorphic) attribute or metaphysical category onto the entirety of natural reality. Some *part* of nature—e.g., personality, the text—gets prioritized and universalized, construed as the "really real," the "ultimate something," the "order of orders," the "mega-trait." As panexperientialists and panpsychists, Whiteheadians are proprietors of priority, in Corrington's judgment. *Regional* features—feeling, decision, the mental pole—are "stretched way beyond their appropriate scope and provenance" and then "discovered" everywhere in the universe. Whitehead likens metaphysical speculation to the flight of an airplane, taxiing on the ground of particular observation, soaring into the thin air of imaginative generalization, and landing repeatedly for renewed investigation.[4] But what Whiteheadians *actually* do, rues Corrington, is "ride the hobby horse of their truncated metaphysics all over nature," ripping pervasive but local traits (mind, experience) out of their native habitats and declaring them omnipresent.[5]

Second, process thought is guilty of romanticizing and anthropomorphizing both nature and the divine, according to Corrington. While claiming consonance with evolutionary theory, Whiteheadians envision a nature that Darwin would hardly recognize, a nature that is witness to an endless growth in beauty, novelty, value, intensity, and wholeness, a nature that is ascending, inexorably, toward the more and more complex, a nature that is replete with ubiquitous final causes and "magically appearing wellsprings of teleology." In the Whiteheadian scheme, the chaos, randomness, waste, destruction, irrationality, indifference, inertia, predation, and repetition of nature have been domesticated, and the prevalence of efficient causality and the entropic march toward heat death covered up with a "cosmology of optimism." Process thinkers, Corrington thunders, wax poetically about reality's web-like relationality,[6] but conveniently forget that a web "is derived from a creature that uses it primarily as a finely-tuned killing machine."[7] They extol "the creative advance," but fail to recognize how costly and rare creativity actually is in the universe. They imagine a grand *telos* goading entities "to live, to live well, to live better,"[8] but ignore the fact that nature evidences no intentionality, no consciousness, no superpurpose, save perhaps extinction. And reinforcing such nature romanticism is a romantic (and anthropomorphic) picture of God, an omnibenevolent, personal being whose lures and aims "are gentle, persuasive, and always (ultimately) congenial to our needs." This deity further blunts the tragedies of temporal existence by ensuring that reality's perpetual perishings are not *really* perpetual, objectively immortalized in the divine consequent nature. Process philosophy and theology, in short, succumb to wishful thinking, in Corrington's telling, attempting to cast "nature into pleasing shapes" and to make "the sacred palatable to our narcissistic longing."[9]

Third, Corrington surmises that the God of Whiteheadianism is not only too personalistic and too nice, but also "too big." Process theologians, in other words, are pan*en*theists whose deity is within *and slightly transcendent of* the natural sphere. And over against David Ray Griffin,[10] Corrington contends that panentheism is not genuinely naturalistic, since it postulates a divine agent that is in and yet somehow above, beyond, and other than nature.[11]

However overstated and ax-grinding, Corrington's criticisms are potent, incisive, and deserving of serious attention. But before Whiteheadians jump ship and convert to ecstatic naturalism, I wish to point out that not all process thinkers are panentheists, personalists, nature romantics, or even panpsychists. As it happens, there is another trajectory *within* the Whiteheadian tradition that is *thoroughly* naturalistic, a trajectory overlooked by Corrington and, more regrettably, by the majority of process theologians. I am talking about the *empirical* school of process philosophy and theology, which stretches from the mid-20th-century Chicago schoolers Henry Nelson Wieman, Bernard Meland, and Bernard Loomer, to a handful of contemporary theologians and philosophers, most notably, William Dean, David Conner, Nancy Frankenberry, and Donald Crosby. In what follows, I will seize this Whiteheadian alternative, as it were, calling for a retrieval of the empirical option in process thought. The Whiteheadian empiricists, this essay argues, remove, or at least reduce, many of the lingering traces of anthropocentrism and anthropomorphism within Whiteheadianism, presenting a process philosophy and theology truly befitting of an ecological civilization.

SEIZING A WHITEHEADIAN ALTERNATIVE:
A RETRIEVAL OF THE EMPIRICAL OPTION IN PROCESS THOUGHT

Three decades ago, Bernard Lee identified two distinctive camps of Whiteheadianism, a "rational" camp and an "empirical" camp.[12] Process empiricists have quite a bit in common with their rationalist counterparts, joining them in endorsing most of the basic Whiteheadian tropes: reality is made up of instances of becoming or the flux of events and processes; concrete phenomena are composed of their relations and interconnections with the world; each droplet of experience is shaped but not determined by the past occasions from which it arises; creativity, novelty, change, and even temporality are metaphysically primordial.[13]

So what distinguishes process empiricists from process rationalists—or "left-wing" Whiteheadians from "right-wing" Whiteheadians, to use Conner's more provocative and fitting labels?[14] To generalize,[15] empirical/left-wing Whiteheadians appropriate Whitehead critically and are allergic to any sort of Whiteheadian orthodoxy or scholasticism. They emphasize the overarching principles of a processive and relational metaphysics over unwavering adherence to the technical and often overreaching categories of *Process and Reality*. They read Whitehead empirically rather than rationalistically, appreciating his *relentlessly* empirical insistence on concreteness, applicability, and exemplification and his *radically* empirical accent on the dim, rich, massive, unclear, and indistinct recesses of experience. They prefer James to Hartshorne, preoccupied less with systematic and logical coherence than with experiential adequacy. They look to the whole communion of process-relational saints, from Bergson to Dewey, instead of insisting on Whitehead alone. And, perhaps most crucially for the purposes of this essay, they deny all ultra-speculative, unempirical abstractions—including the anthropomorphic and quasi-naturalistic components of Whiteheadianism exposed by Corrington.[16] As I shall now show, process empiricists carefully nuance (or even limit) the presence of mentality, feeling, subjectivity, etc. in nature, have no truck with panentheism or personalism, and refuse any sort of teleology or theology that softens or sugarcoats the disorder, impermanence, and ambiguity of the cosmos. On the contrary, all of them are cosmological *realists* and religious or theological *naturalists*. Some of them are *emergentists* and *pantheists*. And yet *none* of them ever ceases to be a process-relational thinker.

BEYOND PANPSYCHISM: TOWARD AN
EMERGENTIST PROCESS ONTOLOGY

Let us begin by considering Whiteheadianism's so-called "panpsychism." Whitehead hypothesized that "mental activity is one of the modes of feeling belonging to all actual entities in some degree," even if it only amounts to "conscious intellectuality" in some. The same goes for decision and self-determination. Every occasion—be it human or subatomic—"completes the self-creative act by putting the decisive stamp of creative emphasis upon the determinations of efficient cause," although "consciousness will be a factor" only in certain decisions.[17] Most process empiricists accept Whitehead's "panpsychist" hypothesis about the universality of mentality, but endeavor to purge the doctrine of any sort of anthropomorphic undertones. Sounding the most Whiteheadian, Loomer clarified that "subjective experience" points to "a synthetic process of unifying the several forms of vectorial energy derived from past occasions," while "self-creativity" simply refers to the manner of response to what an actual entity has received—that is, its "howness" of becoming.[18] Frankenberry agrees, adding that Whitehead was *not* a panpsychist. He merely taught that each event is "a locus of receptivity as well as a center of reactivity, not at all conscious or mental, except in societies of human occasions."[19]

Conner is also critical of attributing "panpsychism" to Whitehead, favoring the designation "pan-mentalism." Conner upholds the dipolarity of physicality and mentality, but very quickly qualifies (contra Corrington) that what Whitehead termed "the mental pole" is a way of accounting for, *not prioritizing or universalizing*, human consciousness. To affirm the "ubiquity of mentality" is simply to state that physical events, at every level of nature, are capable of *receiving, retaining, and conveying information*. Hardcore materialists peremptorily dismiss such non-physicalist viewpoints as hopelessly anthropocentric and anthropomorphic. However, Conner counters that panmentalism is backed by mounds of empirical evidence, elegantly explaining both the existence of pattern and structure in the universe and the emergence of purposiveness and freedom in complex organisms.[20]

Dean, unlike Conner and Frankenberry, gladly sails under the banner of panpsychism, construing it as a type of *naturalistic historicism*.[21] In the Whiteheadian system, *all* phenomena, "from the present atom to the human thinker, are interpreting subjects."[22] That makes the cosmos radically *historical*, in Dean's account.[23] Dean looks to Darwinism and to recent developments in quantum physics to support Whitehead's historicist cosmology. Scientists from Charles Darwin to John Wheeler imply that the world is not mechanistically determined or subjectively arbitrary, but interactional, participatory, changing, indeterminate, and historically contingent, a "chain of interpretations"[24] or a "historical series of observer-observed, relational events . . . that could have taken a different course at innumerable junctures."[25] In short, they thoroughly historicize natural processes, talking "not primarily of objective worlds or of subjective readings but of how innovations initially 'proposed' by a nonhuman entity are then 'accepted' generally in a space-time location or in an environment."[26]

Fellow historicist Sheila Greeve Davaney applauds the attempt to formulate a "historicized naturalism," but warns that portraying the natural sphere as "a chain of interpretations" anthropomorphizes nature and, ironically, reinscribes the very linguisticism and humanism Dean desires to overcome.[27] Of course, it is very important to keep in mind that, for Dean, "interpretation" or "interpreting subject" do not denote "the conscious elucidation of meaning," as Davaney herself concedes, but responsiveness or reactivity to environmental stimuli. And Dean forthrightly acknowledges that the responses and reactions of nonliving and nonconscious phenomena are *"analogous to* observation and decision—that is, interpretation."[28] Thus, such statements as, "organisms at the simplest levels in some way experience and decide about how to react to environments,"[29] are meant to be taken *loosely*, not literally. *Something like* interpretation occurs in physical and biological processes.

Even so, I think Davaney, Corrington, and others are right to be wary of the anthropomorphic connotations of paninterpretation-ism, panpsychism, panmentalism, and panexperientialism, although empirical process thinkers like Dean, Conner, and Frankenberry do significantly temper anthropomorphism by qualifying what is meant by "the interpreting subject" or "the mental pole." I would simply ask: are mentality, subjectivity, freedom, interpretation, and the like defined so generically as to become nearly vacuous? Indeed, the contention that nature utilizes and traffics in information, or that nonhuman organisms react to and alter their environments, is hard to refute. But what is the philosophical value of describing such processes as "mental" or "interpretational"? For example, what is recognizably mental about electrons possessing mass, spin, and charge, or natural laws displaying mathematical uniformity?[30] Or what is legitimately interpretational about E. coli randomly mutating and transforming their relation to the environment from an inhospitable to a hospitable one?[31] This objection is more than just terminological, because even if trafficking with information and responsiveness and history somehow go all the way down to "nature's ground floor,"[32] mind, sentience, feeling, interpretation, purposiveness, and decision do not. Neither does life, in my perspective, Whitehead's "philosophy of organism" notwithstanding.

Personally, I find Crosby's "emergentist" ontology more empirical, more parsimonious, and more processive than any variety of panpsychism, panmentalism, or panexperientialism, however nuanced. Crosby is skeptical of the panpsychist/panexperientialist/panmentalist theories of Whitehead, Hartshorne, and other process thinkers, rejecting the idea that every constituent of the universe, including the most elemental units of matter, bear the marks of feeling, mentality, and self-creation, even if only in a diminished or nonconscious manner. The notion that something as evolutionarily recent as mind or experience inheres in every single occasion strikes Crosby as anthropomorphic and empirically implausible, regardless of how broadly these traits are interpreted. Inwardness, decision, self-directed innovation, and the power to choose between alternate possibilities are not "omnipresent" or "primordial" but "emergent," arising "only with the development of relatively high levels of biological organization, especially with the formation of complex central nervous systems and brains."[33]

Interestingly, Crosby jettisons panexperientialism and panpsychism for *process* reasons. "Complexity of organization is the key to sentience and subjectivity, not the positing of experiential entities at every level of reality. It is ironic that neither Whitehead nor Hartshorne seems to have grasped this point, given their common insistence on the workings of real chance, real novelty, and real creativity in the world."[34] Hartshorne, for his part, should have drawn such an emergentist conclusion, since he repudiated Whitehead's doctrine of eternal objects and maintained that potentialities arise and perish with actualities. This means, for example, that feeling need not be present in rocks, because it can *emerge* with the actualization of novel and "previously nonexistent possibilities" (e.g., the evolution of complex central nervous systems and brains).[35] Indeed, the processive character of reality entails that *no* trait or principle, no matter how ostensibly fundamental, is universal or permanent; even the laws of thermodynamics are outcomes of the "innovative and destructive processes of nature that never cease." Crosby thinks that *all* of reality's features, from mentality to entropy, are local, emergent, and fleeting *precisely because* nature is an unrelenting flux of constant change, infinitely bringing new possibilities, even new universes, into and out of being over vast expanses of time.[36]

To be very clear, in Crosby's version of empirical process naturalism, subjective experience, feeling, and even mind reach *deep* down into the natural world, even if not *all the way* down. Not everything in nature is alive, nor is every life-form consciously aware or purposive. Nonetheless, *all* living beings, from the very primitive (e.g., amoebae) to the neurologically complex (e.g., birds, fish, reptiles, and mammals), possess inwardness—i.e., the ability to "identify, adapt to, and in many cases alter their environments by actively drawing on resources within themselves."[37] And *multitudes* of species, not just *Homo sapiens*, exhibit varying degrees of sentience, mentality, emotion, preference, intentionality, and consciousness; even *self*-consciousness is found in some nonhuman creatures (e.g., in great apes and dolphins).[38]

Yet, for Crosby, the continuity of biological evolution is sufficient for explaining the profusion of sentience in nature and the eventual emergence of mind—no panpsychist or panmentalist ontology required. Human self-consciousness is the product not of a primordially mental cosmos, but of an evolutionary one, made possible by "a gradually increasing capacity for sentient awareness and cognitive capability" in other living beings, which in turn emerged out of potentialities already ingredient in the "essential inwardness" of life itself.[39]

In sum, Crosby allows that subjectivity, experience, mentality, feeling, etc. are rampant in reality, while stopping far short of pan-psychism/panmentalism/panexperientialism and nudging process ontology in the direction of emergentism. Yet even the Whiteheadian empiricists who push feeling, sentience, life, mind, or interpretation further down into nature are not simplistically projecting human traits onto the universe but attempting to give a robust account of the world as we *empirically* find it, a world that is both receptive and reactive (Loomer and Frankenberry), physical and informational (Conner), given and altered (Dean).

BEYOND ROMANTICISM: TOWARD A REALIST PROCESS COSMOLOGY

In addition to moving beyond an unqualified and blatantly anthropomorphic panpsychism, process empiricists dispense with nature romanticism. Their cosmology is processive, relational, and identifiably Whiteheadian but not teleologically bloated or naively optimistic.

For starters, the Whiteheadian empiricists trim the teleological excesses of conventional process philosophy and theology. Empirical process thought, Frankenberry grants, does permit a "modicum of teleology" insofar as it recognizes that evolutionary processes are "ordered" and "characterized by . . . a creative synthesis which is productive of novel emergents"—or what Dean refers to as a "tropism toward greater complexity."[40] Be that as it may, no process empiricist believes that nature evinces a grand *telos* or a "superpurpose," in Corrington's sense of the term. As Conner hazards, while purpose is in some measure elemental,[41] "there is no encompassing goal or unified teleology that guides the entire cosmos at once."[42]

Crosby is even more teleologically conservative than Conner, asserting that purpose is an *emergent* rather than a primordial reality. Teleological behavior and actions are relatively recent products of a long history of evolution, which eventually brought about biologically and cognitively complex organisms capable of having intentions, setting and achieving goals, aspiring toward specific ends, generating purposes, and so on.[43]

The rejection of process panentheism and theological personalism in Whiteheadian empiricism, which we shall discuss shortly, further curbs those "magically appearing wellsprings of teleology" derided by Corrington. Once again, Crosby is instructive. By Crosby's reckoning, persons, intentions, consciously aware beings, and purposes exist *in* nature, but nature itself *has* no personality, intentionality, consciousness, or overarching purpose. Nor is there any personal, intentional, conscious deity that bestows purpose upon nature from without—e.g., a panentheistic God tenderly and patiently luring the world by some primordial vision of beauty, value, and goodness.[44] To be sure, there are lures toward the beautiful, the valuable, and the good *within* the universe but, *pace* most process theologies, they are not "*consciously* intended or directed."[45]

And not all lures are beautiful, valuable, and good, according to process empiricists. Nature, on the contrary, is an *entanglement* of beauty and horror, value and disvalue, goodness and evil. The concrete world, Loomer famously argued, is utterly *ambiguous*. Becoming, he declared, is metaphysically ultimate, but "the creative advance" is not so much an "adventure toward perfection" as it is a "struggle toward greater stature" or what he later dubbed "size," namely, the capacity to take in and sustain intense relationships, contrasts, tensions, and ambiguities.[46] Moreover, relatedness is metaphysically primary, Loomer realized, but the web of life comprises "a diversity of forces, many of which are either noncreative or destructive."[47] Frankenberry concurs with Loomer, indicating that the creativity and qualitative structure of the universe are "confounded by the simultaneous interweaving in nature of less than creative processes," processes "that are confused, tragic, contradictory, disorderly, and, at best, ambiguous."[48] What is more, Frankenberry, Loomer, Dean, and Crosby all suggest that ambiguity is somehow ontologically necessary, because good and evil, creativity and destruction, etc., are intertwined and even interdependent.[49] Crosby supplies empirical examples:

> We would not be here were it not for the vast extinctions in evolutionary history that preceded us. Our solar system would not exist without the cataclysmic explosion of a

supernova star. Many of earth's wonders have resulted from stupendous earthquakes, floods, storms, and fires . . . Gravity mercifully holds us to the surface of the earth, but it can also kill us . . . When we eat, we usually destroy some previously living thing.[50]

In brief, the natural world is ambiguous—inescapably ambiguous. For empirical process thinkers, there is nothing within or beyond nature that invariably and unambiguously urges each occasion toward the good or that saves the world from the calamities and ambiguities of existence. I am obviously referring to the primordial nature of God, which I alluded to above and to which I shall briefly return later, and the consequent nature of God, which every process empiricist renounces. For one thing, the consequent nature of God is not very empirical and not even very Whiteheadian.[51] Conner notes that the concept lacks any observable referent or testable consequences in the real world. And although the divine consequent nature has become a "soteriological or eschatological cornerstone" of conventional process theology, Whitehead wrote about it in only one text (namely, *Process and Reality*) and relegated his analysis of it to the final section of the book, a section, Conner reminds us, "marked more by poetic reverence than by philosophical precision."[52]

More problematically, the consequent nature of God, as Crosby bemoans, runs roughshod over the very real evils and ambiguities of existence. The idea of a deity who everlastingly remembers all occasions of experience and "enjoys" them with the greatest possible intensity and harmony trivializes and defangs "the disharmonious and ugly devastations, sufferings, disappointments, setbacks, and losses of the world."[53] The consequent nature, in truth, represents a failure to follow through on a radically processive worldview. Wieman noticed, in 1936, that it was invented to soften a harsh truth to which *Whitehead himself* pointed, to wit, that "time is a perpetual perishing," and that all virtue, beauty, and value eventually "sink into oblivion," swallowed up "in the fading past." By positing "an all-conserving

Cosmic Consciousness," Whitehead, objected Wieman, "indulged in a speculation, driven to it by the awful tragedy" and "wastage" left behind in the relentless march of temporal process.[54] Frankenberry makes the same point in Jamesian terms:

> empirical theologians, although not without natural piety, are willing to say with William James that the last word is not sweet, that all is not "yes, yes" in the universe, and that the very meaning of contingency is that ineluctable no's and losses form a part of it, with something permanently drastic and bitter always at the bottom of the cup. Therefore, they find little or no warrant for process theology's claim that the divine totality preserves whatever is good as everlasting and immune to perishing ... The principle of the primacy of becoming over being leads empiricists to an appreciation of the intrinsic value of radical contingency and temporality, not to an expectation of its everlasting duration, even for God.[55]

Empirical process thought, then, is honest about and accepting of the unavoidable endings, sorrows, brutalities, traumas, and ambiguities of life, offering up, in the words of Crosby, "no pap, no panaceas, no empty promises."[56] This is *not* the comforting, sentimental, death-defying romanticism that Corrington excoriates, but a candid, raw, gritty realism.[57]

BEYOND PANENTHEISM: TOWARD A NATURALIST PROCESS THEOLOGY

Lastly, the process empiricists not only refuse to psychologize, teleologize, and romanticize the world; they also refuse to anthropomorphize, supersize, and sanitize the sacred, ditching the personalistic and panentheistic God of conventional process theology. An *empirical* process theology, in contrast, is a *naturalistic* and, in some cases, a *pantheistic* process theology.[58]

Perhaps the staunchest and sharpest critic of traditional process theism is Conner. Process theologians such as John Cobb and Marjorie

Suchocki attribute anthropomorphic qualities (e.g., compassion) and activities (e.g., persuasion) to God, forgetting that Whitehead, except for the occasional hiccup, eschewed theological personalism. Whitehead did speak *metaphorically* of a divine "poet of the world" and a "great companion," a "fellow-sufferer who understands."[59] However, Whitehead's God, Conner adamantly persists, is "an ontological structure," not a being who has a will, an experiencing subject who endures through time, or a unitary divine person with consciousness, intentionality, feelings, knowledge, and the like. As Robert Neville likewise avers: "On most interpretations of process theology, God is ascribed the intentions to be just and bear suffering with sympathy. Whitehead himself knew too much of the vast expanse and natural depth of the cosmos to relate God's cosmic function to the scale of human affairs in any but the most poetic sense."[60] Conner suspects that process theologians are motivated by an "unstated concern for religious relevance"—e.g., by a desire to philosophically buttress the New Testament affirmation that "God is love" or "the conventional theology of, say, Wesleyan Arminianism."[61] But whatever its *religious* relevance, personalistic theism, including standard process theology, is "very difficult either to illustrate naturalistically or to defend empirically."[62]

Furthermore, most Whiteheadians regard process theology as a form of panentheism, according to which "God's being somehow contains and surpasses the world." Catherine Keller, to illustrate, notes that process theology does not *identify* God with the cosmos, "as in pantheism ('all is divine')," but takes the panentheistic view that "all is *in* God."[63] Conner retorts that panentheism is more of a Hartshornian doctrine than a Whiteheadian one.[64] Whitehead himself often sounds more like a pantheist than a panentheist.[65] At the very least, Whitehead's God is not as ontologically distinguishable from the world as process theologians imply.[66]

None of the other process empiricists want any part of personalism or panentheism either.[67] In fact, Frankenberry points out that two of the issues that divide Chicago-school empirical theology and Claremont-style process theology are (1) the applicability of personalistic or agential models of God, and (2) the evidential warrants of a universe-encompassing panentheistic deity. Process empiricists lay bare the profound metaphysical limitations of anthropomorphic theological language—for instance, what could divine love, justice, or even personhood possibly mean on a cosmic level?—and conceive of God as "one kind of process included within nature" rather than of "nature as included within God."[68]

In actuality, only *some* process empiricists conceive of God as *one* kind of process within nature; others, including Frankenberry herself, take the pantheistic route and conceive of God as the *totality* of nature. Of course, *every* process empiricist, pantheist or otherwise, is an out-and-out *naturalist*. Wieman, Meland, Loomer, Dean, Frankenberry, Conner, and Crosby all repudiate supernaturalism, embed human life squarely and fully in the natural world, insist that the one nature, with its immeasurable potentialities, is all there is, and disavow any appeal to transcendent realities, causes, principles, or justifications.[69] And it is this shared commitment to a full-orbed naturalism that ultimately drives each of the empirical process theologians to discard panentheism and to take up a theological or religious naturalism. If there is nothing in addition to, other than, or even slightly transcendent of nature, then "God" or "the sacred" must be either identified with or included within the natural world itself.[70] And the process empiricists are split virtually down the middle; Frankenberry, as well as Loomer, Dean, and myself, opt for a process pantheism, whereas Wieman, Meland, and Conner consider only an aspect of the world divine.[71]

Wieman blurred the Whiteheadian contrast between God and creativity. In Wieman's empirical process theology, God *is* the creative event in nature that augments "qualitative meaning" or, simply, "the good" (human as well as cosmic), the tendency in the universe wherein "the several parts of life are connected in mutual support, vivifying and enhancing one another in the creation of a more inclusive unity of events and possibilities."[72] Wieman agreed with Whitehead that God is not the creator of the world (in the traditional sense of *creatio ex nihilo*); but neither is God the poet or the savior of the world.[73] Rather, the divine is more like the *poetry* or the *salvation* of the world (i.e., the growth of qualitative meaning). As Frankenberry helpfully explains, Wieman's argument is not "that wherever God is manifest, there is creative transformation, but precisely the opposite—wherever one finds creative transformation, *there* one finds what has been meant by 'God.'"[74] Meland found "God" in essentially the same place, speaking of "the Creative Passage" that participates "in events which move toward qualitative attainment."[75] As he remarked in *Fallible Forms and Symbols*, God is "the ever-present interplay of *creativity, sensitivity*, and *negotiability* that gives dynamic possibilities to each nexus of relationships imparting to each a creative intent, enabling it to live forward and to participate in the élan of existing."[76]

With Wieman and Meland, Loomer associated God not with a personal being that is somehow distinct from the world but with the processes of the world itself. But against Wieman and Meland, Loomer divinized even the *destructive* processes of nature. He opted for a full-blown *pantheism*, equating God with the *totality* of the natural realm.[77] God is none other than "the organic restlessness of the *whole* body of creation." And if God *is* the world, then God must embody all the ambiguity actually found therein, "all the evil, wastes, destructiveness, regressions, ugliness, horror, disorder, complacency, dullness, and meaninglessness, as well as their opposites."[78] His God was commensurate with his realist cosmology.

Loomer took issue with Whiteheadian efforts to circumvent the ambiguity that characterizes the concrete sphere of nature and to dissociate the divine from evil. Whitehead himself does this by "ontologically separating God and creativity" and imagining "an aesthetic form of persuasiveness that is pitted against the coercive and inertial powers of the world." Loomer harshly judged that this "unambiguous structure or character can be derived only by a complex abstractive process, the end result of which has no counterpart in reality."[79] Wieman improved upon Whitehead by urging that "the being of God is not other than the being of the world." But Wieman identified God with only "one aspect of the world or one kind of process," namely, the part of nature that is generative of good and worthy of worship.[80] Therefore, no less than Whitehead's deity, Wieman's deity (and presumably Meland's deity, too[81]) is defined by pure goodness and, as such, is too "clean" and "perfect," too "unsullied" and "orderly," to be concretely real; it is a bloodless, unempirical abstraction from a cosmos that is inescapably ambiguous.[82] Loomer would probably have similar words for Conner. Though a metaphysical principle rather than an intentional agent, Conner's God still performs the basic process functions. Akin to Whitehead and most conventional process theologians,[83] Conner assures us that God's aims for all actual entities, whether viruses or humans,[84] always "point in the same general direction of enhanced intensity, complexity, etc."[85] Loomer, by contrast, held that God's activities are "not wholly or even primarily identified with the persuasive and permissive lure of a final cause or a relevant and novel idea . . . God is also a physical, efficient cause that may be either creative or inertial in its effects." If "the size of God" embraces nothing less than nature in its mysterious, ambiguous wholeness, then the divine lure is not just Eros but Thanatos; it "may exemplify itself as an expansive urge toward greater good" *or* a "passion for greater evil."[86]

Loomer's pantheist mantle has been taken up by his students, Frankenberry and Dean. In good Loomerian fashion, Frankenberry questions whether Wieman's empirical process theology, especially the claim that the creative event is "entirely trustworthy" and "unqualified in its goodness," is empirically observable or verifiable.[87] Pantheists, on the contrary, notice that "nature is often indifferent to human desires and deaf to our moral urgencies" and frankly interpret it as "a sign . . . of the remorselessness of the divine nature." In Frankenberry's pantheistic perspective, the religious ultimate and the metaphysical ultimate are one and the same; "God," that is, is "coincidental with . . . the whole of reality."[88]

Dean has been just as dogged as Frankenberry and Loomer about the thoroughgoing ambiguity of the divine, recognizing that creativity is supportive of the human good *and*, at the same time, leading toward the extinction of our species.[89] He blasts process theologians and fellow religious naturalists for hedging about the sacred's complicity in evil, for clinging to an omnibenevolent God far removed from "the dark side" of life. Such a God is fundamentally *ahistorical*, because "social and natural history evince nothing that is perfectly good . . . In history . . . every 'good' is contextual and perspectival, so that, for example, what is good for a blood-sucking mosquito is bad for its victims."[90] So rather than theologically zeroing in on the "better part" of reality and treating "the ambiguities of history as though the sacred does not relate to them," Dean puts forward a "historicist pantheism," accepting that "ultimate meanings refer to everything in history," even "history's evils." A pantheistic God is a God connected with, implicated in, and tainted by the entirety of nature, even its atrocities and tragedies.[91] As Dean searchingly asks:

> Must God not be . . . not only the fascinating but also the *tremendum*: the overpowering, the abyss, that which is repulsive to our moral sensibilities? We liberals believe that God is immanent in history. But where is the tipping point, where the immorality so pervasive in history suggests something about the morality of the God also pervasive in history?[92]

To summarize: process theology is not synonymous with panentheism and personalism. There is such a thing as *naturalist* process theology, even *pantheist* process theology.

THINKING ECOLOGICALLY IN THE TRADITION OF PROCESS
EMPIRICISM: FOUR CONCLUDING PROPOSITIONS

In conclusion, not all process thought is anthropocentric and anthropomorphic. There are seizable Whiteheadian alternatives, and the
particular option I wish to retrieve is a thoroughly empirical and
naturalistic process metaphysics that is emergentist in its ontology,
realist in its cosmology, and pantheistic in its theology.

As a closing move, I want to explicitly address the theme of this
anthology and very briefly explore what it might mean to think ecologically within the tradition of process empiricism. I put forward
four provisional propositions for discussion and debate.

I.   Emergentism inculcates a reverence for nature in both its
      stunning variety and its biohistorical continuity. Cobb and
      indeed all process thinkers are rightly critical of the all-too-
      human penchant "to subdue nature and make it serve us."[93]
      Yet Whiteheadians, as Corrington charges, metaphysically
      generalize from human experience and, in so doing, end
      up foisting human-like features onto the entirety of
      reality, ironically perpetuating the very anthropocentrism
      they wish to overcome. This makes Whiteheadianism, in
      Corrington's telling, surprisingly tribalistic, even colonialistic,
      if "colonialism" is understood to connote the tendency "to
      impose one region and its power on another."[94] However, an
      emergentist process ontology, much like Corrington's "ordinal
      phenomenology,"[95] is non-anthropocentric, anti-tribal, and
      post-colonial, respecting the autonomy, particularity, and
      irreducible plurality of nature's attributes and functions[96] and
      regarding traits such as life, mentality, feeling, subjectivity,
      and conscious awareness as emergent rather than omnipresent.
      That being said, emergentists like Crosby underscore the
      wide (if not ubiquitous or uniform) dispersement of life,
      mentality, feeling, subjectivity, and conscious awareness

throughout nature, a fact that carries far-reaching implications for environmental ethics and the cultivation of "I-thou" relationships between humans and the other sentient species to whom we are evolutionarily related and on whose survival we are dependent.[97]

2. Exchanging panentheism for pantheism eliminates the superfluous "en" that diverts our attention and energy away from nature itself. Positively put, to sacralize or even divinize the world rather than posit a God that is somewhat transcendent of and somehow distinct from the world is to make *the world itself* the object of religious devotion and ethical concern, a world that is steadily becoming too warm and too overpopulated to sustain human life and the ecosystems on which it relies.

3. The rejection of a divine consequent nature, which putatively salvages perpetually perishing goods and/or aesthetically redeems the losses of the world,[98] lends greater urgency to our ecological endeavors and deepens the tragic import of impending catastrophe. The preciousness of the here and now, the weight of our decisions, the necessity of immediate and radical action, and the plea to protect the planet are all *intensified* by forgoing an immortality-conferring deity and embracing the unconquerable finitude and inescapable ambiguity of existence.

4. The ultimacy, immensity, and ambiguity of nature—i.e., its metaphysical and religious supremacy; its lack of consciousness, personality, grand *teloi*, or divine supervision; its pervasive extinctions, predations, sufferings, evils, and disasters—invite a spirituality that is part Calvinistic and part Arminian. On the one hand, this cosmological and theological realism compels us to acknowledge our littleness, impotence, and relative insignificance vis-à-vis a natural realm that is utterly sovereign, unimaginably vast, destructive as well as creative,

capricious and ambiguous, and indifferent—sometimes even inimical—to our purposes, projects, and plans. And yet on the other hand, this very same acknowledgment, even as it calls us to stand in awe, humility, gratitude, and holy terror before the majesty and mystery of nature in its sacred totality, also drives us to work out our own salvation with fear and trembling. In other words, we realize that it is *up to us* to save our species and to preserve the ecology of our home planet. Of course, reality is in process, which means that the earth and its endless forms most beautiful *will* inevitably come to an end, maybe sooner rather than later. Regardless, we must *try* to build an ecological civilization and accept that our efforts are goaded not by primordial urges but by *human* interests, empathies, and penances. If there is no omnibenevolent, unambiguous, personal deity that "wills" or "lures" or "desires" our survival, then we must make the most of whatever technological ingenuity, political savvy, cultural wisdom, moral insight, and prophetic courage we can manage to muster. But this is not works righteousness, because the capacity to think, choose, and innovate and the ability to develop humanistic and ecological ethics and to discern and honor the intrinsic value of all things are nature's (God's) gifts to us.[99] Wieman was right: God (nature) *is* the source of human good (albeit not *only* that). And the unique goods we have been given place special obligations on us. To quote Crosby: "We humans have the privilege and responsibility of drawing upon our distinctive natural gifts to protect the integrity, beauty, diversity, and providingness of the earth and its creatures."[100]

ENDNOTES

1   See John B. Cobb, "Seizing an Alternative: Toward an Ecological Civilization," http://www.ctr4process.org/whitehead2015/wp -content/uploads/2014/07/SEIZING-AN-ALTERNATIVE2.pdf. Accesssed May 9, 2015.

2   John B. Cobb, "Whitehead as the Philosopher of an Ecological Civ-
      ilization," http://www.ctr4process.org/whitehead2015/philosopher
      -of-eco-civ. Accessed May 9, 2015.

3   The following analysis of Corrington is slightly adapted from Demian
      Wheeler, "American Religious Empiricism and the Possibility of an
      Ecstatic Naturalist Process Metaphysics," *Journal for the Study of
      Religion, Nature and Culture* 8, no. 2 (2014).

4   Alfred North Whitehead, *Process and Reality: An Essay in Cosmology*,
      Corrected Edition, eds. David Ray Griffin and Donald W. Sher-
      burne, eds. (New York: The Free Press, 1978), 5.

5   See Robert S. Corrington, *Nature and Spirit: An Essay in Ecstatic
      Naturalism* (New York: Fordham University Press, 1992), 1, 4–5, 21,
      25–26; Corrington, *Ecstatic Naturalism: Signs of the World* (Bloom-
      ington and Indianapolis: Indiana University Press, 1994), 14–15,
      56–57, 61; Corrington, *Nature's Religion* (Lanham: Rowman and
      Littlefield, 1997), 137, 155; Corrington, "Empirical Theology and Its
      Divergence from Process Thought," in *Introduction to Christian Theol-
      ogy: Contemporary North American Perspectives*, ed. Roger A. Badham
      (Louisville: Westminster John Knox Press, 1998), 169; Corrington, *A
      Semiotic Theory of Theology and Philosophy* (Cambridge: Cambridge
      University Press, 2000), 3, 8–9, 12, 14–15, 29–30, 103; Corrington,
      "My Passage from Panentheism to Pantheism," *American Journal of
      Theology and Philosophy* 23, no. 2 (2002), 130, 134, 148; Corrington,
      "An Appraisal and Critique of Alfred North Whitehead's *Process
      and Reality* and Justus Buchler's *Metaphysics of Natural Complexes*,"
      http://www.users.drew.edu/rcorring/publications.html (2009), 7, 9, 13,
      22–23, 26, 33–36; Corrington, "Evolution, Religion, and an Ecstatic
      Naturalism," *American Journal of Theology and Philosophy* 31, no. 2
      (2010), 124–26; Corrington, *Nature's Sublime: An Essay in Aesthetic
      Naturalism* (Lanham: Lexington Books, 2013), 13–14; Corrington,
      "Guest Editor's Introduction: Ecstatic Naturalism and Deep Pan-
      theism," *Journal for the Study of Religion, Nature and Culture* 8, no.
      2 (2014), 142–44; Robert S. Corrington and Leon J. Niemoczynski,
      "An Introduction to Ecstatic Naturalism: An Interview with Robert
      S. Corrington," *Kinesis* 36, no. 1 (2009), 74–78, 93–94.

6   See, for example, Catherine Keller, *From a Broken Web: Separation,
      Sexism, and Self* (Boston: Beacon Press, 1986).

7   Corrington, *Nature's Religion*, 97.

8   See Alfred North Whitehead, *The Function of Reason* (Boston: Beacon Press, 1958), 8.

9   See Robert S. Corrington, "Ecstatic Naturalism and the Transfiguration of the Good," in *Empirical Theology: An Handbook*, ed. Randolph Crump Miller (Birmingham: Religious Education Press, 1992), 213; Corrington, *Ecstatic Naturalism: Signs of the World*, 6, 22, 51; Corrington, *Nature's Religion*, 8–9, 99, 103; Corrington, *A Semiotic Theory of Theology and Philosophy*, 14, 28–29, 40, 48, 138, 207; Corrington, "My Passage from Panentheism to Pantheism," 130; Corrington, "Three Conventional Notions Ignore the Fullness of Nature," *Research News and Opportunities* 3, no. 10 (2003), 20; Corrington, "An Appraisal and Critique of Alfred North Whitehead's *Process and Reality* and Justus Buchler's *Metaphysics of Natural Complexes*," 7–8, 12, 14, 18, 20, 25–26, 30–31; Corrington, "Evolution, Religion, and an Ecstatic Naturalism," 125–28, 134–35; Corrington and Niemoczynski, "An Introduction to Ecstatic Naturalism: An Interview with Robert S. Corrington," 74, 77–78, 91.

10   See David Ray Griffin, *Religion and Scientific Naturalism: Overcoming the Conflicts* (Albany: State University of New York Press, 2000); Griffin, *Reenchantment without Supernaturalism: A Process Philosophy of Religion* (Ithaca: Cornell University Press, 2001).

11   Corrington, "Empirical Theology and Its Divergence from Process Thought," 169–71; Corrington, "My Passage from Panentheism to Pantheism," 149; Corrington, "Deep Pantheism," *Journal for the Study of Religion, Nature and Culture* 1, no. 4 (2007), 505; Corrington, "Guest Editor's Introduction: Ecstatic Naturalism and Deep Pantheism," 140.

12   Among the process rationalists mentioned by Lee are John Cobb, David Ray Griffin, Schubert Ogden, and, of course, Charles Hartshorne. Bernard J. Lee, "The Two Process Theologies," *Theological Studies* 45, no. 2 (1984), 311–15.

13   See, for instance, Henry Nelson Wieman, *The Source of Human Good* (Atlanta: Scholars Press, 1995), 68; Bernard Loomer, "The Size of God," in *The Size of God: The Theology of Bernard Loomer in Context*, ed. William Dean and Larry E. Axel (Macon, Georgia: Mercer University Press, 1987), 23–35; William Dean, "Deconstruction and

Process Theology," *The Journal of Religion* 64, no. 1 (1984), 1–19; William Dean, *American Religious Empiricism* (Albany: State University of New York Press, 1986), 48–49; William Dean, "Historical Process Theology: A Field in a Map of Thought," *Process Studies* 28, no. 3–4 (1999), 255–59; Nancy Frankenberry, "Major Themes of Empirical Theology," in *Empirical Theology: A Handbook*, ed. Randolph Crump Miller (Birmingham: Religious Education Press, 1992), 37; Donald A. Crosby, *A Religion of Nature* (Albany: State University of New York Press, 2002), 17–42.

14 David Emory Conner, "Whitehead the Naturalist," *American Journal of Theology and Philosophy* 30, no. 2 (2009)," 182–85.

15 The following generalizations are drawn and modified from Lee, "The Two Process Theologies," 311–16, and Conner, "Whitehead the Naturalist," 182–85.

16 In addition to panpsychism, cosmological optimism, nature romanticism, and panentheistic theology, empirical Whiteheadians undercut several other Whiteheadian abstractions as well. Dean, for instance, makes quick work of Whitehead's overreliance on speculative reason. See Dean, *American Religious Empiricism*, 49. And Crosby, to cite another example, bristles against Whitehead's "principle of relativity," according to which *every* prior actuality is involved in each new concrescence, thereby guaranteeing the "solidarity of the universe." Gone, for Crosby, is any "all-comprehending" perspective that can "explore, affect, be affected by, or relate to every aspect of the world," or some absolute oneness that reconciles the world's ineradicable pluralism. Nor is there a "totalizing divine vision capable of formally deducing from the inexhaustible diversity of past attainments a single valuative meaning." Taking a cue from William James, Crosby rejoins that interconnections *and* disconnections persist in nature, and the order, harmony, unity, and relationality of the world are partial, not complete. Crosby, in brief, is a relationalist but not a *pan*relationalist. See Donald A. Crosby, *Living with Ambiguity: Religious Naturalism and the Menace of Evil* (Albany: State University of New York Press, 2008), 67–74; Crosby, "God as Ground of Value: A Neo-Whiteheadian Revision," *American Journal of Theology and Philosophy* 13, no. 1 (1992), 41–43, 51–52.

17 Whitehead, *Process and Reality*, 56, 47, 43.

18   Loomer, "The Size of God," 26.

19   Communicated in an email Nancy Frankenberry sent to the author on May 1, 2013.

20   Conner, "Whitehead the Naturalist," 18–81. See also Conner's essay in this volume, "Beyond Emergentism."

21   I discuss naturalistic historicism at considerable length in my forthcoming *Religion within the Limits of History Alone: Pragmatic Historicism and the Future of Theology* (Albany: State University of New York Press), especially Chapters 1–2.

22   William Dean, *History Making History: The New Historicism in American Religious Thought* (Albany: State University of New York Press, 1988), 132.

23   See especially Dean, *American Religious Empiricism*, 51–55; Dean, *History Making History*, 100, 130–33; Dean, *The Religious Critic in American Culture* (Albany: State University of New York Press, 1994), 113–25. See also William Dean, "Humanistic Historicism and Naturalistic Historicism," in *Theology at the End of Modernity: Essays in Honor of Gordon D. Kaufman*, ed. Sheila Greeve Davaney (Philadelphia: Trinity Press International, 1991); Dean, "Historical Process Theology: A Field in a Map of Thought."

24   Dean, *The Religious Critic in American Culture*, 65.

25   Dean, *American Religious Empiricism*, 52.

26   Dean, *The Religious Critic in American Culture*, 114.

27   Sheila Greeve Davaney, *Pragmatic Historicism: A Theology for the Twenty-First Century* (Albany: State University of New York Press, 2000), 201, note 41.

28   Dean, *The Religious Critic in American Culture*, 123–25, emphasis added.

29   Dean, *The Religious Critic*, 124.

30   These are two of the several pieces of evidence that Conner offers up to substantiate panmentalism. See Conner, "Whitehead the Naturalist," 180–81; Conner, "Beyond Emergentism," 211–12.

31   See Dean, *The Religious Critic in American Culture*, 124–25.

32   Conner, "Beyond Emergentism," 214.

33 Donald A. Crosby, "Metaphysics and Value," *American Journal of Theology and Philosophy* 23, no. 1 (2002), 39–42, quote on 40. See also Crosby, "Emergentism, Perspectivism, and Divine Pathos," *American Journal of Theology and Philosophy* 31, no. 3 (2010), 197–99. Robert Neville is another process naturalist who views mind as emergent instead of universal: "Thus, rather than claiming, with Hartshorne, to be a pan-psychist for whom material nature is a special case, I would claim to be a pan-naturalist for whom cases run from mere matter with no psychic developments to psychically subtle nature in which matter is no longer 'mere.'" Quoted in Corrington, *A Semiotic Theory of Theology and Philosophy*, 29.

34 Crosby, "Emergentism, Perspectivism, and Divine Pathos," 198.

35 Crosby, "Emergentism," 197–98.

36 Crosby, *A Religion of Nature*, 39–40.

37 Donald A. Crosby, *The Thou of Nature: Religious Naturalism and Reverence for Sentient Life* (Albany: State University of New York Press, 2013), 23.

38 Crosby, *The Thou of Nature*, 19–35.

39 Crosby, *The Thou of Nature*, 19–21, 24, 26.

40 Frankenberry, "Major Themes of Empirical Theology," 41; Dean, *American Religious Empiricism*, 60.

41 Several passages in "Beyond Emergentism" imply that purpose is primordially inherent in nature. To mention just one, Conner suggests that once the idea of a physical-informational dipolarity is accepted and examined closely, "notions of primitive, primordial intentionality and valuation follow closely behind" (193).

42 Conner, "Whitehead the Naturalist," 180.

43 Donald A. Crosby, "A Case for Religion of Nature," *Journal for the Study of Religion, Nature and Culture* 1, no. 4 (2007), 497. See also Crosby, *Novelty* (Lanham, Maryland: Lexington Books, 2005), 52.

44 See Whitehead, *Process and Reality*, 346.

45 Crosby, "A Case for Religion of Nature," 490; Crosby, *A Religion of Nature*, 146–51. Here, Crosby echoes Corrington: "we have providingness but no provider, natural grace but no bestower of grace,

sheer availability but no intentionality, and a seed bed for consciousness with no consciousness in the seed bed." Corrington, *Nature's Religion*, 103.

46 Loomer, "The Size of God," 21, 42, 51; Loomer, "S-I-Z-E," *Criterion* 13 (1974), 6. See also Gary Dorrien, *The Making of American Liberal Theology: Crisis, Irony, and Postmodernity, 1950–2005*, 3 vols., vol. 3 (Louisville: Westminster John Knox Press, 2006), 129.

47 Loomer, "The Size of God," 40.

48 Frankenberry, "Major Themes of Empirical Theology," 41.

49 See Frankenberry, "Major Themes," 49; Loomer, "The Size of God," 51; William Dean, "Dean Replies to Zbaraschuk," *American Journal of Theology and Philosophy* 31, no. 3 (September 2010), 262; Crosby, *A Religion of Nature*, 85–87, 124, 132–45; Crosby, *Living with Ambiguity: Religious Naturalism and the Menace of Evil*, ix, 22–33, 36, 74–77, 79–90.

50 Crosby, "A Case for Religion of Nature," 499.

51 The primordial nature of God, on the other hand, *is* very Whiteheadian but still not very empirical. See Dean, *American Religious Empiricism*, 49.

52 Conner, "Whitehead the Naturalist," 177–78.

53 Crosby, "Emergentism, Perspectivism, and Divine Pathos," 203–05. Such "disharmonious and ugly devastations, sufferings, disappointments, setbacks, and losses" obviously include *ecological* predicaments and calamities like global climate change, the endangerment of numerous species, the destruction of ecosystems, and so forth.

54 Henry Nelson Wieman and Bernard E. Meland, *American Philosophies of Religion* (Chicago and New York: Willett, Clark & Company, 1936), 238–39.

55 Frankenberry, "Major Themes of Empirical Theology," 52.

56 Crosby, *Living with Ambiguity: Religious Naturalism and the Menace of Evil*, 108.

57 See, for example, Crosby, *The Thou of Nature: Religious Naturalism and Reverence for Sentient Life*, 135–37.

58 Corrington also replaces panentheism with a type of pantheism,

a "deep pantheism." See especially Corrington, "My Passage from Panentheism to Pantheism," Corrington, "Deep Pantheism," Corrington, "Guest Editor's Introduction: Ecstatic Naturalism and Deep Pantheism," and Corrington, "Neville's 'Wild God' and the Depths of Nature," *American Journal of Theology and Philosophy* 36, no. 1 (2015).

59 Whitehead, *Process and Reality*, 346, 351.

60 Robert Cummings Neville, *Ultimates: Philosophical Theology*, 3 vols., vol. 1 (Albany: State University of New York Press, 2013), 279.

61 According to Conner, Marjorie Suchocki is an example of a process theologian who blends Whiteheadianism with Wesleyanism. Conner, "Whitehead the Naturalist," 171, note 10. Another is Catherine Keller, who practically equates Whitehead's initial aim with Wesley's notion of prevenient grace. See Catherine Keller, *On the Mystery: Discerning God in Process* (Minneapolis: Fortress Press, 2008), 100.

62 Conner, "Whitehead the Naturalist," 170–72, 174–76; Conner, "The Plight of a Theoretical Deity: A Response to Suchocki's 'The Dynamic God'," *Process Studies* 41, no. 1 (2012), 111–23; Conner, "Beyond Emergentism," 216, 227–28, , note 82.

63 Keller, *On the Mystery*, 53.

64 Hartshorne was not only a panentheist but also a kind of personalist. In response to Tillichian ground-of-being theology, he writes: "Overlooked by Tillich is the consideration that . . . God can be, not simply *a* being, but *the* being, essential to all, strictly unique in status. For this being is universally relevant, the Subject to whom all individuals are infallibly known objects, and upon whom all individuals depend." Charles Hartshorne, *Omnipotence and Other Theological Mistakes* (Albany: State University of New York Press, 1984), 32.

65 For example, Whitehead's theology of "mutual immanence," spelled out in the last chapter of *Process and Reality*, can be interpreted pantheistically. Conner, "Whitehead the Naturalist," 179, 184. See Whitehead, *Process and Reality*, 348.

66 Conner, "Whitehead the Naturalist," 171, 178–79; Conner, "Beyond Emergentism," 216.

67 For instance, Loomer, akin to Conner, contended that the divine

is not "an enduring individual with a sustained subjective life," nor is the world "an organismic unity within the concrete actuality of God (panentheism)." Loomer, "The Size of God," 42, 39.

68 Frankenberry, "Major Themes of Empirical Theology," 52. Incidentally, Corrington also professes that nature includes and transcends the divine instead of vice versa. "Nature turns out to be greater in scope than God . . . and as a natural complex, God must be related to other complexes but not to all complexes." Corrington, "Guest Editor's Introduction: Ecstatic Naturalism and Deep Pantheism," 152. Or, as he more tantalizingly puts it elsewhere: "Nature is the genus of which the sacred is a species," the logical entailment of which is that "there are innumerable nonsacred orders that lie outside of the holy." Corrington, *Nature's Religion*, 2, 10.

69 See, for example, Wieman, *The Source of Human Good*, 6–8, 36, 72; Bernard E. Meland, *Fallible Forms and Symbols: Discourses on Method in a Theology of Culture* (Philadelphia: Fortress Press, 1976), Part One; Loomer, "The Size of God," 22–25; Dean, *History Making History*, 1–22, 124–44; Frankenberry, "Major Themes of Empirical Theology," 37–40; Conner, "Whitehead the Naturalist," 180; Crosby, *A Religion of Nature*, Part 2.

70 Loomer, "The Size of God," 22–23.

71 Crosby is an anomaly. He follows Loomer, Frankenberry, and Dean in deeming the metaphysical ultimate (i.e., the whole of the natural sphere) *religiously* ultimate (see especially Part 3 of *A Religion of Nature*). Nevertheless, Crosby dispenses with any form of theism, *including pantheism*: "nature is sacred but not divine." Crosby, *Living with Ambiguity: Religious Naturalism and the Menace of Evil*, 63. I have argued elsewhere that Crosby, although denying the pantheist label, still operates within the *theo-logic* of pantheism. Wheeler, "American Religious Empiricism and the Possibility of an Ecstatic Naturalist Process Metaphysics," 171. See also Wheeler, "Is a Process Form of Ecstatic Naturalism Possible? A Reading of Donald Crosby," *American Journal of Theology and Philosophy* 37, no. 1 (2016), 95.

72 Wieman, *The Source of Human Good*, 7, 56.

73 See Whitehead, *Process and Reality*, 346.

74 Nancy Frankenberry, *Religion and Radical Empiricism* (Albany:

State University of New York Press, 1987), 124.

75 Bernard E. Meland, *Essays in Constructive Theology: A Process Perspective*, ed. Perry LeFevre (Chicago: Exploration Press, 1988), 228, 241; Meland, *Higher Education and the Human Spirit* (Chicago: The University of Chicago Press, 1953), 162. The "Creative Passage" is actually only one of several names Meland reserved for God. Among the other names were: "Creative Order," "Creative Matrix," "Matrix of Sensitivity," "Sensitive Nature within Nature," "Depth of Mystery," "Cosmic Presence and Intent," and "Ultimate Efficacy within Relationships." Dorrien, *The Making of American Liberal Theology: Crisis, Irony, and Postmodernity, 1950–2005*, 3, 127.

76 Meland, *Fallible Forms and Symbols*, 45.

77 Why call the world "God?" Loomer replied: "The justification for the identification is both ontological and pragmatic in the deepest Jamesian sense. In our traditions the term 'God' is the symbol of ultimate values and meanings in all of their dimensions. It connotes an absolute claim on our loyalty. It bespeaks a primacy of trust, and a priority within the ordering of our commitments . . . It signifies a richness of resources for the living of life at its depths . . . It symbolizes a transcendent and inexhaustible meaning that forever eludes our grasp. The world is God because it is the source and preserver of meaning . . . and because it contains yet enshrouds the ultimate mystery inherent within existence itself. 'God' symbolizes this incredible mystery. The existent world embodies it. The world in all the dimensions of its being is the basis for all our wonder, awe, and inquiry." Loomer, "The Size of God," 42.

78 Loomer, "The Size of God," 40–43.

79 Loomer, "The Size of God," 50, 38.

80 See Wieman, *The Source of Human Good*, 54–83. Wieman claimed that "life may be a valley of frustration, but nothing can prevent ultimate, absolute, and complete regnancy of supreme value, somehow, sometime, somewhere, although the human mind cannot know how this may be" (82–83).

81 Like Wieman, Meland argued for divine omnibenevolence, pointing to "a religious discernment which attends to the qualitative events within the concrete structures of experience giving intimation of

God's grace and goodness." Meland, *Higher Education and the Human Spirit*, 166. Gary Dorrien comments that Meland *did* emphasize tragedy, ambiguity, and dissonance. In Meland's estimation, "there is no human life of any depth or vigor that is without its tragic sense." But Meland never went as far as Loomer in affirming that God's being includes the world's evil, exclaiming on one occasion that he was not willing "to make a devil out of God." Dorrien, *The Making of American Liberal Theology: Crisis, Irony, and Postmodernity, 1950–2005*, 3, 128–31.

82 Loomer, "The Size of God," 21, 40, 48–50.

83 For example, Catherine Keller takes the standard Whiteheadian position that the "divine Eros" is "a cosmic appetite for becoming, for beauty and intensity of experience." The content of the initial aim for each occasion is "that moment's best possibility." Keller, *On the Mystery: Discerning God in Process*, 99–100. Is there any observable difference between Keller's interpretation of the initial aim and Conner's?

84 Conner complains that conventional process theologians like Marjorie Suchocki assume that God's goals for *all* things include "adventure, truth, beauty, zest, and peace," overlooking the fact that "such goals are a great deal more applicable for human beings than they are for animals or plants, not to mention non-living societies and entities." By Conner's reckoning, this reveals that Suchocki is not engaged in objective metaphysics but is in thrall to unacknowledged religious motives, confessional biases, and anthropocentric interests. Conner, "The Plight of a Theoretical Deity: A Response to Suchocki's 'The Dynamic God'," 115.

85 Conner, "Whitehead the Naturalist," 176. See also Conner, "The Plight of a Theoretical Deity: A Response to Suchocki's 'The Dynamic God'," 118, 120.

86 Loomer, "The Size of God," 41.

87 Frankenberry, *Religion and Radical Empiricism*, 126.

88 Nancy Frankenberry, "Classical Theism, Panentheism, and Pantheism: On the Relation Between God Construction and Gender Construction," *Zygon* 28, no. 1 (1993), 40, 29.

89 William Dean, "Second Thoughts," *American Journal of Theology*

and Philosophy 29, no. 3 (September 2008), 301.

90 Dean, "Dean Replies to Zbaraschuk," 262.

91 Dean, *The Religious Critic in American Culture*, 69–70, 75–79, 82–83, 140–48. Besides nature itself, Dean looks to a number of other sources for "evidence" of an ambiguous God, including the Judeo-Christian scriptures, the thought of Luther and Calvin, contemporary liberation theologies, and most recently, the poetry of Wallace Stevens. See William Dean, *The American Spiritual Culture: And the Invention of Jazz, Football, and the Movies* (New York and London: Continuum, 2002), 161–65; William Dean, "Even Stevens: A Poet for Liberal Theologians," *Journal of Religion* 92, no. 2 (April 2012).

92 Dean, "Second Thoughts," 302.

93 Cobb, "Whitehead as the Philosopher of an Ecological Civilization," 16.

94 Corrington, "An Appraisal and Critique of Alfred North Whitehead's *Process and Reality* and Justus Buchler's *Metaphysics of Natural Complexes*," 33. See also Corrington and Niemoczynski, "An Introduction to Ecstatic Naturalism: An Interview with Robert S. Corrington," 74–78.

95 See especially Corrington, *Nature and Spirit: An Essay in Ecstatic Naturalism*, 1–39; Corrington, *Nature's Sublime: An Essay in Aesthetic Naturalism*, 1–32.

96 See Crosby, *A Religion of Nature*, 20–21, 23–26, 32.

97 See Crosby, *The Thou of Nature: Religious Naturalism and Reverence for Sentient Life*.

98 See Conner, "Whitehead the Naturalist," 177; Crosby, "Emergentism, Perspectivism, and Divine Pathos," 203.

99 See Crosby, "A Case for Religion of Nature," 139–41, 165.

100 Crosby, *The Thou of Nature: Religious Naturalism and Reverence for Sentient Life*, 128.

⇒ 8 ⇒

PROCESS POLYTHEISM

Eric Steinhart

ABSTRACT: *I develop a version of process theology inspired by Hartshorne. This development aims to reconcile Hartshorne both with recent science and with analytic metaphysics. It posits an endless series of ever-greater cosmic epochs. Each cosmic epoch is a subcomputation in a divine organism. Each divine organism is like a phoenix. Just as new cosmic epochs are born from the ashes of old cosmic epochs, so new deities are born from the ashes of old deities. The result is a process polytheism.*

WHAT FOLLOWS is a version of process theology inspired by Charles Hartshorne, but the version developed here will differ from his process theology in several ways. This version of process theology is a novel kind of polytheism. It posits many deities. However, unlike older polytheisms (such as Greek or Norse polytheisms), these deities do not inhabit our universe. On the contrary, there are many universes, and each deity produces its own universe. There are many deity-universe pairs. Each universe gets exactly one deity, and each deity gets exactly one universe. Versions of this *process polytheism* have been discussed by John Leslie, Peter Forrest, and myself.[1]

PROCESSES AND FOUR-DIMENSIONALISM

This presentation of process polytheism begins with a discussion of processes. Hartshorne endorses the thesis that persisting things are processes, which are time-ordered sequences of distinct instantaneous stages.[2] His philosophy, "like that of the Buddhists or of Whitehead . . . regards enduring individuals as somewhat abstractly conceived sequences of events."[3] The events which compose a process are not identical. Things are not enduring substances which remain self-identical through time. Hartshorne rejects identity through time.[4] The relation between events is genidentity.[5]

Among contemporary theories of persistence, the one that comes closest to the theory in Hartshorne is known as *four-dimensionalism*.[6] According to this theory, there are three ordinary dimensions of space, and there is a fourth dimension of time. A persisting thing is a four-dimensional series of three-dimensional stages. While the persisting thing is temporally extended along the fourth dimension of time, its stages are merely spatially extended along the three dimensions of space. So the instantaneous stages of persisting things are like three-dimensional pages of a four-dimensional book. The stages in any process are temporally ordered from earlier to later. While each stage is identical with itself, it is not identical with any earlier or any later stages.

The process theology developed here involves a specific kind of four-dimensionalism. It is known as *exdurantism*, also known as *stage-theory*, and also known as *temporal counterpart theory*. Suppose Mary is a middle-aged woman in 2016. Her life is a process containing many past stages and many future stages. All those stages exist in their own times on the temporal dimension. Of course, they do not exist at the same time. Her past stages are earlier than her future stages; her future stages are later than her past stages. To say that Mary *is* middle-aged means that Mary has a present counterpart (namely, herself) who is middle-aged. To say that Mary *was* born in 1960 means that Mary has a past counterpart who is born in 1960.

Mary's past counterparts never pass out of existence; each just *exists* in its own time. To say that Mary *will* die in 2050 means that Mary has a future counterpart who dies in 2050. Mary's future counterparts never come into existence; each just *exists* in its own time.

THE SEQUENCE OF COSMIC PHOENIXES

Process metaphysics contains an early multiverse theory.[7] For Whitehead, physical reality at the largest scale is a series of cosmic epochs. Hartshorne also acknowledges the division of the total physical process into distinct epochs.[8] Distinct cosmic epochs have their own beginnings and ends. Hence "the present quantitative system of the cosmos is doomed."[9] The end of our cosmic epoch will be the heat death of our universe.[10] These epochs have their own laws. Since these epochs are isolated and have their own physical laws, it is reasonable to refer to them as universes. Hence physical reality at the largest scale consists of an ordered series of universes.

Every universe (every cosmic epoch) has an organic unity; it is a cosmic organism. Hence each universe resembles a living body.[11] The laws of physics are to each universe as a genotype is to an organism. So the laws of physics are the genetic program of the universe. But the laws of physics are not eternal. As an old universe changes into a new universe, the old laws change into new laws. The old cosmic genotype changes into a new cosmic genotype. Hence the cosmic genotypes evolve. After our cosmic epoch, there will be a new epoch with its own genotype, its own laws of physics.

It appears that each universe resembles an organism which is born, lives, and dies. After its death, a new universe is born. This cosmology resembles the old Stoic cosmology in which each universe ends in a fiery conflagration (*ekpyrosis*).[12] After its *ekpyrosis*, a new universe is born from the ashes of the old universe. The Stoics also thought of universes as living organisms. Since universes are organisms that die in flames and that then produce their successors, each universe resembles a cosmic *phoenix*, which is born, lives, bursts into flames, and is then reborn out of its own ashes.[13] Each phoenix has the power to create its successor.

DIGITAL INTELLIGENCE

Our universe is an organism; but organisms are animated by minds. Hartshorne believes our universe is animated by a cosmic mind, which he calls *God*. He says God is to the universe as a mind is to its body.[14] He accepts mind-body dualism.[15] His mind-body dualism is not defensible. Perhaps the only way to use Hartshorne's analogy is to invert it: *God is to the universe as a body is to its mind*. This inversion rejects mind-body dualism in favor of epiphenomenalism. According to this epiphenomenalism, minds are not distinct substances from their bodies; rather, they supervene on their bodies (mostly on their brains). The mind supervenes on the brain much like the image of a face supervenes on a pattern of colored pixels on a video screen. Or the mind supervenes on the brain like a gene supervenes on a sequence of DNA base-pairs.

One of the benefits of this inverted analogy is that it can be correlated with defensible contemporary ways of thinking about minds. One idea is that the mind is to the brain as software is to hardware. This is the *computational theory of mind*. On this theory, the brain is an organic computer. Although the brain does not have the same structure as an artificial digital computer, the functionality of the brain is equivalent to the functionality of an artificial digital computer. The way the brain works can be exactly simulated by any digital computer. So the brain runs a program or algorithm which transforms earlier digital patterns of neural activity into later digital patterns of neural activity. But these digital patterns encode thoughts; thoughts supervene on those patterns.

It seems likely that Hartshorne himself would object to this digital conception of the mind. He says our brains are at least "thinking machines."[16] But he also says that they are "far more than thinking machines."[17] Unfortunately, he never clarifies the ways our brains exceed thinking machines. One of the greatest objections to Hartshorne's thought is its mystification of mentality. His concept of the mind is obscure. The computational theory of mind has at least the benefit of clarity. Moreover, it reconciles panentheism with contemporary science and philosophy. And it allows several other aspects of Hartshorne's cosmology to be scientifically recovered.

COMPUTATIONAL PANENTHEISM

According to this inverted analogy, just as the mind supervenes on the body, so the universe supervenes on God. And, according to the computational theory of mind, the mind supervenes on the body as software supervenes on hardware. Thus the universe is to God as software is to hardware. This means that our universe is a software-process running on a divine hardware substrate. This divine hardware substrate is God. God is a cosmic computer and the physical universe is an informational pattern running on that computer. God generates the universe by computing it into existence. The idea that our physical universe is running on an underlying computer is supported by many contemporary arguments in philosophy and physics.[18] Hence this way of thinking about the God-universe relation is also supported by those arguments.

This way of thinking about the God-universe relation is panentheistic: the universe is a proper part of the divine computational activity. God has parts and is complex.[19] Some but not all of these parts compute the cosmos.[20] Thus God is a divine body which thinks because it computes. Part of its thinking is the universe. By treating the divine body as a computer, and by treating the divine mind as a process which supervenes on the divine body, much of Hartshorne's philosophy can be recovered.

This computational panentheism dovetails nicely with Hartshorne's organic conception of the cosmos. He said that the laws of physics are to each universe as a genotype is to its organism. But genotypes are like programs. So the cosmic genotype is the program being run by the cosmic computer. This genetic analogy further supports the thesis that God is to the universe as a body is to its mind. After all, the genotype belongs to the body, and, by running its genotype, the body produces the mind. God is a living entity. And just as living things have the power to produce offspring, so God has the power to produce offspring. If each cosmic epoch is like a phoenix, then it has the power to create its successor. But that power is divine creative power.[21]

THE SEQUENCE OF DIVINE PHASES

There is a sequence of cosmic epochs. Each cosmic epoch has an organic unity; it has its own genotype. Hence the stages in every cosmic epoch are very tightly bound together. Each epoch is like a distinctive software-process running on its own computational substrate. At some point in time, the cosmic epoch ends, the cosmic organism dies, the software process halts. When this happens it seems appropriate to say that the hardware substratum also ends in some significant sense. After all, when an organism dies, it does not continue. But this end need not be total.

Once more the metaphor of the phoenix is apt: the sequence of cosmic organisms is analogous to a sequence of distinct phoenixes. As any phoenix burns up, its ashes form a cosmic egg. From this egg, the next phoenix is born. Of course, each next phoenix is not totally new, but inherits much of its nature from its predecessor. These cosmic phoenixes are all genetically linked, like parent and offspring. By analogy, as any cosmic epoch ends, it begets the next cosmic epoch. Each dying cosmic epoch computes a new genotype, which is the cosmic program for the next epoch. The stages in distinct epochs are bound together. However, since they are not bound by the same laws, they are not bound together as tightly as those in a single epoch.

Each stage in the life of each phoenix is a stage in the life of God. All the stages in the life of God are unified. But the unity of stages in each single cosmic epoch is greater than the unity of stages in distinct epochs. Hence the life of God is divided into segments or phases by the death of each previous phoenix and the birth of the next phoenix. These phoenixes are relatively isolated segments of the life of God. These phoenixes are divine lives within the greater divine Life. They might be referred to as gods or deities, but those terms have their own connotations. So, to avoid confusion, they will be referred to as *titans*. Each of these titans is born, lives, and dies. As it dies each previous titan gives birth to the next titan. This confirms Hartshorne's idea that there is "a kind of 'begetting' in the divine life."[22] Each new titan generates its own new universe, with its own laws and contents. On this view, God is a sequence of organically unified titans, and each titan is a sequence of stages. Each titan creates the next titan.[23]

THE PROGRESSION OF DIVINE STAGES

For process theologians, God is a process. Thus God is a time-ordered series of stages. For Hartshorne, God is perpetually self-surpassing. The later stages of God are divinely greater than the earlier stages. He says that "God cannot conceivably be surpassed or equaled by any other individual, but He can surpass himself, and thus His actual state is not the greatest possible state."[24]

Hartshorne analyzes the greatness of any divine state in terms of aesthetic value. To be greater is to have more aesthetic value. There is an endless progression of ever greater degrees of such value: "Aesthetic value is the most concrete form of value. Everything can contribute to and increase it."[25] But there is no maximum of this aesthetic value.[26] Hence there is no maximum of value: "The most concrete form of value has no upper limit; there can always be additional values."[27] Hartshorne defines aesthetic value in ways that seem to include greater degrees of complexity. So his concept of value can be correlated with computational concepts of complexity.[28]

There is no maximum of divine perfection: "Take any conceivable number. A greater can be conceived. How do we know this is not true of 'beings'?"[29] Thus the divine life has at least the structure of the positive integers. As time goes on, the stages of divine life grow in value: "The only change [in God] must be in increase in whatever aspects of value are incapable of an absolute maximum, these being summed up in the idea of enjoying the beauty, the aesthetic harmony and richness, of creation."[30] For Hartshorne, the later stages of God are greater than the earlier stages.

Hartshorne often says that God is the self-surpassing surpasser of all.[31] On the present interpretation, this means that God is a sequence of divine phases. Each phase is a titan. It is an organically unified segment of the divine life. But each titan subdivides into divine stages. Hence God can also be identified with the class of all the divine stages in all the titans. These stages satisfy at least these two axioms: there is some stage of God; every stage of God is surpassed by some greater stage of God. And God, as the class of all stages, surpasses every stage. Thus, for Hartshorne, God surpasses every stage like the class of all positive integers surpasses every positive integer.

THE REGRESSION OF DIVINE STAGES

For Hartshorne, the later stages of God are greater than the earlier stages. If this is right, then the earlier stages of God are also *lesser* than the later stages. There is a regression of ever lesser stages of God. According to Hartshorne, this regression is infinite. He says that there is no beginning of time.[32] Thus time runs infinitely far back into the past.[33] As time runs back, so the cosmic epochs also run back. Since time also runs forwards without end, Hartshorne affirms that there is a two-way infinite series of cosmic epochs.[34] Consequently, the series of stages of God has at least the structure of the integers: it runs infinitely forwards in time like the positive integers and it runs infinitely backwards in time like the negative integers.

There are two ways in which the series of divine stages can involve an infinite regression. The first way associates every integer with some divine stage. Each stage has a degree of perfection proportional to the integer itself. Hence the zeroth stage has zero perfection and the negative stages have negative perfections. Perhaps an exactly simple thing has zero perfection. But it seems absurd to say that any divine stage has negative perfection. Hence this first way of regressing fails.

The second way also associates every integer with some divine stage. But now the zeroth stage has exactly one unit of perfection. Every next stage has twice as much perfection and every previous stage has half the perfection. So, on the negative integers, perfections decrease like the fractions ½, ¼, ⅛, and so on. The objection to this fractional regress is that it makes little sense to talk about fractional degrees of perfection. For instance, if the divine stages are organic, then they have some complexities. But it makes little sense say that the complexity of an organism can be perpetually divided in half. At some point, dividing the perfection of an organism by half results in something which is not an organism. Organisms are not infinitely divisible. They are composed of discrete structures. Hence this second way of regressing fails.

The divine life is not infinitely regressive in the same way that the integers are infinitely regressive. On the contrary, the stages of the divine life must contain an order like the structure of the ordinal number line. The ordinal number line starts with the finite natural numbers (0, 1, 2, 3, and so on). But it then continues beyond the finite numbers into infinite numbers. The ordinal number line is infinitely long, and infinite ordinals do indeed have infinite regressions behind them. But those regressions bottom out in the initial number zero. For the sake of mathematical coherence, the stages of the divine life must be organized in a similar ordinal way.

Moving backwards into the divine past, the divine greatness ultimately decreases to an initial minimal value. This is the degree of perfection of some initial stage. This initial stage is correlated with the ordinal number zero. Just as earthly life begins with an initial self-replicator, so divine life begins with an initial self-surpasser. This initial stage is the necessary simple first cause. It is the minimal cosmic organism, the initial titan. It seems plausible to say that the perfection of any simple thing is zero.

TO INFINITY AND BEYOND

Hartshorne is aware that, just as there is no greatest finite number, so there is no greatest infinite number.[35] Hartshorne is aware that mathematicians posit an endless sequence of ever greater infinities: "There are in standard mathematics many infinities unequal to one another, but no highest infinity."[36] He is aware that the phrase "greatest possible number" does not refer to any number.[37] The ordinal number line progresses without any end. And he is aware that there is no maximally inclusive class; but then, there is no greatest possible class. There is no "class of all classes."[38]

Hartshorne now appears to argue like this: the concepts of greatest possible number and greatest possible class are paradoxical; since they are paradoxical, they are not instantiated; but the concept of a greatest possible value is analogous to those mathematical concepts; reasoning by analogy, the concept of greatest possible value is likewise paradoxical and not instantiated.[39] Hartshorne says "It is arguable that even an infinite richness may be open to increase."[40]

These arguments suggest that the degrees of perfection are organized like the ordinal number line. The ordinal number line runs through all the finite ordinal numbers, and then it runs out into the infinite. Just so, the titans and their universes progress through all the finite and infinite degrees of perfection. For every ordinal number, there exists some titan whose perfection is proportional to that ordinal. And that titan contains a universe whose perfection is proportional to that ordinal.

At this point the computational theory of the titans can help provide these ideas with some scientific precision. Computer scientists have defined endless ranks of infinite computers. These computers have infinite memories. They perform infinitely complex operations on infinitely rich informational patterns. And these endless ranks of infinite computers define endless ranks of infinite minds.[41] Those infinite minds can run infinite universes which contain infinitely complex physical bodies.[42]

THE ENDLESSLY RAMIFIED TREE OF TITANS

The series of titan-universe pairs suffers from two problems. The first problem is that the series of titan-universe pairs has an unattractive contingency: why does only this sequence exist, rather than some other series? It is certainly possible that there are others which are at least as divine. The second problem is that, since there is only one series of universes, they do not constitute mutual alternatives, and the class of these universes does not serve the needs of quantified modal logic or temporal logic. It does not yet provide an adequate account of the actualization of possibility.

The needs of the logic of possibility (modal logic) can be met by continuing the biological analogy. Just as ordinary organisms can make many offspring, so cosmic organisms can make many offspring. Every cosmic organism is a titan, but every titan is a phoenix. When a phoenix burns up, its ashes form an egg. From each egg, a new phoenix is born. The offspring relation organizes the titans into a divine tree of life, which resembles the earthly tree of life. Following Hartshorne, each offspring titan surpasses its parent titan. Within any lineage of titans, the stages of the divine life are perpetually self-surpassing. Lesser titans evolve into greater titans. More precisely, for every titan, for every possible way it can be surpassed by a greater titan, it produces some offspring titan which surpasses it in that way. Since this principle incorporates possibility, the resulting class of titan-universe pairs can serve as an adequate domain of quantification for modal logic (e.g., for counterpart theory).

Perhaps Hartshorne would agree that the *relative side* of God can be analyzed into an endlessly ramified tree of titans, each of which is the unity of its own cosmic epoch (or universe). Nevertheless, he might further insist that the *absolute side* of God includes and transcends all the lives of these titanic deities. Perhaps this is consistent with his neo-trinitarianism, which permits there to be infinitely many Holy Spirits.[43] Thus the titans are analogous to these universe-bound spirits. Of course, this reference to Christian theology is not necessary. The absolute God is merely some pantheistic unity. It is the whole of which the titans are parts, or it is the class of which they are members. But since this absolute God has little resemblance to any traditional God, it seems odd to keep the name. Since the endlessly ramified tree of titans defines all physical universes, and since the titans themselves are conceived of here in naturalistic terms (as divine organisms), it seems more accurate to refer to this tree as *nature*.

Some may say there is little difference between using the term "God" pantheistically (or panentheistically) and using the term "nature." But Crosby wisely says that "God" has so many anthropomorphic connotations that it cannot be used without unconscious misinterpretation.[44] Following Crosby, at least until the term "God" becomes purified of its anthropomorphic connotations, process polytheism prefers to use the term "nature" to refer to the tree of titans, and to say that *nature is the self-surpassing surpasser of all*. Since this absolute side of nature transcends the tree of titans, and exists in an eternal completeness, it can be thought of as nature natured (*natura naturata*).

CONCLUSION

It is easy to use Hartshorne's process theology to motivate a process polytheism involving many titanic deities and many universes. Each universe is associated with its own deity. According to this process polytheism, the divine life is not the continuous activity of any single divine individual; on the contrary, it is a vast ecological enterprise, the actualization of all the many divergent possibilities of divine life. And just as there does not exist any single organism which supports all the distinct organisms on earth, so also there does not exist any single deity which supports the distinct titanic deities. Process polytheism really is polytheistic, and not some kind of cryptic monotheism. Moreover, just as there are many species of earthly organisms, with their own natures, so there are many species of deities, with their own natures too.

Nevertheless, to say that the great tree of titans actualizes all the possibilities of divine life suggests that there exists some life which has those possibilities. However, since that life is not the continuous activity of any single divine individual, it must be an energy which flows from earlier divine individuals to later divine individuals. It flows from every titan to its offspring. This energy drives every titan to surpass itself. It is the power of self-surpassing. This energy resembles the Stoic *pneuma*, which drives a cyclical process of cosmic creation and destruction. Or perhaps it resembles the Hindu Brahman or the Aztec *teotl*.[45] However, as the power which brings all biological and thus all psychological entities into being, this energy has neither any biological nor psychological attributes. It is genderless, mindless, uncaring, and utterly impersonal. It has no feeling, no consciousness, no desire, no purpose. This ultimate creative power can be thought of as nature naturing (*natura naturans*).[46]

Process polytheism posits many titanic deities and many kinds or species of titanic deity. The deities are not made in the image of any single species. They are not made in the image of humanity. Process polytheism helps to overcome the anthropomorphic conception of the divine. When the deities are thought of more biologically, they become more highly naturalized. They cease to be above and beyond the world of life. Since the titanic deities evolve, process polytheism values evolution; it declares that evolution is divine; evolution is holy. Since process polytheism posits many diverse species of deity, it likewise declares that biological diversity is divine; biological diversity is holy. The earthly tree of life mirrors the divine tree of life.

If theology deals with our ultimate concerns, then a more biological conception of the divine can help to integrate life itself into the structure our ultimate concern, and may thereby help humanity to see itself as unified with earthly life. Theology tells us what we ought to ultimately be concerned about. It defines our highest values. Process polytheism affirms that evolution and ecological diversity are among our highest values. We ought to care for those most deeply in our lives on earth. We ought to act to ensure that the self-surpassing of earthly life is as rich as possible. We ought to act to ensure that the self-surpassing of earthly life sustains itself for as long as possible.

ENDNOTES

1　Multiverse polytheism posits many universes with at least one god at each. It has been discussed by John Leslie, *Infinite Minds: A Philosophical Cosmology* (New York: Oxford, 2001), and by Peter Forrest, *Developmental Theism: From Pure Will to Unbounded Love* (New York: Oxford University Press, 2007). It has been extensively developed by Eric Steinhart in "On the Plurality of Gods," *Religious Studies* 49, no. 3 (2013), 289–312, and in Eric Steinhart, *Your Digital Afterlives: Computational Theories of Life after Death* (New York: Palgrave Macmillan, 2014).

2　Charles Hartshorne says persisting things are processes. He analyzes these as time-ordered sequences of stages. See his *The Logic of Perfection and Other Essays in Neoclassical Metaphysics* (LaSalle, IL: Open Court Publishing, 1962), 41–42, 66, 119–22, 218–21. And see his *Omnipotence and Other Theological Mistakes* (Albany, NY: State University of New York Press, 1984), 104–06.

3　For the rejection of identity through time, see Charles Hartshorne, *Anselm's Discovery: A Re-Examination of the Ontological Argument for God's Existence* (LaSalle, IL: Open Court Publishing, 1965), 51.

4　Hartshorne rejects identity through time. See his *The Logic of Perfection,* 119–22.

5　Hartshorne, *Anselm's Discovery,* 50–51.

6　The theory of four-dimensionalism in contemporary analytic philosophy is closest to Hartshorne's theory of persistence. Four-dimensionalism is discussed by Katherine Hawley in *How Things Persist* (New York: Oxford University Press, 2001), and by Ted Sider in *Four-Dimensionalism: An Ontology of Persistence and Time* (New

York: Oxford University Press, 2001).

7   Leemon McHenry uses contemporary cosmology to develop the early multiverse theory found in Whitehead. See McHenry's "The Multiverse Conjecture: Whitehead's Cosmic Epochs and Contemporary Cosmology," *Process Studies* 40.1 (2011): 5–25.

8   For cosmic epochs, see Hartshorne, *Omnipotence and Other Theological Mistakes,* 92–94. More recently, Donald Crosby affirms Hartshorne's idea that physical reality is a series of cosmic epochs. See Crosby, *A Religion of Nature* (Albany: State University of New York Press, 2002), 35–44.

9   Hartshorne, *The Logic of Perfection,* 215.

10   Hartshorne also develops his theory of cosmic epochs in his *Man's Vision of God* (Chicago: Willett, Clark, & Co., 1941). For heat death, see 201.

11   For Hartshorne's discussion of his theory that the universe is a cosmic organism, see Ibid., 180–02, 200–01, 262–63.

12   See Michael Lapidge, "Stoic Cosmology," in *The Stoics*, ed. John Rist (Berkeley: University of California Press, 1978), 161–87.

13   For universes created by birds, see Hume, *Dialogues Concerning Natural Religion* (New York: Penguin, 1990), 87.

14   Hartshorne, *Man's Vision of God,* 176; *Omnipotence and Other Theological Mistakes,* 59.

15   Hartshorne, *Man's Vision of God,* 175, 185–93.

16   For brains as thinking machines, see Hartshorne, *Omnipotence and Other Theological Mistakes,* 92.

17   For brains as exceeding thinking machines, see Hartshorne, *Omnipotence,* 92.

18   The thesis that our universe is running on a computer is discussed by Steinhart in his *Your Digital Afterlives,* chapter 5.

19   Hartshorne, *Anselm's Discovery,* 28.

20   Steinhart, "On the Plurality of Gods."

21   Hartshorne, *Man's Vision of God,* 230–32.

22   Hartshorne, *The Logic of Perfection,* 122.

23 Charles Hartshorne, *The Divine Relativity: A Social Conception of God* (New Haven: Yale University Press, 1948). For divine creativity, see 30.

24 Hartshorne, *The Logic of Perfection*, 35.

25 Hartshorne, *Omnipotence and Other Theological Mistakes*, 10.

26 Hartshorne, *Omnipotence*, 10, 31.

27 Hartshorne, *Omnipotence*, 10.

28 Value is complexity. Many computer scientists and mathematicians analyze complexity in terms of an abstract quality known as *logical depth*. Steinhart argues that intrinsic value is logical depth in his *Your Digital Afterlives*, secs. 72–74.

29 Hartshorne, *Anselm's Discovery*, 27.

30 Hartshorne, *Omnipotence and Other Theological Mistakes*, 110.

31 Hartshorne, *The Divine Relativity*, 20; *Anselm's Discovery*, 28–32, 135–36.

32 Hartshorne, *Man's Vision of God*, 233–34; *Omnipotence and Other Theological Mistakes*, 75.

33 Hartshorne, *The Logic of Perfection*, 123; *Anselm's Discovery*, 129, 188.

34 Hartshorne, *Man's Vision of God*, 230–32.

35 Hartshorne correctly rejects the idea of a greatest infinite number. See his *A Natural Theology for Our Time* (La Salle, IL: Open Court, 1967), 19–20.

36 Hartshorne, *Omnipotence and Other Theological Mistakes*, 7.

37 Hartshorne, *Natural Theology*, 19–20; *Omnipotence and Other Theological Mistakes*, 7.

38 Hartshorne, *Omnipotence and Other Theological Mistakes*, 3–4.

39 Hartshorne, *Natural Theology*, 19–20; *Omnipotence and Other Theological Mistakes*, 3–4.

40 Hartshorne, *Omnipotence and Other Theological Mistakes*, 7.

41 For infinite computers and infinite minds, see Eric Steinhart, "Supermachines and Superminds," *Minds and Machines 13* (2003), 155–86.

42 Steinhart, *Your Digital Afterlives*, chapters 8 and 9.

43 Hartshorne, *The Logic of Perfection,* 122.

44 Crosby argues that the term "God" is so "hopelessly anthropomorphic" that it must be rejected. See his *A Religion of Nature,* 9.

45 James Maffie discusses Aztec *teotl* in chapter 2 of his *Aztec Philosophy: Understanding a World in Motion* (Boulder, CO: University Press of Colorado, 2014).

46 Crosby, in his *A Religion of Nature,* provides an extensive discussion of nature naturing as an ultimate creative and destructive power.

PART THREE

EMERGENCE, PANPSYCHISM
AND DEEP ECOLOGY

❧ 9 ❧

ARISTOTLE AND WHITEHEAD:
EMERGENCE, PROCESS, AND THE
IMPORTANCE OF IRRELEVANCE

Lawrence Cahoone

ABSTRACT: *Process philosophy and emergence arose as fellow-travelers during one of the most creative periods of Western philosophy of nature, 1900–1930, soon to be eclipsed by the splitting of philosophy into the "two cultures" of analytic and continental philosophy. Process and emergence were part of a revolt against 17th century mechanism and dualism, but also against the substance metaphysics and fixed species of Aristotle that seem to lay behind them. But I will argue that Aristotle shares something with emergence: the renunciation of the belief that our metaphysical problems will be solved by our conception of the smallest or most comprehensive domains of nature. There are independent, qualitatively distinct, weakly related or completely unrelated macroscopic systems and processes in nature. In effect, this is a refusal of the metaphysical primacy either of physics or the Whole. Aristotle is the premodern philosopher most congenial to this emergentist conception of nature, in some ways more so than Whitehead.*

WHAT WE CALL PROCESS PHILOSOPHY and what we call emergence arrived on the scene as fellow-travelers during one of the most creative periods of Western philosophy of nature, roughly 1900–1930, a period rivalled in the West only by the 17th century and ancient Greece. Its flowering was curtailed after 1930 when the iron curtain of the separation of analytic and continental philosophy descended, philosophy's version of "the two cultures," C.P. Snow's term for the segregation of the natural and human sciences.

Emergence and process were part of what might be called a revolt against a revolt against Aristotle, albeit not thereby an Aristotelian counter-revolution. Seventeenth-century physics was a revolt against Aristotle; so was evolutionary thought in the mid-19th century, and, in another way, the new logic of the end of the century and beginning of the next. One might say Darwin, Frege, and Russell complete the 17th-century project. While the new naturalism of 1900–1930 primarily attacked 17th-century mechanism, the rebels saw Aristotle's substance metaphysics as the regressive *ancien régime* behind mechanism. The needed corrections, they felt, would be new concepts of process and relativity, by no means a reincorporation of Aristotle.

But I will argue the emergence of the 1900–1930 rebellion shares something with Aristotle after all. Emergence implies a renunciation of the belief that our major metaphysical problems will be solved by our conception of the smallest *or* most comprehensive domains of nature. The middle matters just as much, maybe more. And Aristotle is *the* metaphysician of the middle. There are independent, qualitatively distinct, weakly related or completely unrelated macroscopic entities in nature. Aristotle is admittedly not an emergentist, because to be an emergentist you have to accept an evolutionary view of nature; emergence is a product of evolution (in both senses). Nevertheless, Aristotle has a claim on being the premodern philosopher most congenial to an emergentist conception of nature, in some ways more so than Whitehead, fellow traveler of emergence though he may be. It is in this middle that we find the objects of ecology, the domain of the greatest emergent complexity.

Let us begin by defining emergence. Following the work of philosopher of biology William Wimsatt, when a system property cannot be reductively explained as an aggregate of properties of the system's parts and the interaction rules governing those parts, it is emergent.[1] Differently put, emergence obtains when the organization of the system makes a difference to the contribution its parts make to the whole system. The underlying issue is, to what must we refer in order to explain the system's properties? If we must refer to the system's interaction with comparable systems, we may call that a *systemic* explanation; if we must refer to the role the system plays in a larger environment and its processes, it is a *functional* explanation; if the system's parts and their interactions are sufficient, it is a *reductive* explanation. Explaining the dent in your fender by the impact of the other car is not reductive, it is systemic. Systemic and functional explanations are both emergent, because non-reductive.

Now, virtually all natural systems have properties that depend on the nature of their components, and cannot be explained without reference to them and their interaction rules. But few systems are such that *all* their properties can be explained that way. In science we commonly cobble together functional, systemic, and reductive explanations to explain the totality of a system's properties. The point is that emergence and reduction are not antithetical; each is a matter of degree, and most natural systems require multiple explanatory strategies.

Emergence has little significance without downward causation. (The combination of the two is what some call "strong emergence.") Lots of people, and scientists, who are indifferent to emergence still accept downward causation. If one believes the distal, higher-level cellular and inter-cellular processes are sometimes necessary to explain movements of macromolecules within cells, or that global neural communication across the brain is sometimes necessary to explain the firing of local and/or lower level neural areas, that is downward causation. If emergence is to have significance, some emergent properties must be downwardly causal, making reductive explanation inadequate for the property in question.

Once we accept emergence with downward causation, we have a *hierarchical* conception of nature—"hierarchy" not in the sense of degrees of importance or reality, but in the sense of wholes, parts, and scale. Natural systems can have different properties, processes, and structures at different levels of composition and scale. Take a whitetail deer. It is simultaneously a system, or entity, interacting with comparably sized macroscopic material and biological systems (water sources, terrain features, vegetation, predators, offspring, conspecifics); it is a member of an ecosystem, a set of organ systems and tissues in interaction, a collection of millions of living cells, a swarm of 10^{27} molecules or atoms, etc. Each level has its own processes, structures, and properties, and, depending on the situation, the explanation of what happens at one level requires reference to any number of other levels. We cannot expect to explain a phenomenon always by reduction to the lowest level, nor through functional explanation from the most encompassing level either. There are mechanisms at every level of nature; pursuing neuroscience and biochemistry and engineering models at one level is not tantamount to the denial of higher level properties or downward causation. That is, a right understanding of emergence leads us to abandon the methodological wars of reduction vs. emergence, part vs. whole, mechanism vs. organicism, process vs. substance, external vs. internal relations, etc. Neither is prior in general.

Now to history. We can find large chunks of modern science previewed in the three great ancient Hellenic metaphysicians: Democritus, Plato, and Aristotle (with some apologies to the Hellenist Plotinus). Democritus made reality out of unchanging material simples in space, devoid of their own principle of change, but whose movements could conform to law. The smallest components are "eternal"; everything else is a consequence of their motions and combinations. Atomism returned in the 17th century and was only confirmed at the dawn of the 20th century. While today's atoms are not simples, we have new *simplests*, quarks and leptons. As field quanta these are not Democritean simples, but quantum mechanics still insists on their discreteness or particulate character, hence the construction of nature from tiny constituents.

Plato, on the other hand, asserted the primacy of the *eidos* or idea, hence the qualitatively distinct form, and saw mathematics as metaphysics' closest cousin. The Demiurge in his *Timaeus* fashioned soul and the world in arithmetic ratios and geometrical shapes. The 17th century confirmed that physics had to be mathematical. Twentieth-century physics, particularly general relativity and the standard model, have pressed the mathematicization of nature much further, ontologically converging on complex mathematical structures. As Howard Stein once argued, in a real sense these areas of physics have come to agree with Plato that ultimate reality is forms and not entities.[2]

At any rate, we can say that the spirits of Democritus and Plato are simultaneously honored in contemporary science and philosophy of science. And for good reason; they have much in common. Both seek the most fundamental or ultimate domain of reals regarding which nothing else is constitutive or determining. Both are attempts to find the ultimate causes of all natural events in the *simplest realities*, whether simple components or mathematical structures. In that sense both Democritus and Plato were doing what we today call *physics*. Whitehead cites the *Timaeus* and Newton's "General Scholium" as *the two* great Western cosmological schemes, and both took mathematics as the key to nature.

Aristotle was different. We may start with that part of Aristotle's philosophy which can readily be appropriated by contemporary anti-mechanist philosophies of nature, namely, his biology and psychology. (Indeed, one of Aristotle's virtues is that he recognized psychology cannot be separated from biology.) *On the Soul* is perhaps the most important work until Darwin on the psychic and its relation to biology. All organisms possess *psyche* or soul, and the essence of soul is *entelechia*, which can be translated as *being-at-work-staying-itself*.[3] Aristotle accepts that life comes in levels. All organisms are *auto-determining* in the sense that they maintain their living bodies and manipulate their relations with environment to achieve ends. This is metabolism, sensitivity, growth, and sex. All *biota* are, we might say, *teleonomic agents*, following a purposive program, without what we moderns call mind. Aristotle rightly put plants as this level; we would add bacteria, fungi, and protists. At the next level there are animals which desire, perceive what they desire, and act to obtain it. They have a moving or passionate *psyche*. We could call these, as he would, *teleological agents*, meaning capable of minded purpose (using the term "mind" in our sense, not Aristotle's, and ascribing it only to some, not all, animals). Last is the human mind, the only true "mind" (or *nous*) for Aristotle, which incorporates rationality and speech. We might call this *moral agency*.

In metaphysics Aristotle distinguished that which has existence or being in the most primary sense of the words "exist" or "to be" from all else that can be said to have it.[4] What exists primarily is *things* or entities (*res* in Latin, or "substances" in traditional English translation), making all other beings dependent on those entities as the former's properties. Once we add Aristotle's distinction of primary from secondary substances, we have a tripartite categorization: things, properties of things, kinds of things. This roughly corresponds to the order of discovery of practical human life, which is why Aristotle has sometimes been called a "common sense" philosopher. Homo sapiens do not start with phenomenology or physics: the order of discovery begins with the identification of publicly recognized, relatively invariant systems with causal powers, or entities. Probably natural selection primed our perceptual recognition processes to be biased toward entity distinction first of all.

That we may be natively biased in that direction, however, does little for metaphysics. Nobody in philosophy seems to want a substance metaphysics any more. There are plausible reasons for this. Evolution requires that secondary substances, i.e., species and kinds, are not fixed but develop out of others. The origin of the universe for contemporary physics is virtually devoid of anything Aristotle could call a substance.

Aristotle's criterion for entity-hood was independence, which some feel has been discredited, since no entity fails to depend on or have internal relations to other entities. Any thing remains an entity only through a particular span of time and environmental conditions (e.g., low velocity and low heat). Indeed, the naturalist revolt of 1900–1930 was partly an attempt to replace substance with either process, or those very insubstantial-seeming things, fields. There has been, since the early 20th century, an urge to dispense with entities.

But this reaction is overblown. It is true there is no entity that can remain what it is if everything else were different. This does not mean there is no independence, only that independence and relation, hence entification, are matters of degree. There *are* macroscopic entities in the world, that is, systems with causal powers which maintain their character and stability across some span of environmental conditions over significant lengths of time, hence across changes of relations to other systems and properties. If there were not, our world would not be the world it is. While it is true than any entity must have some internal or constitutive relations to some other things, it does not and cannot have such relations to *all* other things. That is, *irrelevance is crucial* to allowing the thing's persistence. The world contains not only internal relations, but also external relations, *and* the utter absence of relation in any meaningful sense of the word. This does not mean entities are ontologically primary, but they are as real as anything else.

One thing to notice about Aristotle's primary substances is they are inherently *complex.* How many kinds of substances are there for Aristotle? He doesn't tell us, and we cannot count them. For Aristotle, reality is constituted by an indefinitely large number of different kinds of metaphysically distinct beings. Furthermore, a primary substance cannot be simple. It must have components or matter, a structure or form or what it is to be that thing, a process by which it came to be so, and an intrinsic tendency toward some state. (Thus Aristotle formulated the most complex historical theory of causality we know, for which each thing has four causes.) The fact that an entity is composed does not make it less real than its components; the fact that it is formed does not make it less real than its form.

Nevertheless 17th-century physics was right to revolt against Aristotle. Physics, which is to say the understanding of *its domain* of nature, could not advance with his substances, substantial forms, and final causes. The scientific revolution was mainly a physics revolution, and modern physics could not live with Aristotle (although, as noted, Aristotle's views remained plausible in chemistry, biology, and logic for a long time after). Then, from the viewpoint of the early 20th-century philosophy of nature that is our interest, the 17th-century mechanist view of nature as a whole (not just the physical) had to be opposed. But that opposition did not rehabilitate Aristotle, for it seemed his mistaken substance metaphysics had been refashioned into atoms and served as the background for mind-body dualism. Fixed species, evolution, and absence of internal relations were (and still are) Aristotle's failings. If so, the apparent remedy seemed to be evolution with internal relations, or the relativity of beings to their environments.

Enter Whitehead. Whitehead was the most metaphysically and physically comprehensive member of the Golden Age of early 20th-century anti-dualist and anti-mechanist realism, including names like Gottlob Frege, Charles S. Peirce, Bertrand Russell, Ernst Mach, Edmund Husserl, Henri Bergson, William James, John Dewey, Conwy Lloyd Morgan, Samuel Alexander, Roy Wood Sellars, and George Herbert Mead. From Darwin they accepted that human mind must be continuous with animal mind and non-mental life, and that nature is evolutionary. Also from Darwin, they faced the problem of how qualitative novelty and complexity could arise by chance. From Frege, Peirce, and Russell's new logic, they recognized that relations and meanings are as real and as logically fundamental as entities. Later, from Einstein, they learned that objects in general hold their character and properties (e.g., location, velocity, volume, shape, mass) in objective relations to other things; they are dependent on relations to objects, not subjects. All sought a new kind of realism in perception (vs. representationalism), in metaphysics (vs. idealism), and in their realist view of relations.

Whitehead explicitly mentions as kindred spirits Bergson, James, and Dewey, the American and English "new" realists (including Alexander), the critical realists (which included A.O. Lovejoy and Sellars), and neutral monism, which had been invented by Mach and James and endorsed by Whitehead's student Russell. Another party to the conversation was that outgrowth of American new realism, *objective relativism*—the claim that real objects have multiple objective characters in relations to multiple other real objects, a human perceiver being one such object—which, to my knowledge, Whitehead does not mention, although ironically he was considered one of its prime exemplars by others.[5] Whitehead and G.H. Mead knew of each other's work, and much of Mead's later philosophy is a response to Whitehead.[6] My point is, while it may be difficult to find sources for Whitehead's unique system, he was, and knew he was, contributing to a major international conversation that took him seriously.

Whitehead was familiar with emergence. In *Science and the Modern World* he admitted he was "especially indebted" to Samuel Alexander's *Space, Time and Deity* and Lloyd Morgan's *Emergent Evolution*.[7] Victor Lowe found that, of Bergson, James, and Alexander, the last has the strongest claim of influence on Whitehead—although still not a formative influence, Lowe believed.[8] Whitehead employed the notion of emergence in allowing that patterns of complex societies of actual occasions manifest properties not seen in their components, e.g., "The emergent enduring pattern is the stabilization of the emergent achievement so as to become a fact which retains its identity throughout the process."[9] A.H. Johnson noted that Whitehead admitted to him that he, Whitehead, should have introduced a category of "Emergence of Novelty" in *Process and Reality*, while pointing out that "he had noted the fact of 'pattern of society'—the pattern being not an element in any one component AE [Actual Entity]".[10]

But as we know, Whitehead does *not* use emergence as the tool was designed, to establish the arising of life and mind in nature from constituents utterly lacking those properties.[11] He ascribes proto-vital and proto-mental traits to the simplest, smallest, most evanescent, real constituents of nature, actual occasions. His aim is clear: features of the organic have to be present at the most primitive level. And with this, all ultimate realities must be related to all other ultimate realities—and indeed to all possibilities as well, at least as these are maintained by God. Internal relations to the rest of the constituents constitute each constituent as it becomes.

We could say that Whitehead admirably combines Democritus and Plato. He is, first of all, an atomist. To be sure, his atoms are unlike anyone else's, for they are equally describable as processes or events, and they are internally related to all other atoms or events. Whitehead called his mature system a "philosophy of organism," and his atoms are nicely constituted for the purpose. All the major types of processes we must account for among complex actualities are present in the smallest of all actualities. Hence the lowest (smallest, most fundament) level is the most important level for explaining anything. He conjoins his process atomism with a Platonic notion of possibilities, or properties, which ingress into actualities (not to say that forms or eternal objects are the source or cause of the later). So all everyday things are *endurances*, or societies of endurances, constituted by *occurrences*, the fundamental event-atoms, and *recurrences*, or forms. As much as any metaphysician in history, Whitehead seeks to solve the problems of metaphysics by positing unobservable constituents with the properties necessary to solve all higher level problems. Rather than abandoning dualism, he puts it in motion, making former antipodes into poles for a dipolar becoming. He invented a philosophy of organism, but his living drops of actuality ("primary organisms" or "primates" in *Science and the Modern World*, "actual occasions" or "actual entities" in *Process and Reality*) play the role of elementary particles. Whitehead was, after all, a mathematician and, in effect, a mathematical physicist (constructing his own theory of general relativity surely qualifies him for that title).[12] Whitehead is doing physics by incorporating organicism into it.

But it is still physics. It is important to recognize what a unique science physics is. It became commonplace among philosophers in the early 20th century to call all sciences other than physics the "special sciences." But it is physics that is special. Physics is not a science of matter; that honor goes to chemistry. Spacetime, electromagnetic fields, and the quantum vacuum are not matter. Physics is a science of: (a) the rules of dynamics (explaining the motion of inorganic entities under forces); (b) the smallest components of everything else, or microphysics (today, quantum theory and the standard model); (c) the background context in which everything interacts, or spacetime; and (d) the rules by which energy evolves, or thermodynamics. The objects of fundamental physics (b, c, and d) are in principle simpler than the objects of all other sciences (excluding mathematics), since chemical compounds, planets, weather and ocean systems, and biological forms presuppose them, but also require methods that go beyond physics. Chemistry has 118 elements; thousands of substances, or natural kinds; and a smallest possible chemical entity, the atom or ion. In biology there are thousands of natural kinds, or species, and a smallest living entity, the cell (or the virus). Physics does not have or need lists, or natural kinds, and has no smallest or largest object *in principle*; it keeps stretching the boundaries of what those are. Physics is the only science (other than mathematics) that can avoid listing types of entities.[13]

Are the features of nature constituted or determined by the smallest and largest? It would be premature to say so. There is a Sydney Harris cartoon of an older male astrophysicist and a younger female astrophysicist walking away from their observatory after a night's work.[14] He says to her "I study the largest and smallest things in the universe—superclusters and neutrinos. I'd like you to handle everything in between." Her job, "everything in between," is not a subject matter, because dozens of methodologically distinct disciplines have had to evolve to study that "everything." And in the last forty years the other natural sciences have been discovering more interesting types of complexity in it. "More is different," as Philip Anderson argued; meaning, complex material systems obey their own rules that cannot be derived from microphysics.[15] Richard Feynman, one of the greatest of microphysicists, wrote,

> We have a way of discussing the world, when we talk of it at various hierarchies, or levels . . . at one end we have the fundamental laws of physics . . . if we go higher up from this . . . we have properties of substances—like 'refractive index' . . . [then] . . . we get to things like muscle twitch or nerve impulse. . . . Then come things like 'frog.' . . . And then . . . we come to words and concepts like 'man,' and 'history.' . . . Which end is nearer to God? . . . I do not think either end is nearer to God. . . . To stand at either end . . . hoping that out in that direction is the complete understanding, is a mistake . . . The great mass of workers in between . . . are improving all the time our understanding and in that way we are gradually understanding this tremendous world of interconnecting hierarchies.[16]

The hierarchical view of nature resulting from emergence means that *the level of description that is most fundamental or most comprehensive is insufficient to explain more complex systems.* We are better off attempting to find our best explanations of phenomena starting at scales familiar to us, which we tend to know more robustly through multiple means of access. Then we can move outward to connect the familiar and robust to smaller and larger, or more energetic scales, without claiming the least accessible, hence most speculative orders, constitute the ontology for all reality. We have good reason to remain ontological pluralists, and to use for explanatory purposes the existence of entities, fields, processes, events, states, structures, relations, actualities, possibilities, pasts, and properties. None is prior *a priori*, or in all cases.

A modern, evolutionary metaphysics that is more Aristotelian than Whiteheadian might start with *systems* as a more neutral term for entity. Some systems have a high degree of coherence, making them *individuals*, like most organisms, planets, and atoms. Some have minimal structure, making them *ensembles*, like clouds or ecosystems. Some do not have true components at all, like *fields*. Not everything is a system, of course. While a hydrogen atom is a system, hydrogen itself is not a system, but a kind of system. Triangularity, velocity, and liquidity are not systems, but properties of systems. So, analogous to Aristotle, we could say we have systems, properties of systems, and kinds of systems. But here we might add something that could be regarded as an extension of a Whiteheadian insight. He allowed "actual entities" and "actual occasions" to be equivalent terms; the ultimate constituents of reality are simultaneously events and entities. Since events are processes as t approaches zero, we might say that a system is equally and co-primordially an entity, a set of processes that maintain it, *and* a structure or organization of components.

To say this is not "process" philosophy: *neither entity nor process nor form is prior in general.* In the kinds of systems to which we have the most robust access, not only do we not find systems without structures and not undergoing processes, we also do not find processes without something undergoing the process, or structures without something structured. There is no reason to identify the "actual" or "real" with one of the three. The causal role of each can be more or less important depending on the particular case. The relative independence of entities at different scales is a crucial feature of the middling orders of nature. Indeed, what is called multiple realizability requires that some wholes maintain themselves despite chaos or noise at lower levels, so that the particular set of components or conditions on components are irrelevant to the stability of the system. The pond remains the pond despite molecular chaos, as I remain me despite vast turnover among my cells and my microbial biome. Sometimes God, or the devil, is in the details, but *sometimes the details are noise.* Weak relatedness and unrelatedness are as crucial to nature as strong or internal relatedness. To make the point in human terms: it is one of the conditions for the meaning of my existence that when I die others do *not* die with me, but remain alive. If "The bell tolls for thee" were true, then when one dies all would die. The meaning of my life requires that my relations to others be real but *not so strong* as to erase their ability to survive me.

It should be noted that emergence does not explain; it is the name of an apparent fact, a description. If one asks why is there emergence, I have no answer other than to say that the values of the physical constants of the universe, along with physical laws, have apparently made evolution with novel properties—physical, chemical, and biological evolution—likely. If that seems metaphysically inadequate, I agree. By all means we have the right to push our thought as far as we can in every direction—into the past, future, smallest, largest, even to the divine—but we must avoid holding our relatively more robust understanding of proximate orders hostage to speculations about the ultimate. Our knowledge of the smallest, oldest, and biggest will *always* be far less reliable than our knowledge of more local, robust scales. That does not mean our knowledge of the local will ever be certain or complete, just that our ability to test and reform our knowledge of it will always be greater. We ought not to formulate conceptions of the smallest and largest in order to satisfy a logic or aesthetics of simples or the Whole, then force our accounts of local, complex systems into those conceptual boxes. A holism that regards every thing as an instantiation or part or phase of something comprehensive is not in principle an advance over a reductionism that regards every thing as an artifact or epiphenomenon or result of something smaller. The most complex systems we know, the objects of the Earth sciences, biology, and ecology, are in the middle. The Earth is in the middle. Hence we are in the middle. Which was where Aristotle was. And that's where emergence is.

ENDNOTES

1   William Wimsatt, *Re-Engineering Philosophy: Piecewise Approxima-tions to Reality* (Chicago: University of Chicago Press, 2008).

2   Howard Stein, "Yes, but . . . Some Skeptical Remarks on Realism and Anti-Realism," *Dialectica* 43, no.1 (1989), 47–65.

3   Aristotle, *On the Soul*, trans. Joe Sachs (Santa Fe: Green Lion Press, 2004), 79.

4   Aristotle, *Metaphysics*, trans. Joe Sachs (Santa Fe: Green Lion Press, 1999).

5   Arthur E. Murphy, "Objective Relativism in Dewey and Whitehead," *The Philosophical Review* 26, no.2 (1927), 121–44; Arthur O. Lovejoy, *The Revolt Against Dualism: An Inquiry Concerning the Existence of Ideas* (New York: W.W. Norton, 1930).

6   Gary A. Cook, "Whitehead's Influence on the Thought of G.H. Mead," *Transactions of the Charles S. Peirce Society* 15, no. 2 (1979), 107–31; George Herbert Mead, *The Philosophy of the Present* (LaSalle: Open Court, 1932), and *Philosophy of the Act*, ed. Charles W. Morris (Chicago: University of Chicago Press, 1934).

7   Alfred North Whitehead, *Science and the Modern World* (New York: Free Press, 1953), viii.

8   Victor Lowe, "The Influence of Bergson, James and Alexander on Whitehead," *Journal of the History of Ideas* 10, no.2 (1949), 267–96.

9   Whitehead, *Science and the Modern World*, 152.

10 Alfred North Whitehead, *Process and Reality*, Corrected Edition, ed. David Ray Griffin and Donald W. Sherburne (New York: Free Press, 1979); A.H. Johnson, *Whitehead and His Philosophy* (Lanham, MD: University Press of America, 1983), 53.

11 Arran Gare, "Philosophy and the Emergent Theory of Mind: White-head, Lloyd Morgan and Schelling," *Concrescence: Australasion Journal of Process Thought* 3 (2002), 1–12.

12 Alfred North Whitehead, *The Principle of Relativity with Applications to Physical Science* (Cambridge, UK: Cambridge University Press, 1922).

13 The elementary particles can be listed, but their status as "entities"

is in question; as field quanta, it would be just as legitimate to call them phases or states of fields. The general question of the irreducibility of chemistry to physics is controversial. Chemists surely use fundamental physics, especially quantum mechanics (and all natural sciences employ thermodynamics). Nevertheless, physics is not primarily concerned with matter, certainly not "normal" matter, but chemistry—with the one exception of nuclear chemistry—is. As the science of "the transformation of substances" or the reactivity of the kinds of matter chemistry must employ explanatory devices and concepts very different from those found in physics, like the periodic table. See for example: Hans Primas, "Emergence in Exact Natural Sciences," *Acta Polytechnica Scandinavica* 91 (1998), 83–98; Eric R. Scerri, "The Electronic Configuration Model, Quantum Mechanics and Reduction," *British Journal of the Philosophy of Science* 42 (1991), 309–25; Eric R. Scerri, *The Periodic Table: Its Story and Significance* (Oxford: Oxford University Press, 2007); and J. Van Brakel, "Chemistry as the Science of the Transformation of Substances," *Synthese* 111 (1997), 253–82.

14 Sydney Harris, "I'll be working on . . ." http://www.cartoonstock. com. shr1332. 2016.

15 Philip Anderson, "More is Different," *Science*, 177, no.4 (1972), 393–96.

16 Richard Feynman, *The Character of Physical Law* (Cambridge, MA: MIT Press, 1994), 118–120

⮞ 10 ⮜

BEYOND EMERGENTISM

David E. Conner

ABSTRACT: *Emergentism may be understood as the assertion that sentience, valuation, purposiveness, mind, and life itself have emerged only after millions of years in a natural world that was originally constituted of elements that were purely physical or material. I argue that the contemporary physicalism or materialism that is the starting point of emergentism is implicitly based on three anachronistic presuppositions, namely, (1) Aristotle's notion of static substance as the neutral stuff that undergoes change, (2) Descartes's idea that matter and mind are radically different and are therefore ontologically separable, and (3) the mathematical methods of Newton, which have tended to eliminate factors such as value and purpose from our explanations of physical events (including the phenomenology of mind, purpose, etc.). I briefly analyze the positions of Ursula Goodenough, Terrence Deacon, and Donald Crosby as three examples of emergentist thinking and conclude that all three are philosophically untenable. I then argue that it is more reasonable to assume as Whitehead did that valuation and sentience are cosmologically primordial and thus coexistent with all actuality.*

IN THE SECOND CHAPTER of his very informative book, *The Trouble with Physics: The Rise of String Theory, the Fall of Science, and What Comes Next,* physicist Lee Smolin tells of an unexpected encounter with a group of creationists in the aisle of a transatlantic flight from London to Toronto. Smolin was returning from a conference on cosmology, and the creationists were returning to their Bible college after a mission to Africa, where they had gone partly in order to test some of the tenets of creationism. Upon learning that Smolin was a scientist, the creationists immediately wanted to defend their own beliefs against the theory of evolution. Smolin was not eager to engage in the discussion, but the confined setting on the plane made it hard to avoid. Smolin said, "But of course you accept the fact that we have fossils of many creatures that no longer live."

"No!" the creationists answered.

"What do you mean, 'no'? What about the dinosaurs?"

"The dinosaurs are still alive and roaming the earth!"

"That's ridiculous! Where?"

"In Africa."

"In Africa? Africa is full of people. Dinosaurs are really big. How come no one has seen one?"

"They live deep in the jungle."

When Smolin objected that even in the jungle the dinosaurs would have been observed, the creationists explained that the dinosaurs spend most of their lives hibernating in caves and that the caves themselves are never found because the dinosaurs seal up the entrances in order to protect themselves. Even so, they assured Smolin, "biblical biologists" from their school were at that very moment in the jungle, searching for the caves and the dinosaurs.

"Be sure to let me know if they bring out a live one," Smolin said, and returned to his seat.[1]

THE ACN WORLDVIEW

I begin this essay with Smolin's story not simply in order start with an amusing anecdote but, actually, to illustrate a central feature of the emergentism that I am intent upon critiquing. In this essay, *emergentism* refers to the idea, held by numerous scientists and philosophers, that natural processes, starting with nothing more than matter and energy, have somehow given rise to increasingly structured entities, resulting at length in the genesis of living organisms. Emergentism holds that nature tends spontaneously to assemble simpler parts into increasingly complex wholes which manifest new and unpredictable characteristics. As the culmination of emergence, life itself is said to have emerged from non-living physical predecessors.

Naturally there are various versions of emergentism, and we will discuss three of them in a moment. First, however, it must be acknowledged that the emergentism embraced by scientists and philosophers seems to have nothing whatsoever in common with the irrational or, more accurately, *pseudo*-rational creationism that Smolin was faced with on his flight to Toronto. Obviously, the primary claims of creationism are, as Smolin said, preposterous. There are no dinosaurs living in caves, and Darwinian evolution may not be dismissed peremptorily as an "unproven theory." Behind creationism's specific claims, however, is a more fundamental question pertaining to *method*. Creationism is based on the conviction that the beliefs of a specific religious tradition must be given *a priori* assent as a matter of fidelity to God and church. Creationism's *a priori* confessionalism effectively preempts any ideas, scientific or otherwise, that are at odds with its religious foundations. Frequently a literalistic or plain-sense interpretation of the Bible is a principal touchstone for creationism's arguments. Creationism is therefore often said to be based finally not on science but on *faith*—though I would argue that creationism is not really an expression of *faith* but of *ideology*. At any rate, in contrast to creationism, emergentism—and the science and the philosophy in which emergentism is couched— is based on the criteria of empirical observation and rational inference: in brief, on *experience* and *reason*. Thus emergentism is held to be derived from factors that are objective and scientific and that are therefore, over time, self-correcting. Obviously, then, unlike creationism, emergentism does not involve *a priori*, faith-like assumptions. Or does it?

In what follows I argue that the versions of emergentism that we are poised to examine are based not only on empirical and rational considerations but also on an arbitrary allegiance to certain assumptions. These assumptions may seem to be scientific or empirical, but they are not. They actually are based simply on long-standing intellectual traditions. I am referring to this set of assumptions as *the ACN worldview*. The letters A, C, and N stand for the ideas of Aristotle, René Descartes, and Isaac Newton, the three primary sources of the assumptions now in view. I hasten to add that neither Aristotle, Descartes, nor Newton subscribed to the "ACN worldview." Rather, there are certain aspects of their thinking that became thoroughly entrenched in science after Newton. These aspects of the legacies of Aristotle, Descartes, and Newton obdurately lurk in the underpinnings of emergentist theories.

From Aristotle the ACN worldview receives the idea of enduring substance (*ousia*) as the ground of existence. Though Aristotle was not a pure materialist in the manner of, say, Democritus, it is mainly from Aristotle that we inherit the notion that substance, being static, does not cause itself to move or to change but rather undergoes change under the impact of external forces. In other words, objects in nature are stable because at their core they are based on an enduring substantial essence. The static character of this essence leads to the conclusion that things change only when they are acted upon from the outside. The idea that change comes from without rather than spontaneously from within is what required Aristotle to posit the existence of a Primer Mover—otherwise, it is problematical to explain the constant presence of motion in nature. During the past hundred years the notion of inert substance has been adapted to include

Einstein's discovery that matter and energy are not simply interactive but interchangeable. Nevertheless, even pertaining to sub-atomic transformations many scientists and philosophers retain the image of matter being acted upon by various types of force.

Unfortunately there has been insufficient recognition of the fact that the interchangeability between matter and energy requires us also to include notions such as *pattern* or *structure* in our idea of nature, for matter is energy that has been localized in a structured way, and radiant energy itself is always emitted and transmitted according to specific patterns.[2] And if adherents of the ACN worldview have under-appreciated the primordial character of structure or pattern in nature, there has been even less recognition that the presence of pattern or structure in nature depends on the transmission and utilization of *information*.[3] Indeed, it can be said that *nature traffics in information*. Aristotle acknowledged something very much like this in his doctrine of formal cause. However, instead of updating the notion of formal causation, in the ACN worldview, structure and pattern have been explained away as mere by-products of efficient causation.

Descartes is, obviously, the source of modern philosophy's fundamental metaphysical distinction between matter and mind. Cartesian dualism is nowadays denounced by almost everyone, and the three emergentists whose ideas we will be considering are no exception. It is sometimes not recognized, however, that an element of Cartesian philosophy stubbornly lingers in the implicit assumption, apparently taken for granted by a majority of scientists and philosophers, that *physical nature in its rudimentary state is utterly devoid of anything such as ideas, abstractions, universals, or "mind."* We can refer to this assumption as "the ontological isolability of the physical"; and the contemporary Western form of it is, in its roots, Cartesian. Though Descartes himself firmly accepted the reality of mind as "non-physical substance"—his well-known *"cogito"* is unintelligible without it—almost all contemporary philosophers and scientists jettison that half of his metaphysics. Obviously, universals, types, categories, etc., are allowed in science as *tools used by human beings* in the perception, classification, and analysis of objects; but, it is assumed, the ontology of physical objects themselves does not involve abstraction, ideation, purpose, value, or anything else that is not, in the end, physical. The ontological isolability of the physical is not contradicted by the emergentist proposal that *some* objects, such as living organisms, do manifest purposiveness, thought, etc. In fact, emergentism upholds the notion of the purely physical by claiming that purpose, thought, etc., have *emerged* from a purely physical substrate.

The contribution of Isaac Newton to the ACN worldview consists of the postulate that the present state of the universe has arisen from conditions that can be best be analyzed *quantitatively* or *mathematically*. Due to the influence of Descartes, mechanistic depictions of nature had already arisen in Europe prior to Newton. It was Newton, however, who led the transition from qualitative to quantitative methods. I am not presently referring to the strict determinism that was subsequently espoused by some Newtonians, but simply to the attitude that observations which can be treated quantitatively are somehow more objective, verifiable, trustworthy, and, therefore, more "scientific." No one disputes the wondrous successes of mathematical methods in the sciences, but what is often overlooked is that those methods encourage a general outlook that might just as accurately be described not only as *scientific* but as *metaphysical*. Though Newton himself never embraced a thoroughly mechanistic view of the universe, this did not deter his successors. Robert Neville describes the effects, by the time of Kant, of the Newtonian ideal of mathematical description:

> Given the mathematics of the day and its modes of deployment, this had the immediate consequence that values in nature and society could not be registered in a reductive scientific account. The cultural outcome of this point was to assume that values are subjective and as such matters of human

projection. Another consequence of the mathematical ideal has been that purposes or "final causes" can be given no explanatory power in a reductionist scientific investigation. Only antecedent conditions, or "efficient causes" have explanatory power. ... This mathematical reductionism posed enormous problems of understanding human experience and behavior.[4]

Decades ago feminists pointed out that white-male worldviews often tend to "define women's experiences out of existence."[5] Instead of having actually to refute the claims of feminism, those who were unsympathetic could simply *ignore* those claims under the aegis of a worldview that disregarded women's feelings as being ephemeral, imaginary, or "hysterical," and therefore virtually unreal. As Neville suggests, a parallel point should be made about the role of mathematics in the sciences. This is exemplified, now that the requisite technologies are available, by the current fascination with efforts to connect various thoughts and feelings with detectable activities in identifiable regions of the brain, with the unspoken implication that such observations thereby explain these thoughts or feelings or at least bestow some sort of scientific legitimacy on them, since they are being observed and measured.

To summarize, then, the assumptions of the ACN worldview are (1) that nature, at least as it existed prior to the emergence of life, can be explained solely in terms of the interactions of matter and energy; (2) that matter and energy can and do exist in their primal state utterly divorced from ideas, abstractions, universals, purposes, values, or other non-physical factors; and (3) that science, which is the paradigmatic form of investigation into the nature of things, should rely first and foremost on methods based on external observation, measurement, and, when feasible, mathematical analysis. Introspection, intuition, and other relatively subjective modes of experience are either to be treated statistically as group phenomena or to be minimized and sometimes completely ignored. Any scientist or philosopher who noticeably strays from this pure physicalism is typically dismissed as having embraced an indefensible heresy, often branded as "Platonism," "vitalism," "panpsychism," "mysticism," or by the use of some other label that is intended to be equally marginalizing. Such dismissals constitute a *de facto* attempt to sidestep both the subtlety and the insistent recurrence of the questions involved. The issues are subtle because, for one thing, there are many ways other than Platonism, vitalism, panpsychism, and mysticism to incorporate non-physical elements into one's philosophy of nature. As examples we have only to recall pre-Socratic philosophers such as Thales, Anaximander, Anaximenes, and Heraclitus, all of whom in their various ways perceived in nature a dynamism that transcended mechanistic causation, but who were, obviously, neither Platonists, vitalists, panpsychists, nor "mystics," at least as those terms are defined today.[6]

The tendency of physicalists to lump non-physicalist philosophies together under various disdainful epithets is more than a mere oversimplification; it hints at the kind of self-assurance that is often observed among members of comfortable majorities who see themselves as maintaining time-honored traditions. Whitehead once described a set of assumptions that he called "the Hume-Newton situation," which closely resembles what I am calling "the ACN worldview." He wrote:

> Combining Newton and Hume we obtain a barren concept, namely, a field of perception devoid of any reason for the concurrence of its factors. It is this situation that modern philosophy from Kant onwards has in its various ways sought to render intelligible. My own belief is that this situation is a *reductio ad absurdum,* and should not be accepted as the basis for philosophic speculation. . . . But the Hume-Newton situation is the primary presupposition for all modern philosophic thought. Any endeavour to go behind it is, in philosophic discussion, almost angrily rejected as unintelligible.[7]

As in Whitehead's time, today it is still the case that non-physicalist alternatives usually are deemed simply unworthy of discussion. The peremptory manner in which non-physicalist modes of thought are rejected by many scientists and philosophers points to the faith-like dimension of the ACN worldview that they do espouse. The methods and conclusions of professional scientists and philosophers are extraordinarily impressive both intellectually and practically, and yet the ACN worldview that is normally presupposed in their work manifests an arbitrary, *a priori* quality. Ironically, this type of *a priori* quality is one of the main things that most of these same scientists and philosophers find disagreeable about outlooks like creationism.

In Section II of this chapter I outline three examples of emergentism. These examples are drawn from the work of cell biologist Ursula Goodenough, anthropologist Terrence Deacon, and philosopher Donald Crosby. These three stances are suitable examples because they differ in important ways in their respective approaches to emergentism and yet they also exemplify a common theme. In each case I endeavor to show how a tacit acceptance of the ACN worldview has made the writer's attempt to describe emergentism unnecessarily difficult. Throughout Section II, hints are interspersed as to how the tasks of each writer might be facilitated by jettisoning the ACN assumptions.

There is a *de facto* scientism which, though sometimes denied, is at the heart of the ACN worldview. A major goal of this essay is to show that the ACN premises are not merely unnecessary but untenable, bearing in mind Whitehead's use of the phrase *reductio ad absurdum*. Section III briefly presents several considerations in support of a scientific-metaphysical outlook that avoids the most formidable difficulties of the ACN worldview. I argue, on the basis of both physical evidence and logical analysis—that nature *does* traffic in information, and that once the notion of "information" is examined carefully, notions of primitive, primordial intentionality and valuation follow close behind.

THREE EXAMPLES OF EMERGENTISM

URSULA GOODENOUGH

We begin with Ursula Goodenough's excellent book, *The Sacred Depths of Nature*.[8] The book is not, nor does it intend to be, a thoroughgoing philosophy of nature. Rather, it contains sixteen short chapters[9] consisting mostly of engaging, non-technical descriptions of various biological processes. The focus is on cellular biology, the author's area of expertise, with the important addition that each chapter concludes with a few paragraphs of "Reflections" presenting the author's thoughts and feelings about the meaning and the religious significance of the biology that has just been explained. Goodenough's religious beliefs are not conventional. She rejects supernaturalism and she does not believe in "God" in the traditional theistic sense of a divine Being.[10] Nevertheless, she tells us that she attends a Presbyterian church, sings in the choir, participates in the ritual, and finds this spiritually enriching.[11]

The Sacred Depths of Nature provides us with a good example of emergentist thinking. Goodenough compares biological processes with a Mozart sonata.

> Invoking the concept of emergence, we can say that the music emerges from the notes. But there's an intermediate level of emergence as well. From the notes emerge chords and phrases and tempos and melodies, and from these emerge the sonata as a whole .... In biology it is the same. The biochemistry and biophysics are the notes required for life; they conspire, collectively, to generate the real unit of life, the organism.[12]

Goodenough indicates that emergence entails more than merely getting the "notes" sequenced in the right order. As in music, in biology wholes do emerge that are more than the sum of their parts. However, the parts do not then recede in importance. "Wholes do display properties and behaviors—emergent functions—that the parts cannot, but this does not mean that the parts are somehow irrelevant, or somehow untrue."[13]

Though wholes really do emerge with truly new characteristics, all holism and emergence must ultimately be understood in terms of the interaction of their constituent parts. "Life," Goodenough says, "can be explained by its underlying chemistry, just as chemistry can be explained by its underlying physics."[14] In other words, reductionism is the final truth. The appearance of life on earth may be a mystery, but the components that lead to life, at least, are not. But the workings of life are not mysterious at all. They are obvious, explainable, and thermodynamically inevitable. And relentlessly mechanical. And bluntly deterministic.[15]

Almost fifty years ago physicist David Bohm remarked that it seemed odd that just when physics was moving away from mechanism, biology and psychology were moving closer to it.[16] Goodenough's explanations of cell biology make it clear why Bohm's comment has become even truer today than it was when he wrote it. Enormous advances in biologists' understanding of the functioning of DNA and genes have made mechanistic explanations altogether too tempting.

I am proposing that, as we attempt to understand the evolving complexity of nature, it is immensely advantageous to jettison mechanistic materialism and accept instead the idea that *Nature's fundamental units possess the ability to transmit, receive, and utilize information*—and not merely the type of "information" that is conveyed by physical contacts or physical forces. There is no biological or other purely scientific reason to refuse even to consider this proposal; it is, rather, the arbitrary acceptance of the ACN worldview that stands intractably in the way.

Goodenough encounters the difficulties pertaining to her own metaphysical presuppositions when she considers how to integrate her scientific understandings with her faith stance. Her religious convictions are expressed powerfully, beautifully, and movingly, but her physicalist-reductionist philosophy serves as an ever-present complication. With admirable candor, she admits: "But all of us, and scientists are no exception, are vulnerable to the existential shudder that leaves us wishing that the foundations of life were something other than just so much biochemistry and biophysics."[17] Elaborating, she writes: "Emergence. Something more from nothing but. Life from nonlife, like wine from water, has long been considered a miracle wrought by gods or God. Now it is seen to be the near-inevitable consequence of our thermal and chemical circumstances. . . . And so I once again revert to my covenant with Mystery."[18]

In principle there surely is nothing to be faulted about making a covenant with Mystery. Every theology, if it goes deep enough, eventually becomes apophatic. Moreover, it would be foolish to suggest that *any* metaphysical stance—physicalist, Whiteheadian, Platonic, or otherwise—can simply eliminate the "existential shudder" that relentlessly dogs the steps of human life. On the other hand, worldviews do make a difference, as Goodenough herself confesses (above), when she wishes "that the foundations of life were something other than just so much biochemistry and biophysics."

Confronted with this chronic tension between physicalist reductionism and religious faith, Goodenough falls back on a stark dichotomy dividing facts from faith, asserting that religions and claims about God "are by definition beliefs since they can neither be proven nor refuted."[19] She continues, "As a non-theist, I find I can only think about these experiences as wondrous mental phenomena. But in the end it doesn't matter: All of us are transformed by their power."[20]

What we are now left with is an outlook reminiscent of the "philosophy of As If," articulated a century ago by German philosopher Hans Vaihinger (1852–1933). According to Vaihinger, since religious beliefs and practices are in principle unable to avail themselves of the benefits of scientific or other evidential forms of verification, we affirm them sheerly because it is useful or practical to act *as if* they were true.[21] For Vaihinger this is not simply pragmatism, but rather a proposal that we should treat certain ideas as if they were true even when we feel rather certain that they are *false*. Vaihinger might well have agreed with Goodenough when she says, "in the end, it doesn't matter."

Certainly Goodenough is welcome to embrace faith on any terms she wishes. However, it must be doubted whether many adherents of religions would be willing to relinquish their own faith's claims to truth. I believe Robert Neville is correct in seeking to re-establish the basis for, and the indispensability of, truth claims in philosophical theology.[22] In any case, the point at present is that the divergence between faith and fact in *The Sacred Depths of Nature* is not an unavoidable consequence of biology itself,[23] but of the ACN worldview in which biology and other sciences are so often framed.

TERRENCE W. DEACON

We now turn to the account of emergentism developed by Terrence W. Deacon in his very impressive and noticeably thorough *Incomplete Nature: How Mind Emerged from Matter.*[24] Deacon, a professor of biological anthropology and neuroscience, sets out deliberately to formulate a detailed explanation of the origins of life and mind, referring not only to science but to philosophy. This said, however, Deacon still takes it for granted that science has primary authority; indeed, he describes science as "that collection of theories that presumably come closest to explaining everything."[25] At present it is neither possible nor necessary to give the book the extended analysis that it deserves. Rather, as a means of clarifying his claim to have explained the emergence of life from physical beginnings, we will briefly review four of Deacon's most significant ideas: *absence, homeodynamics, morphodynamics,* and *teleodynamics.*

Deacon begins with the proposal that in order to understand the origins of life we must consider the notion of *absence,* or *absentialism.* By "absence," Deacon means something that has no specifically *physical* attributes. He explains, "Each of these sorts of phenomena—a function, reference, purpose, or value—is in some way incomplete. . . . Longing, desire, passion, appetite, mourning, loss, aspiration—all are based on an analogous intrinsic incompleteness, and integral without-ness."[26]

The idea of absence is central to Deacon's explanation of the origins of emergence itself. Deacon observes that the word *emergence* has been used to refer to many things: "concepts of novelty, unpredictability, ascent in scale, synergy, and so on."[27] In *Incomplete Nature,* absence is intended to refer to the way that structure, self-organization, purpose, and, ultimately, selfhood emerge from initial conditions that are purely physical. The gist of Deacon's argument is that physical conditions proceed through a series of increasingly complex configurations— analogous to the effect of a hollow space inside the mold as plaster is being cast—so that, in the end, purpose and life result.

Deacon's understanding of absence does serve another purpose— an unstated one—that should not escape our notice. "Absence" points to Deacon's unquestioned assumption that things such as meaning, longing, passion, aspiration, etc., are, prior to their emergence in living things, not present in nature; that is, they are "something-that-is-not-a-thing." Thus Deacon's emphasis on absence provides evidence of the ACN worldview that predominates in his analysis.

Deacon's term *homeodynamics* is intended to describe the tendency of some systems to distribute certain properties throughout that system. A paradigm is provided by examples of the second law of thermodynamics,[28] which pertains to entropy. It is helpful to remember that the idea of entropy originated as a description of heat flow; for example, heat always "flows" out of a hot brick into an adjacent brick that is colder, until equilibrium is reached. Though differences in the bricks' *positions* may still be discernible, at equilibrium the two bricks have become indistinguishable based on temperature, and the system is deemed to have become more disordered. In Deacon's thinking, initially the relative *absence* of heat in the cold brick has had a defining effect on the overall properties of the system. Noting that the *arrangement* of the bricks (proximity, shape, etc.) matters greatly in the achievement of thermal equilibrium, Deacon asserts that situations such as this give us a new, physicalized way of understanding Aristotle's concept of formal causes.[29]

Once a system has achieved a homeodynamic state, the next step is *morphodynamics.* Morphodynamics has to do with self-organization. Deacon holds that morphodynamics—structure-like or pattern-like features in a system or a region—are enabled to arise by ongoing "perturbations" of the system. As an example, he describes a large container of gas that is steadily heated on one side—perhaps by sunlight. The gas near the heated side of the tank will be warmer and less dense in comparison with gas on the unheated side, so that the tank as a whole manifests a thermal pattern. This signifies a reduction in entropy.[30] The structured quality of the system arises not as a result of a target or a goal but rather from purely physical conditions. Such "organized" systems constitute a further step in the conditions that lead to the emergence of life.

The next step is what Deacon calls *teleodynamics,* described as "a dynamical form of organization that promotes its own persistence and maintenance by modifying this dynamics to more effectively utilize supportive extrinsic conditions."[31] Deacon's adaptation of the root word *telos* is in harmony with the writings of certain Greek philosophers who sometimes use *telos* to refer not to deliberate purposes but simply to "outcomes" or "end results."[32]

> Teleodynamics . . . is a specific dynamical form that can be described in quasi-mechanistic terms. Although it is the distinguishing characteristic of living processes, it is not necessarily limited to the biological domain. . . . Teleodynamic processes . . . are characterized by their dependence on and emergence from the interactions of morphodynamic processes. Teleodynamics is the dynamical realization of final causality, in which a given dynamical organization exists because of the consequences of its continuance, and therefore can be described as being self-generating. . . . [It] is *a consequence-organized dynamic that is its own consequence.*[33]

Despite his emphasis on externally observable self-organization, Deacon does acknowledge the necessity of describing the nature of the internal *sentience* that seems to be the hallmark of selfhood. At the close of his chapter on teleodynamics and throughout the following chapter entitled "Sentience,"[34] Deacon repeatedly relies on the terms *dynamic* (or *dynamical*) and *supervenient*.

> The core hypothesis of this book is that all teleodynamic phenomena necessarily depend upon, and emerge from, simpler morphodynamic and homeodynamic processes. . . .[35] [T]here can be no simple mapping between ententional and mechanistic (teleodynamic and thermodynamic) properties, even though whatever is ententional has emerged from a statistical mechanistic base. . . .[36] I believe that only by working from the bottom up, tracing the ascent from thermodynamics to morphodynamics to teleodynamics and their recapitulation in the dynamics of brain function, will be able to explain the place of our subjective experience in this otherwise largely insentient universe.[37]

Though *Incomplete Nature* displays considerable strengths, the book also manifests several weaknesses. A major problem is that Deacon's chapters repeatedly seem to be moving toward some succinct conclusion but fail to arrive there. This failure to provide actual explanations often arises because Deacon repeatedly substitutes the *description* of certain conditions for an *explanation* of how these conditions actually bring about the emergence of sentience, purpose, etc. He uses physicalist illustrations without recognizing that such illustrations do not exemplify the type of emergence ("mind," eventually) that he is attempting to explain. For example, Deacon presents a case study based on Rayleigh-Bénard convection, in which heating a thin layer of liquid can cause the appearance of hexagonal-shaped columns of moving liquid. Thus, "[t]he geometric regularity of these currents is not imposed extrinsically, but by the intrinsic constraints of conflicting rising and falling currents slowing the rate."[38] Deacon's point is that *shapes* and *patterns* emerge from sheerly *physical* conditions. But the question at issue is not whether patterns and shapes can arise in inorganic chemistry, geology, etc.—obviously, they do—but how *this* type of physical emergence plays a culminating role or is the final, decisive step in the creation of living organisms. The supposition that thermodynamic sources of structure are in themselves a sufficient cause in the search for the origins of teleology and sentience simply begs the question.

Deacon does state explicitly that there is a circular quality to teleodynamics since teleodynamic patterns, by definition, serve to preserve their own existence. But this obvious observation should not obscure the fact that Deacon's *argument* is also "circular," for we have a sort of chicken-and-egg situation in which certain teleodynamic elements are said to emerge fortuitously (via thermodynamics, etc.) and then happily enable teleodynamic phenomena to occupy or "fall into" a prior "absence"—when actually, in the situation being described, *no previously existing tendency towards teleodynamic behavior has been established.* In fact, as we've already observed, *absence* for Deacon is intended to serve as a means of *avoiding* the idea of any previously existing tendency towards teleodynamics within initial physical conditions—not as a way of *explaining* that presence. Reviewer Colin McGinn writes:

> The whole idea of "incomplete nature" is confused and unhelpful; the only sliver of truth to it is that physics is incomplete as a description of full reality, so that many realities are absent from *it*. Despite his aspirations to producing a new metaphysics, Deacon is clearly no metaphysician. . . . Still less appealing is his contention that absences can be causally relevant to what happens in the world. For how can what is *not* there cause what *is* there?[39]

One could argue that absences do cause certain events, as when the relative absence of air in a vacuum cleaner causes dirt to be drawn out of a carpet. Even then, though, the true cause is actually the higher atmospheric pressure outside of the canister; and in cases of "emergent" teleology, similarly positive causes would be found to replace alleged causation by "absence."[40]

Deacon declares that he has explained "a non-material conception of organism," but he fails to expand upon the ontology of this non-material reality. Even more critically, he fails to develop the closely related concept of *supervenience*,[41] which is the linchpin of his whole line of reasoning—for supervenience refers to the relation between mind (or, more accurately, "ententional phenomena") and matter. Deacon states matter-of-factly that "[t]he ententional features of life cannot be directly mapped to specific physical substrates or chemical processes, and yet they nevertheless *dynamically supervene* on *processes* involving these physical correlates."[42] What exactly is this dynamical supervention, or this supervening dynamism? This question brings us back to the most notorious problem for Cartesian dualism, namely, to explain how mind and matter do interact. Deacon asserts that his solution avoids Descartes's problem,[43] but in the end it is not clear that it really does.

The idea of *dynamic supervenience pertaining to processes* hints at a fleeting similarity between Deacon's ideas and the ideas of process metaphysics. Current versions of process metaphysics would seem to be supportive of Deacon's stance, both in their characteristic denial of naïve materialism and in their affirmation of dynamism in connection with emergent phenomena. But alas! In the second chapter of *Incomplete Nature* Deacon has already dismissed "philosophers of mind" who argue that "an ententional principle is an unanalyzably primitive attribute of all physical phenomena: a basic universal property of things like mass or electric charge."[44] In a cursory two-page rejection of these philosophies, Deacon takes the superiority of his own assumptions for granted, oversimplifies the philosophical positions he is criticizing, and jumps to unsubstantiated conclusions. Next, in chapter three—ominously entitled "Homunculi"—Deacon makes quick work of the philosophy of A.N. Whitehead, the foremost 20th-century exponent of process philosophy. Deacon wrongly identifies Whitehead's philosophy as a variant of panpsychism,[45] which helps us to see why he associates Whitehead's thought with the word "homunculus." Then, after a three-paragraph attempt to summarize intricate Whiteheadian topics such as prehension, concrescence, societies, etc., Deacon concludes that Whitehead's philosophy provides no means of distinguishing between the subjective state of a brain and the subjective state of a river.[46] It is obvious that Deacon lacks an accurate understanding of Whitehead's explanation of structured societies, defining characteristics, social hierarchies, enduring objects, and the indispensable role of sentience in every actual entity as the basis for the ways that societies of actual entities are formed and sustained.

My point is that Deacon has misunderstood and prematurely rejected the types of philosophy that his own stance finally, if only vaguely, begins to resemble. *Incomplete Nature* is in many ways instructive, challenging, and extraordinary. However, its depiction of the conditions leading to selfhood, feeling, consciousness, and meaning is ultimately descriptive rather than genuinely explanatory. The book amounts to a very elaborate and laborious but unsuccessful attempt to reconcile the existence of "ententional" phenomena with the physicalist assumptions of the ACN worldview. I argue in the conclusion of this essay that all such attempts are doomed to failure due to a vicious circularity in reasoning that amounts to a *reductio ad absurdum*.

DONALD A. CROSBY

Our final example of emergentism is encountered in the work of Donald A. Crosby. In distinction from Goodenough and Deacon, Crosby is a professional philosopher; as such he has brought forth a noteworthy series of articles and books focusing especially on the presence of value within nature.[47] Manifestly a major goal of Crosby's work has been to offer a renewed intellectual basis for reverence towards life and also to argue in favor of attendant forms of social, ethical, and environmental commitment. His writings typically are more constructive than critical. Crosby avoids the pitfall—too common among some intellectuals—of engaging in what Whitehead called "brilliant feats of explaining away."

Many of Crosby's writings deal at least partly with emergence, but one of his most focused discussions of this subject is found in his book, *Novelty*. In this book Crosby distinguishes *novelty* from both *creativity* and *emergence*. Crosby indicates that "creativity" often connotes something positive and constructive, whereas novelty denotes sheer newness which often manifests elements of randomness, chaos, and even destruction."[48] Similarly, the word "emergence" often refers to instances of increasing degrees of composition or organization, whereas novelty may result in disintegration. Nevertheless the focus of *Novelty* is on the kinds of novelty that result in growing levels of structure and complexity. Pertaining to all types of novelty, Crosby does not hesitate to use the term "emergence," which he associates with a type of holism, inasmuch as the parts of a whole are in many situations influenced or changed by their inclusion in that whole.

> In all of these types of evolution—cosmological, terrestrial, and biological—we witness the emergence of something new. . . . The result is emergent entities and systems of entities, all of which continue to be embodied and material, but the new character and capabilities of their underlying material constituents and structures need to be taken fully into account.[49]

At this point we must ask what *causes* these evolved realities to emerge. Crosby seems to propose two answers. Sometimes he appears to say that *novelty itself* is the type of reality that can serve as a causal agent. However, a closer reading reveals that Crosby views novelty not as a cause *per se* but as a descriptive term that pertains to all matter, and that matter itself is the cause of novelty.

> Matter, then, in all its manifestations and transformations, is the "really real" of the system of thought being defended in this book. . . . Life and mind, for instance, are real, not

as ontologically separate or entirely different kinds of being but as high level functions of certain kinds of material entities. . . . Whatever is not material or embodied in some way cannot be real in its own right. It is either an abstraction from what is concretely real (i.e., material) or *its operation is wholly dependent upon and derivative from some form of material reality.*[50]

We commonly say that gravity "causes" an object to fall when it is really the massive objects themselves that exert the attractive force. In the same way we may say that novelty "causes things" as a convenient figure of speech, but we are alluding to the fact that instances of novelty are really caused by the material entities involved.

Crosby's confidence in the foundational status of matter does not mean that he embraces a reductionistic worldview. He emphatically rejects reductionism and its corollaries—such as the sufficiency of physical sciences to explain all events, the idea that all forms of agency can be relegated to efficient causes, and the view that matter is an inert stuff that remains essentially unaltered when included in larger wholes.[51] When matter does evolve into increasingly complex forms, it is genuinely changed, according to Crosby. "With growing complexity of organization there is increasing capacity for inwardness, centeredness, and self-direction."[52] Crosby insists that self-direction, purposes, and goals are not instilled by some external source, but become properties of matter itself.[53]

In my view, nature in some shape or form always has been and always will be; hence, it has no need of a transcendent personal and purposive creator. It requires no ground or explanation beyond itself and has no purpose conferred upon it *from without.* . . . Moreover, it has no pervasive *immanent or self-contained* purpose, aim, or goal. I restrict teleological action or behavior to emergent conscious beings, and nature is not a conscious being. These are debatable claims, of course, and I want to remain open to evidence to the contrary.[54]

Matter itself, working in accord with the novelty that is an innate part of its constitution, produces complex wholes, including life. Crosby provides a helpful summary of several major proposals as to how life emerged from matter, though he refrains from endorsing any one theory.[55] Thus, the exact process by which sentience and life emerge remains mysterious.

Crosby's work is a model of nuanced reflection. Unfortunately we cannot now give his ideas the detailed consideration that they merit but must turn instead to a series of questions prompted by his overall outlook. A first question pertains to the term *matter* itself. If matter is as radically dynamic and, by means of that dynamism, as radically prone to novelty as Crosby claims, then why not call it *process* or use some other word that would allude to the novelty that Crosby is emphasizing? As Crosby admits, matter "is often assumed to be something that is unchanging in its basic nature."[56] His decision to retain the word *matter* shows that he does wish to preserve some decisive emphasis on physical stability, mass, solidity, and sameness— despite the fact that such traits can be explained in terms of localized patterns of energy,[57] as Crosby is surely aware.

A second question asks what exactly Crosby does mean by "novelty." Is novelty simply a tendency towards change or inconstancy, like the spontaneous decay of unstable particles? If novelty is an innate property of all matter, is novelty then self-caused (*causa sui*)? Since the changes produced by novelty are not (except in living things) directed by any external or internal *purposes*, how are the contributions of novelty really anything more than another sub-category of mechanistic causation? In a review of *Novelty*, James Haag writes:

> I find Crosby's reliance on novelty puzzling and problematic. If we are to expand efficient causation, we need an expansion that can be as scientifically and philosophically sound as our current notions of efficient causation. Clear and precise definitions of efficient causation cannot be easily aligned with vague and broad understandings of novelty. . . . Where novelty merely means "new" . . . one could legitimately

identify every single instant in the history of the universe as novel. . . . Unfortunately, when everything is novel, nothing is novel.[58]

A third and most telling question is to ask how Crosby's concept of novelty helps to explain the genuine difference that, Crosby admits, exists between the formation of mere aggregates and the formation of organisms, selves, purposes, etc. If experiencing organisms arise simply from complexity *qua* complexity, we must ask why complicated machines don't really achieve self-awareness spontaneously, the way they do in science fiction movies like *The Terminator*? If the answer is that machines up until now have not approached the amazing complexity of the brains of animals, our response must be that it's only a matter of time! The Internet itself stretches around the world, connecting billions of operating programs and memory devices that hold, surely, billions of terabytes of data—and yet the Internet is clearly nothing more than a vast machine. The purposes that it serves are created not by itself but by human beings.

The crucial difference between an aggregate and an organism can be illustrated by comparing a grain of salt with an amoeba. Sodium chloride is often cited as an instance of emergence or holism because the properties of salt are strikingly different from the properties of sodium or chlorine; the taste of salt, for example, emerges from the way that sodium and chlorine atoms bond together. But the emergent flavor of saltiness is *an externally observable* property. In an organism there is an *internal experience of subjectivity*—even though the level of experience may be very primitive compared with human consciousness. Many scientists and philosophers writing about the defining characteristics of life continue to focus on externally measurable properties such as the ability to metabolize food, reproduce, etc. This emphasis on externally observed properties is characteristic of the ACN worldview, with its reliance on "objective" data. But the presence of *internal subjectivity* is what truly defines life. Goodenough points to this subjectivity when she writes, "All creatures evaluate. The amoeba perceives and then moves toward a food source; it perceives and then moves away from a toxin."[59] This process of "evaluation" is defined not by *thinking*, but by *feeling*. How does Crosby's concept of novelty help to explain the definitive differences between the type of holism displayed by salt and the type of holism displayed by an amoeba?

Though Crosby does affirm that life and mind are not epiphenomena, I cannot see how Crosby's explication of novelty allows us to explain *why* they are not, for "novelty," when presented simply as a property of matter, becomes merely another facet of physical, efficient causality. Crosby could have addressed this conundrum by deliberately including an element—even if only a conditional element—of sentience, purpose, or "teleology" in his concept of novelty but, like Goodenough and Deacon, Crosby simply disallows any basic coinherence between matter on the one hand and purpose, feeling, or subjectivity on the other. In contrast to Goodenough and Deacon, Crosby does spell out substantive reasons for rejecting teleology, including (a) the failure of nature to exhibit any consistent evidence of coherent purpose; (b) the problem of evil as a particularly troubling example of this failure; (c) the excessive anthropomorphism of most depictions of God as a purposive Creator; (d) and the near-atheism of alternative, non-anthropomorphic doctrines of God, such as that of Paul Tillich.[60] We may easily sympathize with Crosby's convictions on this point, but that does not mean that we view his reasons as being sufficient to substantiate a neo-materialist metaphysics.

As a philosopher Crosby takes deliberate measures to address the difficulties that attend the ACN worldview—difficulties such as reductionism, mathematicism, and scientism. Despite this, Crosby's unwillingness to abandon the physicalist materialism which is the core of the ACN worldview leads to the result that his description of the origins of life and mind is based finally not on metaphysical explanation but on an appeal to mystery. Crosby acknowledges that there are conceptual difficulties that stubbornly remain in various physicalist attempts to explain life, and he attempts to compensate for these difficulties by portraying novelty as something that is innately wondrous and mysterious. Who would deny that there is much about nature that is marvelous and mysterious? This, Crosby observes, is not necessarily a detriment. In fact, Crosby deems the mystery of nature to be *supportive* of a religious attitude toward nature.[61]

On the other hand, I believe Crosby would also agree that where we can reduce our reliance on mystery in philosophical discussion, we should do so. There are various types of mystery, and these types differ greatly. There is mystery based on the *unavoidable limitations of available methods*; for example, presently we have no means of determining whether there is life in other solar systems. There is mystery based on *actual indeterminacy*, related to such things as quantum uncertainty or to the as yet unformed decisions of human beings in the future. There is a third type of mystery related to what Bernard Meland called *"appreciative awareness,"* the mystery of our own powerful feelings as we respond to life's deepest and most meaningful experiences. It is this type of mystery that Crosby, Goodenough, and others associate—I think, very appropriately—with novelty, nature, and the evolution of life. However, there is a fourth type of mystery: the mystery that is created unnecessarily by *our own flawed reasoning or faulty assumptions*. It is said that someone once asked Augustine why God, an infinitely powerful being, needed to rest on the seventh day after having created the world, and Augustine replied that God wasn't actually resting on that day; he was creating hell for people who ask questions like that one. My point is that the question itself is badly formed, having been based on dubious assumptions about the "perfection" of God's power, about God's role in creation, about the mythological nature of the Genesis creation stories, etc.

I present this little typology of mystery in order to reveal something crucial about Crosby's statement that novelty is inherently mysterious. As we endorse Crosby's affirmation of the third type of mystery, we must not unwittingly introduce an equivocation that mingles the third type with the fourth type—mystery that results from faulty assumptions. The fact that there will always be mysterious and arbitrary dimensions to our understanding of universal Creativity cannot be allowed to become a way of disguising or excusing the puzzles that persistently characterize efforts to explain the emergence of life and mind from initial conditions that are purely physical.

AN ALTERNATIVE TO EMERGENTISM

This discussion would be incomplete if it merely rejected emergentism without suggesting a viable alternative. I have already acknowledged that in this section I shall be relying on the philosophy of Alfred North Whitehead. Unlike more systematic approaches to Whitehead's ideas, the approach employed in what follows is more empirical in orientation. Instead of defining Whitehead's neologisms and explaining their meaning, we focus on the application of Whitehead's ideas to natural processes.

EMPIRICAL CONSIDERATIONS

Process philosophy—or what Whitehead called "the philosophy of organism"—is often illustrated by appealing to various human experiences. Admittedly, human experience often provides the only illustrations that are readily available. Unfortunately the effect of such examples is that the natural world seems to have been anthropomorphized, resulting as we have already noted in the attribution of inappropriate terms such as *panpsychism* and *homunculus* to Whitehead's philosophy. It is not as widely recognized as I think it should be that Whitehead himself ascribed the origins of his philosophy not to social or psychological studies but to his investigations concerning mathematics and mathematical physics.[62] We will now speculate briefly on Whitehead's philosophical response to the discoveries of early 20th-century physics.

It seems remarkable that Whitehead included chapters on relativity and quantum theory in *Science and the Modern World,* published in

1925, while scientists themselves were still formulating interpretations of these discoveries. Relativity and quantum theory both imply strongly that patterns and structure are embedded in the simplest atomic entities rather than merely being attributed to those entities by human interpreters, and that nature itself somehow relies on the transmission and reception of information.[63] We cannot presently argue in detail for these assertions, but a simple list of illustrations is quite suggestive.

A. Throughout the detectable universe, all the electrons of the element with the next higher atomic number build upon the electronic configuration of its immediate predecessor.[64]

B. When an excited electron falls back to its ground state, it always emits energy that is discretely quantized.

C. Particles that are produced by or are members of the same quantum system are "entangled," so that changes in one particle are *immediately* detectable in other entangled particles, even at large distances. Phenomena of this type are referred to as "non-local correlations" because they take place instantly without the physical transmission of matter or energy through intervening space.[65]

D. Throughout the universe, sub-atomic particles or "particle-like entities" such as hadrons and electrons possess consistent properties such as mass, spin, charge, etc., and hadrons (such as protons and neutrons) are created from the structured arrangements of quarks.

E. The theory of relativity suggests that something resembling perspective or viewpoint and some process resembling measurement characterize nature at its simplest levels.

F. The very fact that all so called laws of nature are uniform and mathematical implies that structure and pattern are built into nature itself. We are so accustomed to the idea that nature is mathematical that we take this for granted without questioning its basis.[66]

These examples are sufficient to illustrate the natural interplay between matter-energy on the one hand and information on the other. Though the philosophical significance of post-Newtonian physics has sometimes been exaggerated or sensationalized,[67] it is interesting that as 20th-century science developed, several of the most prominent physicists discarded a purely materialist worldview. Einstein did not believe in a personal deity but he did express a quasi-religious faith in the utter rationality of the universe. Erwin Schrödinger displayed an outspoken if not entirely consistent interest in Eastern religions, pantheism, and philosophical monism. Wolfgang Pauli enjoyed a sustained friendship with Carl Jung; the two found common ground between depth psychology and quantum theory, and Pauli believed that Jungian archetypes were present in nature.[68] Pauli and Werner Heisenberg both studied the Greek philosophers. Heisenberg stated that the new physics requires us to adopt a new, non-materialist ontology.[69]

> The atom of modern physics can only be symbolized by a partial differential equation in an abstract multidimensional space. Only the experiment of an observer forces the atom to indicate a position, a colour and a quantity of heat. *All* the qualities of the atom of modern physics are derived, it has no *immediate and direct* physical properties at all, i.e., every type of visual conception we might wish to design is, *eo ipso*, faulty.[70]

Citing Aristotle, Heisenberg used the word *potentia* to describe the ontological status of atoms and other particles that have not been disturbed by external sources.[71] *Potentia* is the Latin translation of for *dunamis* or *dýnamis* (δύναμις). Today we associate "dynamism" with action or energy, but Aristotle often used the term to denote *possibility*,[72] and Heisenberg uses it this way to denote the well-known axiom of quantum physics that the status of entities at the quantum level is indefinite prior to interacting with their environment.[73]

In response to these discoveries, Whitehead developed a metaphysical system in which processes replace stable physical objects as the ultimate building blocks of nature. He wrote, "The process itself is the actuality, and requires no antecedent static cabinet."[74] The processes, however, are not disconnected or random; they acquire pattern, regularity, and uniform structure even at the sub-atomic level, as shown in the examples just given. In some radically simple way this formation of patterns involves the reception and utilization of information by the most miniscule processes of physical reality. When these atomic processes interact with their environment they necessarily become something definite; otherwise there would be no basis for influence. At a metaphysical level, an indeterminate entity or event cannot serve as a cause. This achievement of definiteness allows entities to influence other subsequent processes. Whitehead's "becoming-definite-upon-interaction" corresponds to quantum theory's "collapse of the wave function,"[75] caused in experiments by the act of measurement or observation.[76] Whitehead called this finality or definiteness "concreteness"; the process leading up to it, he called "concrescence."

The idea of atomistic-processes-that-utilize-information contributes powerfully not only to the interpretation of the 20th-century physics that Whitehead was pondering but to a new philosophy of nature as a whole. It is counterintuitive to think that insentient matter can act to sort out and utilize information, but this is not so obviously true concerning *processes*. Whitehead reasoned that each process is intrinsically *dipolar*, manifesting both *physical* and *mental* aspects. The word "mental" unfortunately seems to suggest specifically *human* thinking, but Whitehead meant merely the ability to assess information at some utterly simple level. The mental and physical poles are conceived to be like the two poles of a magnet, mutually necessary to each other. This amounts to a direct denial of the doctrine that I referred to earlier as "the ontological isolability of the physical." This affirmation of mental-physical dipolarity may be thought of as a way of restoring Aristotle's notion of formal cause to contemporary science.

The conviction that mental-physical dipolarity goes all the way down to nature's ground floor makes it possible to explain the fact that increasing physical complexity does lead to more advanced forms of existence, eventually including life and mind. Since rudimentary mentality is included primordially, life and mind *are* plausible as consequences of what Teilhard called "complexification." Whitehead's explanation of these more highly organized phenomena is included in his description of the formation of societies of occasions.[77]

Two other aspects of Whitehead's thought that must be considered, if only briefly. One is the eternal objects. The other is God.

The phrase "eternal objects" was used by Whitehead as a near equivalent to what have in other contexts been called "universals," "abstractions," "generals," "categories," "ideas," "Platonic forms," "prototypes," "archetypes," etc. Unfortunately, Whitehead's own language does occasionally make the eternal objects sound like library books that are being checked out to readers by a cosmic Librarian—a Librarian who, indeed, already knows just which books the reader should read! However, the substance of Whitehead's reasoning does not justify this imagery.

Critics have assailed the eternal object in various ways. The eternal objects do have a Platonic flavor, and Whitehead has often been called a Platonist, not infrequently in contexts where that designation was not intended as a compliment. But Whitehead's eternal objects lack the ontological primacy and the metaphysical eminence that the forms typically have for Plato, and Whitehead is in fact no more a Platonist that he is an Aristotelian. The eternal objects are indispensable, but for Whitehead they are, in the end, mere tools in the hands of nature's real actors. Whitehead writes that "the general Aristotelian principle is maintained that, apart from things that are actual, there is nothing—nothing either in fact or in efficacy."[78] The eternal objects serve as lures for *feeling*; in the least complex forms of life they represent not high-minded goals or sophisticated designs but primal physical urges, appetites, and fears, illustrated by Goodenough's comment about the amoeba.

The eternal objects have also been criticized as being simply unnecessary philosophically. Don Crosby, for example, alleges that the "pure possibilities" constituted by the eternal objects can be jettisoned, since "all the conceivable possibilities of a given time are to be seen as *real* possibilities,"[79] where "real" possibilities are possibilities that arise in actual situations. What I believe Crosby fails to see, perhaps partly because of his materialist orientation, is the extent to which real (situational) possibilities still depend eventually on *pure* possibilities.[80] For one thing, there is otherwise no means by which concrescing entities can envisage the genuine novelty that Crosby so highly prizes, since "real" possibilities are by definition already implicit in existing circumstances. In Whitehead's terms, prehensions would be restricted to phenomena that already exist. I would argue that, at a human level, our experience of creative imagination depends partly on that which is "not real, yet waiting to be realized." The basic difference between Crosby and Whitehead seems to be that Crosby is thinking about practical circumstances and Whitehead is thinking about primordial metaphysical requirements.

Whitehead was a mathematician, and one area of expertise was number theory. It is possible that the analysis of numbers and their relations was an inspiration for Whitehead's idea of eternal objects. A moment's contemplation suggests that as soon as the universe contained more than one thing—presumably, immediately after the "big bang"—all the numbers stretching to infinity became *pure possibilities* and, along with them, so did all the rules of arithmetic, the Pythagorean theorem, algebra, trigonometry, etc.[81] Few people would claim simply that numbers "do not exist," but, on the other hand, it is clear that their ontological status differs from that of physical objects. The analysis of this ontological difference pertains also to Whitehead's eternal objects.

In our current outline of a philosophy of organism, we come at last to the concept of God. Many of Whitehead's interpreters have depicted his idea of God in ways that are inappropriately anthropomorphic, personalistic, panentheistic, or otherwise promoting the sense that God is more distinguishable ontologically from the world than Whitehead's own dipolar understanding of the God-World relation warrants. I have sought to address these problems elsewhere.[82]

In our present discussion, we need something like Whitehead's God because the simple claim that entities traffic in information is not enough. The information must be "informed"; that is, it must be coordinated or ordered or graded in its relevance so that it is appropriate to promote intensity of feeling in each entity's own circumstances. There must be a larger reality that serves this integrative, coordinating function, because (a) we see its emergent effects in physics and cosmology, in the other physical sciences, and, through increasing complexity, in the life sciences, psychology, sociology, and the humanities; and (b) it is hard to imagine that *each single entity* can serve this coordinating function on its own.[83] It is imperative to emphasize once more that Whitehead is not thinking of a God who acts as an independent agent ontologically. Referring to his own theory as one of "organic mechanism," he adds, "In this theory, the molecules may blindly run in accordance with the general laws, but the molecules differ in their intrinsic characters according to the general organic plans of the situations in which they find themselves."[84] There is no divine Mind that intervenes to alter physical laws.

My point is that though the universe does not embrace or promote *particular* values, it does foster the rather amorphous and ambiguous value—if it may be called a value—of supporting the existence and the evolution of goal-seeking, value-realizing creatures.[85] In any case, our interest at present is not religious but philosophical, centering on the question of whether the emergence of life and mind can be explained on purely physicalist grounds. I am arguing that it cannot, and have offered empirical evidence for my counterproposal that the most basic elements of nature are characterized by a dipolar integration of both physical and informational (or mental) aspects. We will now analyze the more purely conceptual side of the emergentist positions that we are disputing.

THE LOGIC OF EMERGENTISM

"A dead nature aims at nothing. It is the nature of life that it exists for its own sake, as the intrinsic reaping of value."[86] The basic challenge to emergentist reasoning is that its physicalist or materialist premises run ineluctably into the pitfalls of Cartesian dualism. Goodenough avoids philosophical dualism by describing life and mind in terms of physical reductionism—though, as we have seen, this forces Goodenough to adopt an "as if" approach to life's deeper experiences. Deacon affirms emergent mind as ontologically distinctive while denying that his approach succumbs to the snares of Cartesian dualism. Crosby seeks a path between Goodenough and Deacon, denying that sentience and mind are distinct from matter ontologically but allowing that increasing complexity alters the parts of wholes "from the top down," so that the qualities of sentience and subjectivity emerge. Crosby believes that his middle way avoids dualism, and he disputes Charles Hartshorne's assertion that emergentism contains an implicit dualism.[87] In Deacon's argument, it is evident that once sentient organisms have appeared this monism morphs into a type of dualism; Deacon's position can be seen simply as an "emergent dualism" in contrast to Descartes's "primordial dualism." But this is dualism nevertheless, for the end result is still that there are two types of reality, and the predicament is still, as it was for Descartes, to explain how these two types of reality interact.

As a way of examining Deacon's and Crosby's positions more closely, let us assume that matter in some crucial moment does become organized to such an extent that something in the organized entity is enabled to *feel* or to *experience* as a subject. Then, having allowed that something has emerged that has the ability to feel, *what is it* that has this feeling? What is the locus of this ability to feel? There seem to three choices. Is it one or more of the *constituent bits* of matter within the entirety? Or, is it *the entirety* of the whole thing at once? Or is it some *aspect* of the whole organized thing? We have seen that Deacon denies that sentience can be "directly mapped to specific physical substrates or chemical processes," but it is obvious that sentience must be restricted in some way to the immediate proximity of the physical processes involved. Therefore what Deacon must now explain is something very much like Descartes's ghost in a machine—in Deacon's own words, "a non-material conception of organism"—which is not matter but remains restricted in location to the vicinity of that matter.

Crosby's approach to emergentism holds that sentience pertains to the interactive processes characterizing the organized entities as a whole. Does this claim obviate the questions just asked? Let us examine the logic of this claim. We have already considered the difference between the holism of a salt crystal and the holism displayed by a living organism. The quality of saltiness is a result not of any one particle but of the interactions of several particles by means of their chemical bonds. Crosby's explanation holds that, as saltiness applies not to sodium or to chlorine but to the wholeness of sodium chloride, by analogy, sentience applies not to atoms or molecules but to cells or organisms. But this analogy fails, because "sentience" is not a property to be externally observed, like the quality of saltiness. Sentience is not a *consequence* that follows structure; sentience is *experience* had internally by a subject. Sentience does not *follow* organism; it *coincides* with it. Salt is an aggregate; organisms are fundamentally different from aggregates.

In a materialist view, only electrons, protons, and neutrons—the physical constituents of matter—are allowed. The taste of saltiness can be explained in terms of the actions of these particles, that is, in terms of chemical interactions of sodium chloride with our taste buds. There is a chemical mechanism to explain saltiness. Selfhood, in contrast, is not a chemical interaction with the external world; it

is an internal experience. If we say that selfhood inheres not in the
electrons, etc., themselves, but in the *pattern* or *organization* that
they create, we must point out that in a materialist metaphysics
pattern and *organization* are, strictly speaking, *not matter*, but rather
abstractions. Is it the pattern itself that experiences subjectivity? If
so, isn't this type of pattern really a new ontological type, despite
the assurances of materialists that it is not? Bonding electrons in a
benzene ring resonate from one carbon atom to another, creating a
pattern that can be depicted as a torus, but this is a physical pattern.
In a materialist theory of emergence, we are forced to say that such
patterns somehow develop sentience and the unity of subjective
experience—even though, by stipulation, they are still essentially a
collection of particles in motion. If we are to be candid, I think we
must admit that this scenario is really not merely counterintuitive but
unconvincing and, in fact, far fetched—an attempted explanation
that it has been forced upon us not by prevailing evidence but by the
underlying presuppositions of the ACN worldview.

Only if a unitary subject has emerged may the item in question
be deemed an organism and have any experience, but it is the having
of experience that defines the presence of subjective unity. If we
consider sentience on the one hand and organism on the other, one is
not a property that emerges from the other after the first (whichever
one is alleged to come first) is formed. This, again, is a chicken-and-
egg conundrum. In the emergentist view, each "emergent"—the
organism that is a subject, and the sentience of that organism—
must be explained by the emergence of the other. If emergentism
claims that both emerge together, then we are thrown back upon
the unsatisfactory image of the ghost-in-the-machine, that is, the
problem of explaining how an assemblage of material has produced
a sentient organism. These questions that keep leading back to each
other constitute a *reductio ad absurdum*.

Organization and organism are not the same thing. Obviously
the ACN worldview makes any philosophy of organism seem patently

implausible. Nevertheless, I submit that it is more reasonable to accept the idea that some primitive form of sentience is primordially inherent in nature than it is to continue to insist that subjectivity somehow emerges from insentient matter.

INTUITION AND SELF-EVIDENCE

Both the ACN worldview and Whitehead's metaphysics are perspectives on the overall character of nature. As such, both involve not only empirical and logical arguments but a type of conviction based on the intuition that one's own position is undergirded by self-evidence. Philosophies of matter and philosophies of process each have their own aesthetic or intuitive appeal.

For many persons, one intuitively appealing aspect of scientific materialism is that it is thought to be mostly and perhaps even entirely unfettered by any dependence on "philosophy." But the truth is that science, despite its frequent claims to be free of metaphysics, is fraught with metaphysical assumptions. This has been markedly obvious in our consideration of emergentism.

Historically, metaphysics by its very nature manifests an unfortunate tendency to degenerate into something authoritarian and grandiose. Whitehead intended metaphysics to be tentative and experimental, and yet at the same time he viewed it as being of immense significance, for metaphysical ideas seep into and permeate the very fabric of human activity, both individually and culturally. An awareness of this fact has been a chief motive behind this essay's attempt to clarify the metaphysical foundations of the origins of life. Once we do question the assumptions of the ACN worldview, the notion that nature traffics in information, and that nature is thus primordially experiential and valuational, is simply more convincing than the attempt to derive life and experience from insentient matter.

Still, beyond metaphysics is the level of religious intuition. Deacon earnestly affirms his commitment to the worldwide relinquishment of our historically exploitive attitudes toward nature,[88] and Crosby and Goodenough are eloquent in expressing the conviction that nature itself has sacred depths and that it therefore merits our utmost ethical concern—a concern grounded in our very reverence for the sacred. In my view, this intuition transcends the differences between materialistic and organismic philosophies. Though I do not concur with the emergentists' arguments, I can only express my wholehearted agreement with their conclusions.

ENDNOTES

1 Lee Smolin, *The Trouble with Physics: The Rise of String Theory, the Fall of a Science, and What Comes Next* (Boston: Houghton Mifflin Company, 2007), 25–26.

2 We return to the subject of sub-atomic pattern and structure in Section III.

3 Some information, of course, may be said to be transmitted by physical contacts, collisions, and forces. There are other patterns, however, that appear in nature that are not explicable solely in terms of physical interaction.

4 Robert Cummings Neville, *Ultimates: Philosophical Theology, Volume I* (Albany: State University of New York Press, 2013), 50.

5 See Anne Wilson Schaef, *When Society Becomes an Addict* (San Francisco: Harper and Rowe, 1988), 108–09. Schaef's point is not that male chauvinism is implicitly a theory of metaphysics but that there is a metaphysical aspect to male chauvinism because it entails convictions that certain things are real (do exist), and other things are not real (do not exist). These ideas are presented in the context of Schaef's discussion of the nature of addiction.

6 See Frederick Copleston, *A History of Philosophy*, Vol. I (Paramus, NJ: The Newman Press, 1947), 27.

7 Alfred North Whitehead, *Modes of Thought* (1938 ; New York: The Free Press, 1968), 135.

8 Ursula Goodenough, *The Sacred Depths of Nature* (New York: Oxford University Press, 1998).

9   Including its introductory sections and the conclusion.

10   Goodenough, *Sacred Depths*, 139.

11   Goodenough, *Sacred Depths*, xi.

12   Goodenough, *Sacred Depths*, 49.

13   Goodenough, *Sacred Depths*, 46.

14   Goodenough, *Sacred Depths*, 28.

15   Goodenough, *Sacred Depths*, 46–47.

16   David Bohm, "Some Remarks on the Notion of Order," in C.H. Waddington, ed. *Towards a Theoretical Biology,* Vol. 2 (Chicago: Aldine, 1968), 34; quoted by Terrence Deacon in *Incomplete Nature: How Mind Emerged from Matter* (New York: W.W. Norton, 2013), 264.

17   Goodenough, *Sacred Depths*, 46.

18   Goodenough, *Sacred Depths*, 28, 29, 30.

19   Goodenough, *Sacred Depths*, 167–68.

20   Goodenough, *Sacred Depths*, 101–02.

21   Vaihinger's proposal of "As if" was based on his 1877 dissertation investigating the philosophies of Kant and Nietzsche. His *Die Philosophie des Als Ob* was published in 1911, appearing in English in 1924 and again in an abbreviated version in 1935. Vaihinger's skepticism was directed not only at religion but at many types of metaphysics; his philosophy has been regarded as sympathetic to logical positivism, though some of the logical positivists themselves were critical of his work.

22   In a time when philosophers and theologians have with good reason become wary of claims to religious truth, Robert Neville refreshingly argues for the importance and the legitimacy of truth in the context of faith. See *Ultimates,* 28, 72–73; 43–44; 96.

23   One well-known example of a biologist who defends the presence of purposes in nature is Charles Birch; see his *A Purpose for Everything: Religion in a Postmodern Worldview* (Mystic, CT: Twenty-third Publications, 1990).

24   Terrence Deacon, *Incomplete Nature: How Mind Emerged from*

Matter (New York: W.W. Norton, 2013).

25 Deacon, *Incomplete Nature*, 1; 146.

26 Deacon, *Incomplete Nature*, 2–3.

27 Deacon, *Incomplete Nature*, 174.

28 Deacon, *Incomplete Nature*, 550.

29 Deacon, *Incomplete Nature*, 230–32.

30 Deacon, *Incomplete Nature*, 247–49.

31 Deacon, *Incomplete Nature*, 272.

32 See F.E. Peters, *Greek Philosophical Terms: A Historical Lexicon* (New York: New York University Press, 1967), 191–92.

33 Deacon, *Incomplete Nature*, 275. Italics are Deacon's.

34 Deacon, *Incomplete Nature*, chapters 15 and 16.

35 Deacon, *Incomplete Nature*, 487.

36 Deacon, *Incomplete Nature*, 488.

37 Deacon, *Incomplete Nature*, 490.

38 Deacon, *Incomplete Nature*, 250.

39 Colin McGinn, "Can Anything Emerge from Nothing?," *The New York Review of Books*, June 7, 2012; soft copy at http://emergence.org/McGinn.pdf; page references vary, depending on format. McGinn's review is caustic almost to the point of an *ad hominem* attack, but it contains several incisive, appropriate criticisms nevertheless.

40 McGinn ("Can Anything") cites the example of a friend not being in a place where one expected to find him; one might say that this absence *caused* one to leave that place. But the fuller explanation of one's leaving is of course that newer goals *replace* the now irrelevant goal of meeting one's friend.

41 Deacon credits C. Lloyd Morgan and Donald Davidson with earlier versions of this concept. *Incomplete Nature*, 165–69.

42 Deacon, *Incomplete Nature*, 488. Italics added.

43 Deacon, *Incomplete Nature*, 487–88.

44 Deacon, *Incomplete Nature*, 40.

45   Deacon cannot bear much blame for this, since many of Whitehead's own supporters have unfortunately characterized his philosophy as a type of panpsychism. This designation is seriously misleading. *Psyche* is the Greek word for "soul" and is still understood today to refer specifically to *human* personality (thus the term "psychology") and its concomitant attributes of mind, will, knowledge, developmental and social challenges, struggle for meaning, etc., none of which is pertinent to Whitehead's individual actual entities. Regarding Whitehead's philosophy, terms such as "pan-mentalism," "pan-experientialism," etc., are more accurate, but even these require nuanced redefinition.

46   Deacon, *Incomplete Nature*, 78–79.

47   Some of Crosby's books are: *More Than Discourse: Symbolic Expressions of Naturalistic Faith*, 2014; *The Thou of Nature: Religious Naturalism and Reverence for Sentient Life*, 2013; *Faith and Reason: Their Roles in Religious and Secular Life*, 2011; *Living with Ambiguity: Religious Naturalism and the Menace of Evil*, 2008; *Novelty*, 2005; *A Religion of Nature*, 2002; and *The Specter of the Absurd: Sources and Criticisms of Modern Nihilism*, 1988.

48   Donald Crosby, *Novelty* (Lanham, MD: Lexington Books, 2005), 2.

49   Crosby, *Novelty*, 6–7.

50   Crosby, *Novelty*, 39. Italics added.

51   Crosby, *Novelty*, 48–49.

52   Crosby, *Novelty*, 49.

53   Crosby, *Novelty*, 50.

54   Crosby, *Novelty*, 52.

55   Crosby, *Novelty*, 51–59.

56   Crosby, *Novelty*, 7.

57   For examples of the idea that matter is actually structured energy, see Lee Smolin, *The Trouble with Physics* (Boston: Houghton Mifflin Company, 2007); Bryan Greene, *The Elegant Universe* (New York: Vintage Books, 2000); Paul Davies and John Gribbin, *The Matter Myth: Dramatic Discoveries that Challenge Our Understanding of Physical Reality* (New York: Touchstone Books, 1992).

58 James Haag, review of *Novelty* in *American Journal of Theology and Philosophy* 30, no. 3 (2009), 340–41.

59 Goodenough, *The Sacred Depths of Nature*, 106.

60 Crosby provides a fine autobiographical description related to the development of his thinking on these points in Chapter 1 of his *A Religion of Nature* (Albany: State University of New York Press, 2002).

61 Crosby, *Living with Ambiguity* (Albany: State University of New York Press, 2008), 55.

62 Whitehead, *Science and the Modern World* (New York: The Macmillan Co., 1927, 219; New York: The Free Press, 1967, 152.

63 The word "information" has various meanings, of course. Some definitions—attempts, to some degree, to reduce the idea of information to the terms of the ACN worldview—are based on physical categories such as thermodynamics, but such definitions are of limited applicability. I follow Whitehead in thinking that information most often possesses both physical and nonphysical characteristics.

64 In an apparent attempt to dismiss the obvious conclusion that information is somehow conveyed to and utilized by electrons as they arrange themselves into orbitals, Deacon says that "orbitals are determined by symmetrical relationships between oscillatory properties associated with specific energy levels and what might be described as resonant symmetries of specific orbital configurations" (*Incomplete Nature*, 233). Jargon such as "oscillatory properties" and "resonant symmetries" must not be allowed to disguise the fact that the orbitals display precise, consistent properties that are not transmitted either by matter in the form of physical contact or by energy. The electrons may indeed "oscillate" or "resonate," but if they emitted or absorbed energy in the basic process by which orbitals are formed, this would violate essential quantum principles and undermine the fundamental stability of the atom, as Bohr initially noted.

65 For the description of a now-classic experiment verifying non-local correlations at a distance of approximately 6 miles, see W. Tittel, J. Brendel, B. Gisin, T. Herzog, H. Zbinden, and N. Gisin, "Experimental demonstration of quantum correlations over more than 10 km," *Physical Review A* 57, no. 5 (1998), 3229–32.

66 In a series of lectures to laypersons, the brilliant physicist Richard Feynman commented on this issue, focusing on the mathematical nature of gravitation. "What does the planet do? Does it look at the sun, see how far away it is, and decide to calculate on its internal adding machine the inverse of the square of the distance, which tells it how much to move? . . . Newton was originally asked about his theory . . . He said, 'It tells you *how* it moves. That should be enough. It tells you *how* it moves, not why.'" (*The Character of Physical Law*, New York: The Modern Library, 1994, 31.) Feynman added, "Every one of our laws is a purely mathematical statement . . . Why? I have not the slightest idea" (33).

67 Deacon rightly calls attention to "unfortunate overinterpretations" of quantum theory (*Inc. Nat.*, 74), which have occasionally been preoccupied with spiritualism, the alleged consciousness of the universe, premature claims that non-local entanglement plays a causative role when further investigation would reveal conventional efficient causality, etc.

68 See *Atom and Archetype: The Pauli/Jung Letters, 1932-1958*, ed. C.A. Meier, trans. David Roscoe (Princeton: Princeton University Press, 2001). See also K.V. Laurikainen, "Quantum Physic, Philosophy, and the Image of God: Insights from Wolfgang Pauli," *Zygon: Journal of Religion and Science* 25, no. 4 (1990), 391–404.

69 Werner Heisenberg, *Philosophical Problems of Quantum Physics* (Woodbridge, CT: Ox Bow Press, 1979), 55–56.

70 Heisenberg, *Philosophical Problems of Quantum Physics*, 38. Italics are Heisenberg's.

71 See Werner Heisenberg, *Physics and Philosophy: The Revolution in Modern Science* (Amherst, NY: Prometheus Books, 1999), esp. chapters II and IX.

72 See F.E. Peters, *Greek Philosophical Terms*, 43. For both Aristotle and in modern English, "potentia" can suggest both the *power* ("potency") to do something and a *possible future state of actualization* ("potential").

73 For a still-helpful analysis of the contributions of relativity theory and quantum mechanics to philosophy, see Ian Barbour, *Issues in Science and Religion* (New York: Harper Torchbooks, 1966), chapter 10.

74 Whitehead, *Adventures of Ideas* (New York: The Macmillan Company, 1933), 356.

75 On the relation of Whitehead's thought to quantum mechanics, see Michael Epperson, *Quantum Mechanics and the Philosophy of Alfred North Whitehead* (New York: Fordham University Press, 2004); and Frank Hättich, *Quantum Processes: A Whiteheadian Interpretation of Quantum Field Theory* (Münster, Germany: agenda Verlag, 2004).

76 See Heisenberg, *Physics and Philosophy,* 50–53.

77 See, for example, Whitehead, *Process and Reality,* Chapter III.

78 Whitehead, *Process and Reality,* 40.

79 Donald Crosby, "Whitehead's God and the Dilemma of Pure Possibility," in *God, Values, and Empiricism: Issues in Philosophical Theology* (Macon, GA: Mercer University Press, 1989), 38. Crosby elaborates on this critique in "Emergentism, Perspectivism, and Divine Pathos," *American Journal of Theology and Philosophy* 31, no. 3 (September 2010),

80 Whitehead uses various terms such as *hybrid physical feeling* or *hybrid physical prehension* for this fusion of pure and "real" possibilities. See *Process and Reality,* 245–52. "[P]otentialities can be analysed into pure abstract potentialities apart from special relevance to realization in the data or the issue, and . . . potentialities entertained by reason of some closeness of relevance to such realization." Whitehead, *Modes of Thought,* 94.

81 Advanced progress pertaining to the assumptions underlying mathematics was achieved by Whitehead and Bertrand Russell in their classic *Principia Mathematica* (1910, 1912, 1913).

82 See David E. Conner, "The Plight of a Theoretical Deity," *Process Studies* 41, no. 1 (2012), 111–32; "Response to Rem B. Edwards," *Process Studies* 43, no. 1 (2014), 97–105; Conner, "Whitehead the Naturalist," *American Journal of Theology and Philosophy,* 30, no. 2 (2009), 168–86; Conner, "A Functional-Empirical Approach to the 'Whitehead Without God Debate,'" chapter 4 in *New Essays in Religious Naturalism,* vol. 2 in the Highlands Institute Series, ed. Creighton Peden and Larry Axel (Macon, GA: Mercer University Press, 1993), 33–48. To summarize and, unavoidably, oversimplify, I hold that Whitehead's God is not a Divine Being who acts upon

the world but rather a natural ontological structure whose primary function is to qualify or inform the initial phase of every actual occasion.

83   See John B. Cobb, Jr., "'The Whitehead without God' Debate: The Critique," in *Process Studies* 1, no. 2 (1971), 99.

84   Whitehead, *Science and the Modern World* (1967), 80.

85   As Whitehead writes, "Every human being is the natural guardian of his own importance." *Science and the Modern World* (1967), 140–41.

86   Whitehead, *Modes of Thought,* 135.

87   Donald Crosby, "Emergentism, Perspectivism, and Divine Pathos," *American Journal of Theology and Philosophy* 31, no. 3 (2010), 197.

88   Deacon, *Incomplete Nature,* 544–45.

❧ 11 ❧

WHITEHEAD'S PANPSYCHISM AND DEEP ECOLOGY

Leemon B. McHenry

ABSTRACT: *This essay examines Whitehead's philosophy of organism as a basis for an ecological ethics. His views are compared with those of deep ecologists, and several problems with his panpsychism are considered in connection with the notion of intrinsic value in nature. In spite of problems raised by critics, this essay concludes that Whitehead's philosophy provides a worldview that offers a corrective to the disastrous course set by views that regard nature as an inert mechanism.*[1]

> *. . . a species of microbes which kills the forest, also exterminates itself.*[2]

IN OPPOSITION to the mechanistic materialism of 17th-century cosmology and Cartesian dualism, Alfred North Whitehead advanced a metaphysics in which the basic units of existence are understood as occasions of sentient experience, i.e., actual occasions. As Whitehead developed his theory of nature in his metaphysical works such as *Science and the Modern World*, *Process and Reality*, and *Nature and Life*, it became clear that the concept of organism was basic in his synthesis of psychology, biology, and physics. The "Concept of

229

Organism" was, in fact, his original proposal for the Gifford Lectures at the University of Edinburgh, which later changed to "Process and Reality" when he delivered the lectures in 1928."[3]

In one of his few surviving letters, he wrote of his project in *Process and Reality*: "I am trying to evolve one way of speaking which applies equally to physics, physiology, psychology, and to our aesthetic experiences."[4] It was in this attempt to capture the rich diversity of concrete experience that he created the psycho-physiological language of the prehensive activity of actual occasions and a vision that revolutionizes our concept of nature.

In this essay I examine Whitehead's philosophy of organism as a basis for an ecological ethics. I compare his views with those of deep ecologists and argue that in spite of problems raised by critics, Whitehead's philosophy provides a worldview that offers a corrective to the disastrous course set by views that regard nature as an inert mechanism. One need only consider the long-term effects of environmental degradation through the depletion of natural resources to see the urgent need to reverse the attitudes that have served the interests of industry but can no longer be sustained on a global scale.

WHITEHEAD'S METHOD AND PANPSYCHISM

As Whitehead described his working hypothesis for arriving at the general principles in pursuit of speculative philosophy, he wrote in *Adventures of Ideas*:

> if we hold, as for example in *Process and Reality*, that all final individual actualities have the metaphysical character of occasions of experience, then on that hypothesis the direct evidence as to the connectedness of one's immediate present occasion of experience with one's immediately past occasions, can be validly used to suggest categories applying to the connectedness of all occasions in nature.[5]

Earlier, in *Science and the Modern World*, he had explained the same method of generalization as follows:

> I have started from our own psychological field, as it stands
> for our cognition. I take it for what it claims to be: the
> self-knowledge of our bodily event. I mean the total event,
> and not the inspection of the details of the body. This self-
> knowledge discloses a prehensive unification of modal
> presences of entities beyond itself. I generalise by the use of
> the principle that this total bodily event is on the same level
> as all other events, except for an unusual complexity and
> stability of inherent pattern.[6]

Before Whitehead, William James and James Ward had adopted
this method in the process of generalization from psychology to
metaphysics. In his *Psychological Principles*, for example, James Ward
had expressed this method as follows: "we must start from individual
human experience; for it is this alone that we immediately know.
From this standpoint we have . . . to reach a concept applicable to
every other form of experience as well as to our own."[7] Similarly, for
William James the introspective method of psychology produced
such innovative concepts as "the stream of consciousness" and "the
specious present" later woven into his pluralistic metaphysics and
radical empiricism.[8]

There is a question of whether Whitehead, James, and Ward
are guilty of the anthropomorphic fallacy or the pathetic fallacy in
their methodology, for the detractors argue that generalizing from
human experience will only produce a view of reality that privileges
what is characteristic of human experience. So, for example, if Alfred
North Whitehead, a Victorian Englishman, generalizes from his
experience, the result is Victorian, English, male actual occasions
instead of features genuinely universal among all of existence. This,
of course, is an exaggeration, but not by much for the critics who
wish to make the point that this method is so flawed that no sensible
person could take it seriously.[9] The idea is that you get something
distinctively human from human experience and nothing else. While
the traditional empiricism of Locke, Berkeley, and Hume focused on
the clear and distinct elements in our visual perception, Whitehead

is trying to find something more basic in our experience that is common to all nature. He called the clear and distinct elements of our experience "presentational immediacy." But as he made it clear in the passage above from *Science and the Modern World*, it is not simply a generalization from consciousness but rather a generalization from *embodied* psychological experience. The vague and inarticulate feelings of our total bodily experience more accurately capture that commonality, a dull throb of existence or a basic feeling of emergence from the immediate past. He called this element in human experience "causal efficacy," and sufficiently generalized causal efficacy becomes the prehensive activity of all actual occasions.

Dorothy Emmet suggested that when Whitehead began working towards a generalized view of organism with an eye for unifying physics and biology, it looked as if physics might be swallowing up biology, but in his later writings, it is biology, or rather psycho-physiology, that is swallowing up physics. In contrast to most philosophers who have created systems of philosophy based on abstractions, Whitehead sought concreteness pervasive in all nature. His recommendation to his students at Harvard, which of course shocked his analytical colleagues, was "meditate on your viscera."[10] The basic principles are not to be found in the high abstractions of human consciousness, but rather in the basic organic functions of lived psycho-physical experience. Our dim semi-conscious experience of half sleep or visceral feelings of well-being, mostly ignored in our every day experience, are more representative of the continuous becoming in the mode of causal efficacy. Note how this plays out in *Process and Reality* when Whitehead turns his attention to the natural world:

> A jellyfish advances and withdraws, and in so doing exhibits some perception of causal relationship with the world beyond itself; a plant grows downwards to the damp earth, and upward towards the light. There is thus some direct reason for attributing dim, slow feelings of causal nexus, although we have no reason for any ascription of the definite percepts in the mode of presentational immediacy.[11]

In other words, nothing of the full conscious experience of human beings or other mammals with a dominant single-line nexus is apparent in the most basic experiences of flora and fauna, but there is every reason to infer sentience in its basic form. Nature is alive with feeling. So the question is not whether generalizing from experience is an acceptable method, but whether the inference passes the test of applicability and adequacy.

While Whitehead did not use the term "panpsychism" to describe his position, and most commentators have preferred "panexperientialism" to "panpsychism," the philosophy he embraced has been aligned with idealism in that he espoused the omnipresence of feeling in a creative universe.[12] As he advanced what he called "the reformed subjectivist principle," he wrote: "apart from the experiences of subjects there is nothing, nothing, nothing, bare nothingness."[13] In other words, if not for the experience of subjects, other kinds of entity-like enduring objects, composites, aggregates, and possibilities ("societies" and "eternal objects" in his terminology) would not exist since they depend on the basic class of entity, the actual occasions. "'Actual entities'—also termed 'actual occasions'—are the final real things of which the world is made up. There is no going behind actual entities to find anything more real."[14] Whitehead avoided the term "panpsychism" because of its literal meaning that all is psyche or consciousness. Consciousness, for him, is rare in the overall scheme of things. In *Process and Reality*, Whitehead thus distinguished between:

- Subjectivity (ascribed equally to all actual occasions in the immediacy of becoming);

- Mentality (ascribed to all actual occasions by the degree to which they can originate novelty);

- Consciousness (ascribed only to a very specific type of highly mental actual occasions based on their capacity for "intellectual feelings").

I shall use the term "panpsychism" in the generic sense of metaphysical idealism.[15] This agrees with Whitehead's view that there is nothing apart from the experience of subjects, and with his protest against the materialist's claim that reality is fundamentally insentient matter. That is, for Whitehead, reality must be conceived as experience from beginning to end; there is no radical emergence of mind or consciousness from mere insentient matter. Consciousness is rather ontologically akin to its rudimentary form in experience. But it should be clear that Whitehead's complete view is more properly described as a synthesis of idealism and realism, panpsychism and physicalism. Subjectivity is basic to all actual occasions in their process of becoming, but once they perish as subjectively immediate, they become objects for the prehensions of future occasions. So, Whitehead's synthesis of idealism and realism, panpsychism and physicalism, is grounded in the temporal relations of past, present, and future. What is subjectively immediate is creative experiencing of the present while what is objectively real and physical is the settled past world.

To understand Whitehead's explanation for different kinds of entities in nature, there is another important aspect of his theory: the dipolarity of actual occasions. Each occasion has what Whitehead calls a "mental pole" and a "physical pole," but given the location of the occasion in different kinds of bodies—mineral, vegetable, and animal, for example—there will be a dominance of one pole over the other. Mere matter has a dominance of the physical pole, which means that the actual occasions composing the body inherit their predecessors with deterministic repetition and thereby provide for the periodicity of nature captured in the mathematical equations of physical laws. Actual occasions of this sort have subjective aims that essentially repeat the patterns of their predecessors and so there is no real potential for novelty. Such low-grade occasions are the basis for physical existence, and, as described above, what they experience is that vague sense of emergence. As we move up the scale to various forms of living organisms, there is more opportunity for intensity of experience. The mental pole of the actual occasions composing such forms provides for more selectivity in the prehensive process, until we arrive at higher organisms with the ability to entertain multiple possibilities and actualize those compatible with their subjective aims. In the case of human consciousness, there is a dominance of the mental pole of the occasions forming what we intimately know as our stream of consciousness or mind. Here, then, is the emergence of rational thought and artistic creativity that Whitehead describes as the "higher phases of experience."[16] So, basically, the dipolarity of actual occasions explains how anything new emerges in the temporal process. Whitehead reinterprets Descartes's dualism of matter and mind in terms of one type of entity, but that entity, depending on its place in the extensive continuum of nature, will have more or less potential for introducing novelty.

Some followers of Whitehead's thought have seen in his panpsychism and relationalism a foundation for an environmental ethics that would address the crisis created from our traditional anthropocentric ethics,[17] but others doubt whether we really are any closer to a satisfactory position with Whitehead's approach. Even the claim that Whitehead has reversed the disastrous anthropocentricism has been questioned.[18] In what follows I shall examine these criticisms and determine to what degree Whitehead's philosophy can be defended against such views.

WHITEHEAD AND DEEP ECOLOGY

Proponents of deep ecology such as Arne Naess, George Sessions, and Warwick Fox seek to radically revise traditional thinking about nature to recognize intrinsic value in nature and our ethical obligations to nonhuman life on Earth.[19] They typically contrast deep ecology with shallow ecology, or superficial environmental ethics that only recognizes value for human beings. For shallow ecologists, preserving an ecosystem would be an ethical obligation only insofar as it serves the interests of people who enjoy it or profit from it, whereas for deep ecologists, our ethical obligation is to preserve the ecosystem for its own sake. Timothy Sprigge, for example, raised the following thought experiment: suppose that there is an ecosystem intensely beautiful yet so fragile that any interference from human beings would destroy its delicate balance. Now, if one holds that this ecosystem must be preserved even if no humans could enjoy it in any practical or recreational way, one would recognize the intrinsic value in nature.[20] We have a duty to preserve nature for *what it is in itself* rather than for *what it is for us*. He regarded this as a sort of litmus test for deep ecology.

Would Whitehead pass Sprigge's litmus test? It is not immediately clear, so I will address this below once I have given sufficient exposition of his views and those of deep ecologists.

Deep ecology is not only a theory of ecological ethics; it is also a movement with a manifesto of eight principles which I quote from Naess's 1986 essay, "The Deep Ecological Movement: Some Philosophical Aspects":

1. The well-being and flourishing of human and non-human life on Earth have value in themselves (synonyms: intrinsic value, inherent worth). These values are independent of the usefulness of the nonhuman world for human purposes.

2. Richness and diversity of life forms contribute to the realization of these values and are also values in themselves.

3. Humans have no right to reduce this richness and diversity except to satisfy vital needs.

4. The flourishing of human life and cultures is compatible with a substantially smaller human population. The flourishing of non-human life *requires* a smaller human population.

5. Present human interference with the non-human world is excessive, and the situation is rapidly worsening.

6. Policies must therefore be changed. These policies affect basic economic, technological, and ideological structures. The resulting state of affairs will be deeply different from the present.

7. The ideological change will be mainly that of appreciating life quality (dwelling in situations of inherent value) rather than adhering to an increasingly higher standard of living. There will be a profound awareness of the difference between bigness and greatness.

8. Those who subscribe to the foregoing points have an obligation directly or indirectly to try to implement the necessary changes.[21]

The deep ecology platform, concisely stated, amounts to three basic principles of action: (1) wilderness and biodiversity preservation, (2) control of the human population, and (3) a directive for living on the planet that involves minimum damage to other forms of life. Boiled down even further to one basic principle, the deep ecology imperative might be formulated as follows: live simply so that others might live at all, including the non-human world and Earth herself. Many advocates of this basic plan, such as John Cobb and Herman Daly, see a steady-state economy that opposes the traditional wisdom of continuous growth as a means to achieving such ends.[22]

Deep ecologists such as Naess and Sessions see in Spinoza's monism and pantheism the metaphysical view that offers the foundation of deep ecology. In fact, for these philosophers, deep ecology is grounded in the metaphysical monism that "all things are ultimately One," whereby the individual dissolves into a web of interconnections. There is only one universal Substance, of which the appearance of individuality and separateness in nature is an illusion. In accordance with Spinoza, the self-interested ego transcends itself to identify with the wider Self of God/Nature as a whole. We become enlightened participants insofar as we develop ecological sensibilities that help us realize our union with nature. In this manner the concept of the self is extended to the whole of nature.[23] Our protection of nature is our protection of ourselves, and our destruction of the natural environment is the destruction of ourselves. We all begin as egoists with only instrumental interests in the preservation of nature, but as we extend the concept of the self beyond the individual ego, we realize the intrinsic value in all of nature. The enlightened egoist therefore understands that the well-being of the whole is his or her well-being as a node in an interconnected web.

Since all forms of life are elements in a single Organism, human beings turn out to be, as Warwick Fox puts it, "just one constituency among others in the biotic community, just one particular strand in the web of life, just one kind of knot in the biospherical net."[24] No single species has more of a right to exist and flourish than any other. While Whitehead is occasionally mentioned as an ally along with Spinoza in the deep ecology movement, Whitehead's recognition of degrees of valuation in the continuum of nature is incompatible with the ecological egalitarianism affirmed by deep ecologists.[25] This is one of the main criticisms of Whitehead's system.

There are, of course, numerous problems that confront proponents of deep ecology. I will here discuss briefly two: the vital needs in Naess's principle #3 and the determinism that is undeniably part of Spinoza's metaphysics and ethics. Regarding the first, where conflicts of interest and/or value come into play, it is debatable what vital needs are. Killing the shark to save the life of the surfer is justified; destroying the tropical rainforest to make room for cattle in the production of hamburgers is probably not. In the latter case, and many others like it, it is the complete lack of moral consideration shown to the environment in which human beings have done the most damage. There is, however, a large middle ground here that inspires contentious debate as to exactly what is a vital need, for example, sacrificing millions of rats, rabbits, monkeys, and dogs for pharmaceutical and product testing. Without a clear concept of vital needs, there is little guidance for action. Moreover, any such concession to vital needs appears to come into conflict with the ecological equalitarianism of deep ecology.

Regarding the second problem for Spinozistic deep ecologists, Spinoza himself writes in Proposition **XXIX** of his *Ethics*: "Nothing in the universe is contingent, but all things are conditioned to exist and operate in a particular manner by the necessity of the divine nature."[26] Given the equalitarianism of all sentient existence within the eternal substance of God-or-Nature (*Deus sive Natura*) in Spinoza's metaphysics, the actions of human beings, like everything else in nature, are completely determined by the iron necessity of what Spinoza calls "divine nature," or what is dictated by the whole *sub specie aeternitatis* to all constituent components. This implies that human beings cannot act independently of God's own activity. We abandon the notion of freedom of choice as we come to understand rationally God-or-Nature as a fixed system of causes and effects. Past, present, and future are merely relative depending on finite point of view, whereas from the perspective of the whole substance of God/Nature, all events are ontologically determinate and eternally present. So, the question for deep ecologists is whether a normative ethics that claims human beings should adopt measures to respect and preserve nature is compatible with determinism. Things simply are, and there is no sense to any claim as to how things should be, because we cannot derive an *ought* from a *can't*. This is not to say, of course, that human beings cannot adopt measures that respect and preserve nature; it is just that they do not do so by any freedom of choice, and therefore there is no moral praiseworthiness of the actions and no real sense to the very idea of normative ethics. This aspect of Spinoza's system has not been emphasized by deep ecologists, but the problem of accepting Spinoza's monism as a philosophical foundation for deep ecology is that it is intimately bound with his determinism. Like Spinoza's enlightened man, it is a matter of moral luck that determines whether the deep ecologist is set on the path of blessedness.

Whitehead did not accept any such Spinozistic monism in which individuals dissolve into the One, but his view of organism has the same practical consequence of recognizing that the environment is our life-support system.[27] Actual occasions grouped together to form macroscopic objects such as plants, animals, and planets are called "societies." A society, as defined by Whitehead, is the massive average objectification of the dominant characteristics, the eternal objects, in the actual occasions forming the society. What he called a "nexus" (plural nexūs) is a togetherness of the basic entities. So-called "empty space" would be a nexus of actual occasions without what Whitehead calls "social order." The things that endure over a period of time, identified as substances in Aristotle's metaphysics or "space-time worms" in relativity theory, are composites of the more basic momentary things. Actual occasions become and perish whereas societies endure. Whitehead explains that the stable structure of matter arises from the actual occasions as a "structured society," that is, as one that includes subordinate societies and subordinate nexūs with a definite pattern of structural interrelations. A molecule, a cell, a planet, a solar system, and a galaxy are all examples of structured societies. Each society is an organism that is harbored within the environment of another larger society, which serves as an organism for another, and so on. The special sciences such as physics, chemistry, biology, geology, astronomy study some layer of society or organisms and their environment—subatomic particles, atoms, molecules, cells, plants, animals, planets, galaxies, to the widest society of actual occasions whose immediate relevance to ourselves is traceable, namely, cosmic epochs.[28]

Whitehead also distinguishes between living societies and non-living societies. A cell or an organism is a living society. A molecule or a rock is a non-living society. The former exhibit a capacity for greater novelty but are also vulnerable to changes in the environment; for example, a living organism will be more responsive to the larger society in which it exists, and it will require special conditions for survival. The latter are largely characterized by pure physical inheritance and exhibit minimal capacity for novelty. Such societies will be relatively unaffected by changes in the environment unless there is catastrophic change or complete destruction of the larger society that harbors the existence of the society in question. This distinction between living and non-living societies, as explained above, is a result of the dominance of the poles of the actual occasions that make up the societies. The occasions that make up living societies have more sophisticated mentality, whereas the occasions that make up non-living societies have mere subjectivity.

Most of the societies that make up the enduring objects of our perceptual experience are "democracies," in the sense that their subordinate societies function together without some central, unified mentality. Cell colonies, plants, ecosystems, and most lower forms of many-celled animals are democracies. These organisms react to stimuli, but there is no central direction or unified control. Higher animals, however, are those with a dominant living nexus of personal order. In the case of the vertebrate animals, the nexus of occasions with a dominance of the mental pole arises out of the complex nervous system, and the intensity of this experience varies from species to species.[29]

PROBLEMS FOR WHITEHEAD'S PANPSYCHISM

As any living society's survival depends on the survival of the larger society that harbors its existence, it is imperative for human beings to ensure the health of Earth that sustains life. This aspect of Whitehead's metaphysics as a foundation for ecological ethics is reasonably well grounded, but his version of panpsychism appears to present a unique problem. Clare Palmer was one of the first to point out that there is a problem for the claim that Whitehead's panpsychism serves as a foundation for an environmental ethics in her book, *Environmental Ethics and Process Thinking*. If, following Whitehead, the fundamental real things are actual occasions, it is unclear what the process approach to environmental ethics could be. She quotes favorably Val Plumwood:

"It is quite unclear what kind of ethical relations could emerge with respect to the homunculi which inhabit 'occasions of experience' or how this esoteric reformulation is supposed to make a difference to our everyday behaviour."[30] Palmer further argues: "The threshold of moral considerability in process thinking is so low that even though something may be morally considerable, its moral significance is negligible. Thus, although technically all actual occasions could be morally considerable, in actuality their significance is so slight, so trivial, that they are not worth consideration."[31]

In other words, each actual occasion has intrinsic value, but the actual occasions that compose nature are bizarre candidates for moral obligation, unless they are of the high-grade type exemplified in human consciousness and in certain nonhuman animals. Palmer, for example, points out that since natural objects as societies of actual occasions have strong physical poles and weak mental poles, they generate little novel or rich experience.[32] Obviously, we cannot hold that all actual occasions are objects of moral consideration since it would be impossible to resolve conflicts of basic interests.

This is puzzling. Whitehead's actual occasions, each with its own intrinsic value, are supposed to be the basis for sentience in nature and the respect that follows from this recognition; yet the kind of actual occasions that compose the greater part of nature are of the sort that seem to deserve no more consideration than mere matter in traditional thinking about nature. This being so we have circled back to something similar to the very view that is the root cause of the failure of respect for nature. No one thought that the atoms of mechanistic materialism were candidates for moral obligation.

Enduring physical objects or "societies" are abstractions in Whitehead's system, but it is the societies, not actual occasions, that should be the entities to which we have ethical obligations for deep ecologists and other environmental ethicists. So, how is it that ecosystems, endangered species, wildlife, wilderness, and planet Earth herself are any better off from the point of view of Whitehead's panpsychism? Even more pressing, how is it that Whitehead's system offers any better solution to the crisis of climate change and global warming if indeed this is a man-made state of affairs? If we focus on his theory of society, of societies and nexūs embedded in higher societies—or organisms and their environments that sustain and nurture them—it appears that we have an interest in preserving the social order that harbors our existence, but this, as noted above, is purely an instrumentalist justification, i.e., superficial rather than deep ecology. Is there also recognition of intrinsic worth in the relevant societies that compose the environment?

Intrinsic worth is intimately connected with the notion of having an inside. This position stands in stark opposition to what Whitehead calls "vacuous actualities" or dead matter of mechanistic materialism.[33] There is something it is like to be a human being, a dolphin, a bat, and a butterfly, but there is nothing it is like to be a rock, a ball of string, or a computer.[34] In the former cases there is a dominant living nexus of personal order of actual occasions, whereas in the latter cases there is not. There is, however, something it is like to be an actual occasion that exists as a member of the societies that compose aggregates and nonliving societies, even if that something is, as discussed above, nothing more than a dull throb of existence and a vague sense of having arisen from the immediate past. Actual occasions as subjectively immediate have an inside. But it appears there is nothing it is like to be structured societies such as ecosystems or the planet Earth.

Palmer and Sessions have also raised the problem about the high-low grade distinction in Whitehead's dipolar theory of actual occasions, because it privileges human consciousness as the highest value of sentience and merely reinforces anthropocentricism that is the source of the ecological problem. Sessions, for example, writes: "the degree of sentience is irrelevant to how humans relate to the rest of Nature."[35] Whitehead's method of generalizing from human experience is the main source for his concept of the actual occasion, but does this just produce another form of anthropocentricism, in that the hierarchy of value in his system gives priority of place to the sort of *intense* experience of human beings and what Whitehead speculates in the experience of God? The very concept of what constitutes "high-grade experience" is in question.

Returning to Sprigge's litmus test for deep ecology, there are hints in Whitehead's writings that point to an answer. In one key passage he writes:

> The western world is now suffering from the limited moral outlook of the three previous generations.
>
> Also the assumption of the bare valuelessness of mere matter led to lack of reverence in the treatment of natural or artistic beauty. Just when the urbanisation of the western world was entering upon its state of rapid development, and when the most delicate, anxious consideration of the aesthetic qualities of the new material environment was requisite, the doctrine of the irrelevance of such ideas was at its height . . . .
>
> The two evils are: one, the ignoration of the true relation of each organism to its environment; and the other, the habit of ignoring the intrinsic worth of the environment which must be allowed its weight in any consideration of final ends.[36]

Whitehead's example in the full passage is the Charing Cross railway bridge, an industrial age fixture in London that defaces the natural beauty of the Thames River. Here he is discussing the need for aesthetic sensitivity with respect to how we mold our environment. This statement occurs in the final chapter of *Science and the Modern World*, entitled "Requisites for Social Progress," which appears to put his statements in the whole context of instrumentalism. Wisdom of sound judgment rather than mere knowledge or industrial know-how is the key to social progress. In fact, the major theme of this chapter is the aesthetic needs of a civilized society against the indoctrination of materialism in the prevailing scientific orthodoxy. Whitehead makes a similar remark when reflecting on the historical importance of his boyhood home in East Kent in southern England that was developed for a golf course: "I feel a sense of profanation amidst the relics of the Romans, of the Saxons, of Augustine, the medieval monks, and the ships of the Tudors and the Stuarts. Golf seems rather a cheap ending to the story."[37]

Whitehead's use of the term "intrinsic worth" in the passage above indicates that he regarded the environment as having both intrinsic and extrinsic value. There is the value of the environment in itself as an object of natural beauty and the value of the environment for those who experience it and make use of it. But this is not the sense of intrinsic worth that recognizes the inner subjectivity of a being for there is nothing it is like to be the environment as a unified whole. Moreover, it remains unclear what Whitehead's answer would be for Sprigge's litmus test. Would Whitehead agree with the claim that the intrinsic values of nature are independent of the usefulness of the nonhuman world for human purposes? In the same chapter cited above, Whitehead writes: "Successful organisms modify their environments" and uses the example of Europeans transforming the North American continent upon their arrival to demonstrate his point of how this principle works on a "vast scale."[38] While most of us would question this example today, especially in light of environmental degradation, overpopulation, and, to put it mildly, disrespect for the indigenous population, the general principle raises further doubt for his connection to deep ecology. The crucial issue for Whitehead is whether the modification of the environment is done with aesthetic sensitivity. John Cobb notes that the deep ecology movement's manifesto for action is quite acceptable to a Whiteheadian.[39] I agree, but I am not convinced, that Whitehead would go quite as far as to embrace the notion that there are intrinsic values of nature that bestow rights to exist independent of humans. Sprigge's litmus test was, after all, not one to determine whether one believes there are intrinsic values in nature, but whether one would be willing to abandon all human interests in the environment for the sake of intrinsic value in the environment. All organisms affect changes to their environments. As noted above, some are better, some are worse.

Insofar as Whitehead gave emphasis to life in nature, such as self-enjoyment and creativity, it is not all actual occasions, but those that compose living societies that are of special significance when it comes to moral consideration. But even here his doctrine of degrees of sentience in various biological organisms, plants, and animals means that moral consideration depends on the strength of the mental poles of the occasions that make up those societies. Sentience, in its basic form of subjective immediacy, of prehending the past, is the foundation from which emerge various orders of society, all oriented toward the production of beauty in nature. Every actual occasion contributes its measure of value to the end result, but beauty does not always win due to the role of contrast and conflict in nature. Where conflict does arise, we are justified in harvesting crops that served as ecosystems for animals, exterminating pests and parasites, defending our homes against hostile invaders, and using chemotherapy to eradicate the advancing cancer. In this connection, Whitehead remarks that "life is robbery. It is at this point that with life morals become acute. The robber requires justification."[40] We are not, however, justified when it comes to the sins of aesthetic sensitivity that human beings have committed on the environment and animals on a massive scale. In the opinion of this writer, that includes vivisection and most of what passes for scientific and medical experiments on animals, factory farming, deforestation, and the collective failures of governments to regulate industries responsible for a wide range of ecological disasters.

CONCLUSION

With regard to the shallow/deep distinction, Whitehead does not quite qualify as a deep ecologist on all points, but neither is he a shallow ecologist when properly understood. Deep ecologists and Whitehead's philosophy of organism share the rejection of substance dualism.

Instead of treating mind and matter as two irreducible and radically different kinds, subjectivity is omnipresent in nature. Deep ecologists and Whitehead also affirm the interdependence in nature rather than seeing in nature separation and independence. For Whitehead, there are genuine individuals, even though the individuals are intimately bound to the environment by their prehensions of it. It is also clear that human beings are not the source of all value; the nonhuman world is not merely of instrumental value to the human world, but human beings are "higher" in moral consideration in virtue of the intensity of experience in which they are capable.[41] This is certainly not the anthropocentricism of Immanuel Kant, according to which only rational agents gain membership in the moral community, but neither is it the equalitarianism of all sentient life espoused by deep ecologists. In this regard, Whitehead's position is a philosophy of the middle way.

So, to conclude, Whitehead's recognition of the problem is clear; what is less clear is the detailed solution as to how his panpsychism serves as a foundation for an ecological civilization. His philosophy was not designed with an ecological ethics in mind. Almost ninety years later, the world has changed, and we see new applications of his thought to address new problems. Whitehead's protest against valueless, dead nature is heard with renewed enthusiasm in those who see the consequences of this view, consciously or unconsciously held by those who have inherited the traditional attitudes and continue on the path of destruction. But whether or not Whitehead's view passes the litmus test for deep ecology or accords with the deep ecology agenda on all points, the change in conceptual framework—from seeing ourselves as apart from an inert, valueless mechanism to seeing ourselves as part of an organic nature—elicits the necessary response. Whitehead's philosophy, with his emphasis on organism and environment and with the relationalism in his theory of prehensions, achieves the same end result without having to adopt the more radical steps of deep ecology.

ENDNOTES

1   This paper is based on a presentation I delivered at the 10th International Whitehead Conference at Pomona College, Claremont, California, in June 2015. I am grateful to Brian Henning and David Conner for critical comments on an earlier draft of this essay.

2   Alfred North Whitehead, *Science and the Modern World* (Cambridge: Cambridge University Press, 1933), 257.

3   Victor Lowe, "Whitehead's Gifford Lectures," *The Southern Journal of Philosophy* 7, no. 4 (1969–70), 330.

4   Letter to T. North Whitehead, March 7, 1928 in Victor Lowe, *Alfred North Whitehead: The Man and His Work,* Volume II: 1910–1947, ed. J.B. Schneewind (Baltimore: Johns Hopkins University Press, 1990), 333.

5   Alfred North Whitehead, *Adventures of Ideas* (Cambridge: Cambridge University Press, 1933), 284.

6   Whitehead, *Science and the Modern World,* 91.

7   James Ward, *Psychological Principles* (Cambridge: Cambridge University Press, 1919), 29.

8   William James, *Principles of Psychology*, Vol. I. (London: Macmillan and Co., 1891), 224–90, 605–42; William James, *Essays in Radical Empiricism* (Longmans, Green and Co., 1912).

9   Clare Palmer, for example, writes: "That this limited representation of human experience should be the interpretative filter through which the entire universe is understood elevates a regional, temporal, species, race-, and gender-specific concept into a universal and eternal principle." *Environmental Ethics and Process Thinking* (Oxford: Clarendon Press, 1998), 221. Also see Edward Ballard, "Kant and Whitehead and the Philosophy of Mathematics," Studies in Whitehead's Philosophy, *Tulane Studies in Philosophy* X (1961), 21.

10   Dorothy Emmet, "Whitehead," Cambridge Philosophers IV, *Philosophy* 71 (1996), 112.

11   Alfred North Whitehead, *Process and Reality,* Corrected Edition, ed. David Ray Griffin and Donald W. Sherburne (New York: The Free Press, 1978), 176–77.

12   Also see my "Whitehead's Panpsychism as the Subjectivity of Pre-hension," *Process Studies* 24 (1995), 1–2.

13   Whitehead, *Process and Reality*, 167.

14   Whitehead, *Process and Reality*, 18.

15   Charles Hartshorne, for example, says that "panpsychism" or "psychi-calism" are terms to describe the case for metaphysical idealism, "to interpret reality in terms of mind." Idealists he says "deny any liter-ally insentient, thoughtless matter taken as more than abstraction from things that in their concreteness, and taken one by one, are at least sentient." *Creative Experiencing: A Philosophy of Freedom*, ed. Donald Wayne Viney and Jincheol O. (Albany: State University of New York Press, 2011), 55.

16   Whitehead, *Process and Reality*, 266.

17   Susan Armstrong-Buck, "Whitehead's Metaphysical System as a Foundation for Environmental Ethics," *Environmental Ethics* 8, no. 3 (1986), 241–59.

18   Bill Devall and George Sessions, *Deep Ecology* (Layton, Utah: Gibbs and Smith, 1986), 236.

19   See for example, Arne Naess, "The Deep Ecology Movement: Some Philosophical Aspects," *Philosophical Inquiry* 8 (1986), 10–31; George Sessions, "The Deep Ecology Movement: A Review," *Environmen-tal Review* 11, no. 2 (1987), 105–25; Warwick Fox, "Deep Ecology: A New Philosophy of our Time?" *The Ecologist* 14 (1984), 194–200. Also see Timothy Sprigge, "Are There Intrinsic Values in Nature?" *Journal of Applied Philosophy* 4 (1987), 21–28; for Sprigge's Spinozistic monism and his connections to various principles of deep ecology, see his *The Vindication of Absolute Idealism* (Edinburgh: Edinburgh University Press, 1983).

20   Timothy Sprigge, Lectures in Metaphysics, University of Edinburgh, 1983; also see "Are There Intrinsic Values in Nature?" 22. What Ses-sions regards as the "deep ecology norm of 'ecological egalitarianism in principle'" similarly calls for a test for what qualifies as "deep" in ecological thinking. Sessions, *Deep Ecology*, 236.

21   Naess, "The Deep Ecology Movement: Some Philosophical Aspects," 13.

22   Herman E. Daly and John B. Cobb, *For the Common Good: Redirecting the Economy toward Community, the Environment, and a Sustainable Future* (Boston: Beacon Press, 1989)

23   Naess, "The Deep Ecology Movement: Some Philosophical Aspects," 29.

24   Fox, "Deep Ecology: A New Philosophy of our Time?" 195.

25   John B. Cobb, Jr., "Deep Ecology and Process Thought," *Process Studies* 30, no. 1 (2001), 114.

26   Baruch Spinoza, *Ethics* in *The Philosophy of Spinoza*, trans. R. H. M. Elwes (New York: Tudor Publishing Company, 1934), 63.

27   It is in this connection that *pando populus,* the oldest and largest living organism, became the model for a Whiteheadian approach to ecological civilization at the 2015 10ᵗʰ International Whitehead Conference, "Seizing an Alternative." The delicate balance in the environment that has sustained the *pando populus*, like planet Earth, is now threatened by human activity.

28   Whitehead, *Process and Reality*, 91.

29   Whitehead, *Process and Reality*, 103–04.

30   Palmer, *Environmental Ethics and Process Thinking*, ix; Val Plumwood, *Feminism and the Mastery of Nature* (London: Routledge, 1993), 130. For replies to Palmer, see John B. Cobb, Jr., "Palmer on Whitehead: A Critical Evaluation," Timothy Menta, "Clare Palmer's *Environmental Ethics and Process Thinking*: A Hartshornean Response," and Clare Palmer, "Response to Cobb and Menta," *Process Studies* 33, no. 1 (2004), 4–70.

31   Palmer, *Environmental Ethics and Process Thinking*, 96.

32   Palmer, *Environmental Ethics,* 97.

33   Whitehead, *Process and Reality*, 29.

34   This is sometimes called "phenomenological consciousness." It is the view that, for an experience, to *be* is to *feel* in a certain way, or what makes a state phenomenally conscious is that there is something "it is like" to be in that state. Timothy Sprigge and Thomas Nagel made this point independently of each other. See Timothy Sprigge, "Final Causes," *Proceedings of the Aristotelian Society*, 1971, 166–68;

Thomas Nagel, "What is It Like to Be a Bat?" *Philosophical Review*, 1974, 435–50. See also Nagel's acknowledgment to Sprigge in *The View from Nowhere* (New York: Oxford University Press, 1986), 15n.

35 George Sessions, "Spinoza, Perennial Philosophy and Deep Ecology"; unpublished paper presented at the "Reminding" Conference ("Philosophy, Where Are You?"). Dominican College, San Raphael, California, June 19–July 4, 1979, 34 pages.].

36 Whitehead, *Science and the Modern World*, 243–44.

37 Alfred North Whitehead, *Science and Philosophy* (New York: Philosophical Library), 11.

38 Whitehead, *Science and the Modern World*, 256.

39 Cobb, "Deep Ecology and Process Thought," 113.

40 Whitehead, *Process and Reality*, 105.

41 Brian Henning argues that while Whitehead does affirm a hierarchical conception of reality and value, it is not the traditional anthropocentricism that permits mistreatment, subjugation, and destruction of others. He writes: "What both critics and proponents of Whitehead's work frequently misunderstand is that, although a Whiteheadian ethic *does* recognize, rightly in my estimation, that the depth of value achievable by individuals varies, the depth of value achieved by an individual *does not*, as it does in traditional systems, *directly determine* that individual's moral significance." "Trusting in the 'Efficacy of Beauty': A Kalocentric Approach to Moral Philosophy," *Ethics & The Environment* 14, no. 1 (2009), 113.

PART TWO

WHITEHEADIANISM, NATURALISM, AND THE WISDOM OF AN ECOLOGICAL CIVILIZATION

12

TRANSCENDENCE, IMMANENCE, AND ANTHROPOCENTRISM

Donald A. Crosby

ABSTRACT: *A fundamental shift toward a radically immanental view of reality and of the place of the human species in reality is required as an essential part of an appropriate response to the ecological crisis of the present day. I discuss and defend this view under three headings: the concept of a radically transcendent God and the concept of humans and the world in relation to such a God; Alfred North Whitehead's concept of a transcendent-immanent God and its accompanying view of humans in their relation to God and the world; and the outlook on humans and their role in the world set forth in the version of religious naturalism I call Religion of Nature. I argue that this last metaphysical (and religious) option is better suited than the other two to counter the entrenched anthropocentric attitude and the practices stemming from it that are lamentable traits of our time.*

We notice that a great idea in the background of dim consciousness is like a phantom ocean beating upon the shores of human life in successive waves of specialization. A whole succession of such waves are as dreams slowly doing their work of sapping the base of some cliff of habit: but the seventh wave is a revolution—"and the nations echo round." In the last quarter of the eighteenth century, Democracy was born, with its earliest incarnations in America and in France; and finally it was Democracy that freed the slave. ~Alfred North Whitehead[1]

THE "GREAT IDEA in the background of dim consciousness" of which Whitehead speaks is the idea of democracy and liberty, the idea that all humans, regardless of ethnicity, gender, or socio/economic background or level, are equally entitled to self-governance, equality before the law, equality of opportunity, and freedom from slavery and oppression. The roots of this idea lay in the dim past, for example, with Christianity's notion that every human being is a cherished child of God and that, in the words of one of Paul's New Testament letters, "[t]here is neither Jew nor Greek, there is neither slave nor free, there is neither male nor female, for you are all one in Christ Jesus" (Galatians 3:28).[2]

But the institution of slavery was for thousands of years the unquestioned basis of economics and society, an institution it seemed impossible for a labor-intensive society to do without. As Whitehead notes, the ideas of democracy and freedom that began to surge with developments in philosophical thought in the 17th and 18th centuries were furthered by the Industrial Revolution. They reached political expression in the American and French revolutions and the abolishment of the slave trade and slavery by England and the United States in the 19th century. But there was much beating of the waves against an adamantine cliff before it began to crumble and give way at last to the persistent force of the battering waves.

A similar strongly resistant, long-established cliff of habit today is an uncritical and uncaring anthropocentricism that holds nonhuman animals and their (and our) natural environments in bondage to hegemonic human enterprises, populations, whims, prejudices, and treatments. The slow erosion of this cliff began to occur due to influences of the sciences of cosmology, geology, Darwinian evolution, and ecology that date from the 16th through the 20th centuries—influences that continue in their effects to this day. But a thoroughgoing revolution which "the nations echo round" has yet to take place. Anthropocentricism is still firmly in place, and widespread ecological consciousness and a humble sense of human responsibility for the well-being of the direly threatened planet Earth and its endangered creatures has yet to exert anything like a revolutionary and radically transforming influence.

What are some of the roots of this seemingly implacable anthropocentric outlook among human beings and human institutions today, and how might a revolutionary overthrow of it be furthered? How might a replacement of it with a pervasive earth-centered perspective be advanced? In this essay I argue that, when it comes to thinking about the nature and destiny of human beings and their relation to nature, a major barrier to such a revolutionary transformation is a traditional and long-assumed emphasis on transcendence. The focus needs to be brought to bear instead on cosmic immanence and the unqualified immanence of humans within the natural order. Transcendence and anthropocentricism are close attitudinal relatives, I claim, and radical immanence and serious ecological sensibility are intimately related, as well. In what follows, I discuss under three headings how the second part of this statement holds true, and how a fundamental shift toward an immanental view of reality—and the place of the human species in reality—is required in response to the ecological crisis.

The three headings are: (1) the concept of a radically transcendent God in relation to the world and the concept of humans in relation to such a God; (2) Whitehead's concept of a transcendent-immanent God and the concept of human beings in relation to Whitehead's God; and (3) the concept of nature set forth in the version of religious naturalism I call Religion of Nature and the accompanying concept of the lives and experiences of humans in relation to the world, as envisioned in Religion of Nature. In my view, this last metaphysical option is better suited than the other two to counter the entrenched anthropocentric attitude and the deplorable practices stemming from it that are a fundamental blight on our time.

In his chapters on "Laws of Nature" and "Cosmologies" in *Adventures of Ideas*, Whitehead distinguishes four basic views of the world: the "immanental," the "impositional," the "positivistic," and the "conventional." In this essay, I shall dwell on the first two of these views. Since for Whitehead the impositional view regards the world as having been created by a radically transcendent God, as having all of its basic features conferred upon it by God in a single act of creation, and as being completely ordered and controlled by God, this view of God amounts to a central aspect of what I am calling the radically transcendent outlook on the world.

Whitehead argues that a compromise or blend of the best features of transcendent (he calls it *impositional*) and immanental perspectives on the nature and relation of God and the world is needed for an adequate conception of the cosmos. His own conception of God, as spelled out in *Process and Reality* and elsewhere, is his response to this need. I shall argue instead: 1) that a thoroughgoing immanental perspective alone is best, 2) that there is no need for any version or degree of the impositional or transcendent picture of the world, and 3) that there is no requirement for any conception of God. I will bring out what I regard as destructive and negative implications of the concept of transcendence, not only for the idea of God and of God's relation to the world—most notably, but not exclusively, God's relation to humans in the world—but also for the general outlook on humans and their relations to the natural environment, on their character and comportment in the environment, and on the physicality of the environment. The upshot of these considerations is that a resolutely immanental view of reality is best suited to save us from the unbridled, deeply entrenched anthropocentrism, the destructive and negative consequences of which are becoming evident on every hand.

THE RADICALLY TRANSCENDENT (OR IMPOSITIONAL) VIEW OF GOD AND THE WORLD

A radically transcendent view of God places God entirely outside the natural world and with no essential dependence on the world. God is viewed as pure spirit, is placed beyond space and time, is wholly self-subsistent, and rules the world by sheer, uncontestable, absolute will or fiat. In accordance with the Cartesian and Spinozistic definition of substance, God, and God alone, requires nothing but Godself in order to exist. Every occurrence and detail of the world is determined by the timeless will of God. God created the world and sustains it in its every aspect, moment by moment. In this view of the world, there is no such thing as chance or freedom, if these terms imply any degree of independence or separation from the divine rule.[3] Everything that happens, human or nonhuman, follows necessarily from that rule. God reigns absolutely over all. A central aspect of this concept of God is that of omnipotence. And omnipotence requires omniscience, because nothing can be surprising or unexpected for God. Omnipresence is also required, because there can be no place in the universe hidden from God or beyond God's cognizance and complete control.

The picture of the world derivative from this view of God is that the world as a whole is a machine, cleverly designed by God, set in motion by God, and maintained in every detail by God. This picture, endorsed by Isaac Newton and other scientific pioneers of the early modern era, has proved in many ways to be a boon for fruitful scientific research. All creatures within the world are, by implication if not express recognition, automata, little more than cogs in that machinery. The glory of God and the absolute authority of God are upheld at the price of any degree of autonomy of the world. Deists in the grip of this view may have claimed that the world, once created, runs its course independent of divine interference, but its running is entirely predetermined by God.

Another part of this idea of God is that God dwells in a realm of pure spirit, a realm utterly separate from the changes, uncertainties, and dangers that mark the world as experienced by its finite creatures. What the creaturely "cogs" may view as threatening disruptions or breakdowns in the machinery of the world are from God's perspective necessary outcomes of its relentless running. Genuine safety and serenity reside only in God's separate and timeless realm.

As Whitehead frequently notes, this radically transcendent conception of God is that of a despot or autocrat, a ruler whose subjects are completely in thrall to his whim and rule. This is not a God of care and concern for anything other than the outcomes and consequences of his absolute might. To view such a God as a God of love would be a pitiful misconception. The world is for God a plaything, an artifact, a game, nothing more. And human beings are nothing more than mere pieces on the board of the game called Earth. And yet, paradoxically, they are also the major point and focus of God's creation of the world. Earth is the background or stage for the saga of the human fall into sin and of the divine relegation of some humans to damnation and others to redemption. Such a world has no inherent claim to goodness. Its goodness, if we want to call it that, results from God's willing it to be what it is. Being the result of God's will constitutes the very meaning of goodness; there is no other meaning.

Is there no escape for humans, then? There are only two modes of escape. One is to aspire to affirm with no trace of objection or rebelliousness the absolute power of God and the resultant complete determination of every happening in the world. It is to give up the dream of having even a smidgen of autonomy. The second avenue of escape is the hope for oneself and one's loved ones of being taken up after death by divine will from the Earth into the serene realm of the divine spirit and there to find timeless rest and everlasting peace.

The ultimate salvation of human beings is thus complete removal from the world, not engagement with the problems of the world. There are in fact no real problems, since everything that happens occurs as the inevitable outcome of God's rule. And the only respite from the seeming evils of the world is rest within the everlasting arms of

God, free at least from the illusion of autonomy and from the world's troubles, dangers, losses, and perplexities. If a particular person is fortunate, God will remove that person from the world after death and bring him or her into the paradise of the divine realm. And God will do so by absolute fiat or act of his will. Those less fortunate will suffer the eternal punishment their sinful attitudes and actions on Earth are said to deserve, despite the fact that these, too, stem entirely from God. In either event, whatever happens takes place because of God's eternal decree. It could not have been otherwise.

And for humans, the Earth is a mere steppingstone to their true destiny, which lies in heaven or hell. In the final analysis, it is all about this destiny, not so much about the transitory earthly stage setting. But humans are helpless pawns of God's will, not persons with genuine freedom. Still, behind the scenes there lurks the idea of God, a personal being whose nature resembles in many respects the nature of human beings. In fact, humans are said to be created in the image of God and to be, in their essence, and *in contrast with everything else on earth*, spiritual (even if wholly determined) rather than physical beings. The near exclusive focus on humans and their destiny, and the fact of God's having traits of human life and personality raised to the "nth" degree, show the extent to which the transcendent vision of God and the world is anthropomorphic in its core.

It is true that the idea of the radical transcendence of God as I am describing it here has rarely been taken to such extremes. In order to be religiously and morally plausible it has had to be amended— either by paradoxical, symbolic means, or by attempts at consistent conceptual resolution—with appropriate assertion of aspects of divine immanence. Whitehead's conception of God is a case in point.

WHITEHEAD'S TRANSCENDENT-IMMANENT GOD

For Whitehead, God is a personal being; transcendent in God's primordial nature but immanent in God's consequent nature. God is nontemporal or eternal in one respect but everlastingly immanent in time in another. God and the world are both everlasting; the world did not come into being as a result of God's creation but has always existed along with God. Responsive to events in the world and to human experiences in the world, in God's consequent nature God interweaves this responsiveness with the pure possibilities of God's primordial nature and seeks to guide subsequent events in the world with a passionate tenderness and loving concern. Whitehead's God acts to preserve forever all the attained value of any past situation and to lure the world to maximal value in every present moment. The world has autonomy in relation to God, and humans have real freedom and responsibility. God's power is the power of ardent and compassionate persuasion rather than the power of absolute rule. God is "the fellow-sufferer who understands."[4] Moreover, Whitehead's focus is on nature as well as God, and the two are mutually dependent on one another.

Even without such explicit adjustments in the traditional notion of the radical transcendence of God, theists have continued for the most part to act and react to God in ways implying that God can relate to events in time and be affected and change in response to those events. They have continued to think of God as a God of mercy, forgiveness, and loving-kindness. Only such a God, they have judged implicitly or explicitly, is worthy of worship and faithful, loving service. They have refused to believe in a God who is an absolute tyrant, willing without affect or concern for the sufferings and sorrows of the world. And they have thought of God as giving significant freedom and autonomy to human beings, holding them responsible for their choices and the consequences of their choices.

Humans are thus seen as being able to work with God for the betterment of the world, and God has been seen as relying on humans to do so. Their actions can make a real difference, and God works with them to bring about such differences. This is the God of *practical* religion, a God whose transcendence is entwined with immanence, who interacts with and is affected by changing events in the world.

Theistic religious beliefs, attitudes, and practices, therefore, have tended strongly in the direction of something akin to Whitehead's concept of God: a blending of transcendence and immanence, of awesome majesty and magnificence with loving and wise intimacy and persuasion.

So far, so good. But I think it vitally important to consider pushing the idea of immanence much further than Whitehead does. I think that we should do so, at least in part, in the interest of helping to rid both humans and nature of the scourge of anthropocentrism. Too much potentiality for this scourge lingers in Whitehead's thought, as I interpret it. What features of Whitehead's view of God and the world would need to be set aside in order to bring about a metaphysical approach less prone to anthropocentrism? What picture of humans and the world would be disclosed if this result were achieved? In other words, what would a more radically immanental metaphysics than Whitehead's transcendent-immanent one be like?

Are there practical consequences of sometimes seemingly arcane metaphysical theories and disputes? I believe that there are because all of us tend to live, plan, choose, and act—consciously or unconsciously—in accordance with our fundamental beliefs about the nature of reality and our place as humans in reality. And these beliefs stand always in need of critical reflection, possible revision, and even replacement by more coherent and adequate beliefs. The version of immanence I shall present next is of course also subject to this statement. But I present it in the hope that the reasons I offer in its support will be weighed in balance and carefully considered. Anthropocentricism is a radical outlook that has long been taken for granted, and the alternative to it needs to be radical as well.

A RADICALLY IMMANENTAL VIEW OF HUMANS AND THE WORLD

In this section, I will first discuss the aspects of Whitehead's metaphysics that I think need to be set aside in the interest of avoiding a still too-anthropocentric view of the world and of the place of humans in it. Before doing so, I should take note of the fact that my own thinking over the years has been deeply influenced by Whitehead's metaphysical views and by his system of thought that I regard as a milestone metaphysical achievement of the 20th century. Nevertheless, I believe that to be critical of aspects of this achievement is to think with him, not against him. He was a lifelong foe of the illusion of finality of thought and well aware of possible and inevitable limitations in his own philosophy. He always saw himself as struggling against formidable limitations of imagination, insight, language, and acculturation toward greater clarity of vision. I do the same in his spirit, even though in my admittedly much more limited way. Great thinkers are stepping stones, not stopping places.

I can heartily affirm features of Whitehead's metaphysics, such as: 1) his idea that becoming is prior to being; 2) that the metaphysical status of possibility is a problem requiring investigation along with the status of actuality; 3) that consistency, coherence, and adequacy are the principal goals of metaphysical systems; 4) that for the sake of doing justice to theistic religious practice and experience, the radically transcendent view of God needs to be replaced with a metaphysical view of God that combines transcendence and immanence and allows God to relate meaningfully and lovingly to the world; 5) that adequate metaphysical understanding must reject causal determinism and take fully into account the roles of novelty and freedom in the world; 6) that all the dimensions of experience and all fields of thought must be drawn upon and included within a satisfying metaphysical vision; and, finally, 7) that our emotions and valuative judgments have cognitive significance because we live in a world of value.

However, there are other features of Whitehead's system that I have come to reject in the course of my own thinking, and one basic reason for this rejection is that I believe them to be too anthropocentric. What are these features? One of them is the dipolar nature of actuality in the system. Another is the notion of pure possibility. Still another is the idea that the world is guided by the purposive actions of a divine being. Another is that sad, regrettable, tragic, evil events in the world are somehow compensated for or made less horrible by a putative divine preservation of whatever potential good may lie within them and of the positive good that is achieved elsewhere. All of these features add up to giving prominence to personal traits and acts that are closely akin to the traits and acts of human beings. This is a prominence that reinforces the dangerous delusion of the centrality of human beings in nature and in the whole scheme of things. Let us take a look in turn at each of the features I have listed.

1. *The dipolar nature of actuality.* Whitehead builds mentality, experience, and teleology into the universe in its every aspect with his key conception of the actual entity as dipolar. But in my view, these factors are characteristic only of highly organized living physical systems and do not pertain to earlier, nonliving stages in the evolution of those systems. As I have argued at length in other works, there is novelty everywhere and in every stage of nature's developments. Continuity and novelty go constantly together and neither is possible without the other.[5] But novelty is not the same thing as mentality, experience, and teleology, despite Whitehead's tendency to conflate them with novelty.

To conflate them is to make the mentality, experience, and teleology that are most prominent in humans and only approximated to by other creatures a fundamental trait of reality as such. It is to give undeserved attention to the human mode of life as somehow characteristic of or basic to the universe as a whole. Whitehead's panexperientialism and an outlook of panhumanism are close cousins—much too close, in my view. Many creatures on Earth are capable of experience in some degree, but nonliving nature does not exhibit mind, experience, or teleological orientation and striving. Such features have slowly *emerged* over vast stretches of time. They are not primordial.

Moreover, the physical and the mental are not complementary and coeval, as they are claimed to be in Whitehead's dipolar actualities.

In my view, mind is a function of matter. This view avoids the temptation to regard the human mind as stemming from or reflecting the character of a putative divine mind. It also resists the elevation of mind over matter or any notion of mind or spirit's transcendence over the physical universe. Radical immanence is consistent with a thoroughgoing materialism or physicalism. No kind of panpsychism or panexperientialism is required.

I hasten to add however, that the *matter* assumed here is not confined to what is currently described in the field of physics. The concept of matter needs to be rich enough and sophisticated enough to encompass the new, non-reducible, emergent realities of life and mind that are the fruits of biological evolution and include the history and development of human cultures. Such things as far-from-equilibrium, non-linear complex systems theory; autocatalysis; and autopoiesis must be taken fully into account, as must all the complex, diverse facts of life and phenomena of mind. And the doctrine of the causal closedness of the universe must be rejected. This means that a wide variety of fields of thought and experience must be drawn upon, including the natural and social sciences, the arts, philosophy, religion, moral and legal theory, history, anthropology, and the like. I discuss at length the need for such a revision and deepening of the concept of matter elsewhere.[6]

2. *The notion of pure possibility*. The notion that there are such things as timeless pure potentials or eternal objects and that these need to be located and ordered somewhere is one of the basic motivations for Whitehead's conception of the primordial nature of God. While Whitehead insists that God is not conscious or personal in God's primordial nature, this nature is the conceptual pole which, in conjunction with God's consequent nature or physical pole, allows God to be a fully conscious personal being. But such a role for God is not required if one rejects, as I do, the need for so-called *pure* possibility as an aspect of reality, and opts only for *real* possibility. Real possibilities do not reside in a timeless realm but in the causal past,

in other words, in an entirely immanent worldly and physical realm. A personal God is not needed either to explain their locus or their ordering. This Platonic feature of Whitehead's thought can be safely discarded. Possibilities are present in the past and already ordered in relevance by events of the past. Mathematical, logical, and linguistic systems can abstract from that locus and ordering but should not be thought to point to some kind of wholly transcendent realm of pure possibility or timeless map of all possibilities for the actual world.

3. *Guidance of the world by a purposive being.* So far as I am able to ascertain, there does not appear to be convincing evidence for a universal purpose of the world or for overarching personal guidance of the world as a whole. There are purposive activities of creatures in the world; we humans are examples of that fact, as are many other earthly forms of life in varying degrees. But I contend that all forms of purposive life on earth have arisen through evolutionary emergence of physical systems and are not preceded by, based on, or lured by some kind of ultimate and at least partially transcendent teleology or goal-directedness. To insist that they must be in order to be made intelligible is to introduce once again the jarring note of a tacitly assumed anthropocentrism. It is an all-too-human way of looking at the world, as though it had to be guided in all its events and actions by a cosmic source of purpose and intent strikingly similar to us humans in its personal attributes and purposive character. An outlook of radical immanence rejects the need or rationale for this view. In doing so, it sets aside another anthropocentric tendency in Whitehead's metaphysics.

4. *The preservation of all attained value in God.* Finally, there is the idea in Whitehead's system that the values attained in the world, however partially or inadequately, do not perish but are perpetually preserved in the experience of God. In Whitehead's view, God distills all possible positive values from the events of the world and saves them forever in an experience that is said to be nontemporal, because it is the experience of God as a single, always concrescing actual entity,

an entity that can achieve ongoing satisfaction without ever coming to an end or being closed up moment-by-moment.

The inevitable fading of value with the passage of time in the world is poignant and regrettable for Whitehead, a perpetual perishing that is inevitable in this domain. Also poignant and regrettable for him are the short-changings of possible positive value when actual entities and the systems made up of them fail to achieve the highest values available to them in given situations, a failure that can lead to progressively greater, more flagrant, and destructive amounts of evil in the world over time. But these events are not finally or completely tragic because all achieved positive value, however minimal or deeply marred by evil it might have become, continues to be actual in the everlasting consciousness and endless experience of God. In the meantime, God continues to guide each new unit of concrescing reality in the world, luring it to the maximal goodness of which it is capable—with the intention of contributing through it to the betterment of the world. The enrichment of God's experience by the achieved goods of the world and the possibilities for future goods they provide is an essential aspect of this divine guidance.

In my view, this notion is too mollifying and optimistic. It fails to do full justice to the stark and intractable suffering, tragedy, and loss in the world that can and often does result from the inexorable, unpredictable, and often unforeseen workings of natural law. It fails to do justice to the staggering number of past extinctions or to the pervasive suffering and loss of predatory animal life. It also fails to do justice to the sometimes horrible, inexplicable evils that can result from human prejudice, perfidy, malice, and cruelty—and that can come to characterize human institutions and their often baleful effects. Suffering, tragedy, and loss are characteristics of an ambiguous world. I do not think that this ambiguity can be finally compensated for or resolved. It is here to stay. Systemic natural evils of nature can be reduced or avoided to some degree, and the moral evils of humans can as well. But neither can be entirely done away with so long as nature is what it is and humans are possessed of the freedom to do evil as well as good. Hope must be tempered with realism.

In a fully immanental view of the world, and/or of human acts in the world, this ambiguity is a stubborn, irreducible fact. Humans can strive to do better in the future and inspire one another to do so. They can also be inspired to do as much good as they can in recognizing and honoring the majesty and sacredness of the earth and the community of living beings of which they are a part. Both are crying, urgent needs. But humans should not underestimate for a moment the amount of real, lasting evil in the world; the tendencies toward evil that lie in the human breast; or the amount of evil that resides forever in a fixed and irremediable past. Whitehead's divine preserver of all accomplished value is a romantic ideal that does not, in my view, take sufficient account of these stubborn facts. It is a dream of another world, a world transcending this one, a world with a too wishful human face.

From the immanental standpoint of a Religion of Nature,[7] the world is religiously right and pervasively sacred despite and even because of its natural and moral ambiguities. It is so partly because a supposedly better earthly world, devoid of sometimes destructive but generally supportive natural laws and of creatures that require one another for their sustenance in food chains that progressively channel the energy of the sun, is not really conceivable. And for the world to be devoid of human evils, it would also have to be rid of the indispensable good of human freedom and responsibility, so such a world is not even desirable. Moreover, consequential human freedom would be impossible without the continuity and dependability of unvarying natural laws, along with the dangers sometimes posed by them. Such a non-ambiguous world is neither fitting nor desirable for finite creatures such as we are, creatures living in a radically immanental, pervasively finite, but marvelously capacious, complex, and sustaining world. We are responsible for our actions and inactions, as these affect the world of which we are a part. We are well advised to respect the lives of our fellow nonhuman creatures and the integrity of their environments. We must fervently resist any foolish tendency toward what George Santayana warns against as "the apotheosis of the human spirit."[8]

We humans are not the apex or lords of nature but only humble members of an interdependent community of innumerably distinct and different forms of life. While there may be other forms of life similar to our own elsewhere in the universe, the whole vast universe gives little evidence of being modeled on us in its essential character, created by a being or beings similar to us, or guided by a personal being or beings. We are not pure spirits but physical beings able to function in mental and spiritual ways. As our recent history gives painful evidence, we are capable of doing much damage to this community, particularly when we think, as we too often do, only of ourselves and our short-term interests, or when we fail to attend to the needs of this world by being distracted too much by the expectation of an imagined other world to come. But we are also capable of doing much remedial and continuing good for nature's sake.

There is no human-like God to save us or to compensate or make up for our sins or the consequences of our sins. No other world awaits us; this material, fragile, wonderful world is our natural home and final resting place. This is the kind of immanental, nature-centered, resolutely non-anthropocentric message I believe we need to hear, accept, and learn urgently to work with in a time of ever increasing ecological peril.

ENDNOTES

1   Alfred North Whitehead, *Adventures of Ideas* (New York: Free Press, 1967), 19–20.

2   The translation is from *The Holy Bible: The Oxford Annotated Bible*, Revised Standard Version, ed. Herbert G. May and Bruce M. Metzger (New York: Oxford University Press, 1962).

3   When human freedom is affirmed in this radically transcendent view of God and the world, it is by implication a *compatibilist*

view of freedom, namely, that absolute divine power is compatible with the human being's ability to choose and act out of his or her own inner intentions, motives, and the like, even though the ultimate and sole source of the latter is the absolute will of God. Theologians and others who take the radically transcendent view of God have great difficulty in avoiding the conclusion that what may to all appearances look like rampant evil in the world and in human decisions and actions is actually the inscrutable workings of wholly benign divine purpose and action. There has been much wrangling over this tangled issue in the history of thought, and some thinkers have been content to let the issue rest as an unresolvable paradox.

4   Alfred North Whitehead, *Process and Reality*, Corrected Edition, ed. David Ray Griffin and Donald W. Sherburne (New York: Free Press, 1978), 351.

5   Donald A. Crosby, *Novelty* (Lanham, MD: Lexington Books, 2005); Donald A. Crosby, *Nature as Sacred Ground: A Metaphysics for Religious Naturalism* (Albany: State University of New York Press, 2015); *Consciousness and Freedom: The Inseparability of Thinking and Doing* (Lanham, MD: Lexington Books, 2016).

6   Donald A. Crosby, *The Philosophy of William James: Radical Empiricism and Radical Materialism* (Lanham, MD: Rowman and Littlefield, 2013), chapter 9; Crosby, *Nature as Sacred Ground*, especially chapter 5.

7   I do not want to leave the impression that there are no kinds of transcendence compatible with a fully immanental view of the world. I discuss six kinds in "Transcendence and Immanence in a Religion of Nature," *American Journal of Theology and Philosophy* 24, no. 3 (2003), 245–59. These kinds of transcendence are to be found within the world, not outside of it. Nature transcends or surpasses itself in its character as *natura naturans* ("nature naturing"); it transcends the human species in space and time; events of grace in our experience transcend our ability to predict or manage them; novelty and freedom transcend causal continuity; we can transcend our current selves by our acts of freedom; and nature transcends our puny attempts to fully comprehend the depth and vastness of its mysteries and wonders.

8   George Santayana, *The German Mind* (New York: Thomas Crow-
     ell, 1968), 107. This book was originally published under the title of
     Egoism in German Philosophy.

❧ 13 ❧

SACRA NATURA:
DISCERNING THE IMMANENT SACRED

Jerome A. Stone

ABSTRACT: *Religious naturalism affirms the possibility and desirability of a robust non-theistic religious/spiritual life. Two ideas of Whitehead are explored: the importance of tentative generalization and appreciative discernment. Then the Chinese balancing of Confucian and Daoist traditions is an example of how to learn from wisdom traditions. Some environmental implications of this view are proposed: 1) We treat sacred things with overriding care. What if the Earth and our sibling creatures were sacred? 2) The egalitarianism of Mohism needs to be in tension with the Confucian view of particular responsibilities. This may be extended by a gloss on Zhangzai's Western Inscription about becoming one with heaven and earth. 3) Human distinctiveness needs to be joined with a sense of parity between species. 4) We need to learn selective withdrawal from markets. Markets are mindless and without morals. 5) All this needs to be focused on ecojustice. Finally, there are reflections on how to pontificate responsibly.*

IN THIS ESSAY I wish to set forward a version of *religious naturalism.* Religious naturalism affirms the possibility and desirability of a robust, non-theistic religious or spiritual life.

In this context *naturalism* means a life without reference to a supernatural god or extra-natural angels, spirits, or deities. To articulate what I mean by *religious* in the phrase "religious naturalism," we can start by reflecting on what it means to hold something sacred.

Let me begin by defining *holding sacred*. We hold something sacred when we are overwhelmingly impressed by its worth or significance. To adopt a religious attitude towards something is to hold it as sacred, to hold it of great significance, of overriding importance.

This is neither a subjective nor an objective judgment. Rather it is a *bridge judgment* anchored in both our attitude and the value residing in the object of our attitude. We could say it is a *transaction* between our judgment and the worth of the object.

A *religious naturalist,* in my current approach, holds that the entire universe, and potentially anything in it, is sacred. Certainly living things and their habitats are potentially sacred, that is, of great significance or value.

Let me be very clear. I am not referring just to the nonhuman world. I am not talking about backpacking in the forest, or watching a sunrise, although we may very well hold these sacred. I include inter-human interaction among things which *might* be held to be sacred.

Another caveat. The sacred is always dangerous. To hold something sacred may hinder inquiry and breed fanaticism. We are well aware that the Nazis spoke of the sacredness of "blood and soil." Sacredness has connotations of unapproachability. I would like to make a distinction between ethical and methodological approachability. When we speak of the sacredness of human beings, we normally hold up ethical restraint as a proper attitude of respect. We will not harm, indeed we may protect and care for what we hold sacred. However, when we speak of the sacredness of scripture or priests, we usually mean that we will not question their dicta. This is methodological restraint. I very much wish to shout from the housetops that sacredness, as it should be used today, implies ethical, not methodological restraint. Let us never put a bar to inquiry. This is very important, for the notion of sacredness could easily foster intellectual complacency, dogmatism, and fanaticism.

SOME WHITEHEADIAN THEMES

Let us now to pay homage to the thinker who inspired so many of these essays, the great philosopher, Alfred North Whitehead. I pass over two characteristics of his worldview: the interrelated and the dynamic character of everything. I pass over these because they are commonplace notions today. Instead I wish to highlight two motifs of his thought which are sometimes overlooked.

The first Whiteheadian theme I wish to underline is the tentative character of all human thought. In the *Dialogues of Alfred North Whitehead*, Whitehead comments that

> By 1900 Newtonian physics were demolished, done for. Speaking personally, it had a profound effect on me; I have been fooled once, and I'll be damned if I'll be fooled again! ... There is no more reason to suppose that Einstein's relativity is anything final, than Newton's *Principia*. The danger is dogmatic thought; it plays the devil with religion, and science is not immune from it.[1]

The second Whiteheadian theme I want to stress is what I call appreciative discernment. In *Modes of Thought* and other writings, Whitehead highlighted the significance of a sense of importance and worth. It was his way of overcoming the fact-value dichotomy and has helped me understand the role of appreciation in our engagements with the world.

LEARNING FROM THE WISDOM TRADITIONS

Now, I ask, what is the best way to learn from the great repositories of wisdom to be found in the wisdom traditions of the world? My proposal is that: 1) it is safest to learn from at least two of the world's great religious or wisdom traditions, including those of the indigenous

peoples, and 2) we should learn the contested areas within these tradition, and 3) we should place them in dialogical relationship with
each other and with the contemporary scientific worldview.

First, becoming familiar with two or three of the great religions
will aid in avoiding a parochial outlook. A number of contemporary
philosophers and theologians are doing amazing comparative work. In
the pre-revolutionary days in China, a person frequently balanced the
yang of the Confucian tradition with the yin of the Daoist. Although
I have done no publishable work in this area, I regularly immerse
myself in the Buddhist and the Confucian traditions. Like a second
language, one may not become highly proficient in a second tradition
yet still attain a relative fluency.

Second, the counterpoint between divergent themes within a
tradition should be explored. For instance, we should pay attention to
the divergence between self-power and other-power in Buddhism, or
between grace and works in Christianity, or the divergence between
the Confucian emphasis on the particularity of family responsibility
as contrasted with the Mohist emphasis on universal responsibility
or love for all people. In exploring these counterpoints, we should
examine not only the classical texts but also the later elaboration of
these themes. We need to study Augustine and the Song dynasty
neo-Confucians as well as the New Testament and the *Analects*.

Third, these traditions, with all of their diversity, should be placed
in dialogue with each other and with the contemporary worldview.
The purpose of this dialogue is to challenge the contemporary reader
to learn and to grow. Ideally this is not a one-way street in which either
a preferred religion or contemporary thinking trumps anything else.
I envision, rather, a transaction, a temporary suspension of skepticism
so as to see if there is something which the present can learn from the
past and vice versa. We can learn much from Hans-Georg Gadamer's
notion of a fusion of horizons and also from Paul Ricoeur's work in
hermeneutics.[2] I have also been inspired by Robert Neville's Boston
Confucianism, Sam Harris's use of Buddhist meditation, and Owen

Flanagan's attempt to develop a naturalized Buddhism.[3] Time does not allow me to elaborate on these hints.

ENVIRONMENTAL CONJECTURES

I now propose some environmental implications or conjectures based on this view.

First, perhaps Earth and our sibling creatures are sacred. Then we should treat our fellow creatures and their habitats with great care and respect. Now, of course, this principle does not tell us *how* to treat Earth and our sibling creatures with care and respect. It is a principle that lacks precision. But this is part of its usefulness. It forces us to ask how to live with care and respect. There are no right answers in the back of the book.

There is a possible objection. To live is to eat, which is to kill. But it is possible to kill with respect. It is called sacrifice. Perhaps eating, which does involve death, is a sacramental act. This point is not meant to settle the question as to whether vegetarianism is morally preferable.

Second, to treat all creatures, great and small, with care and respect, is in tension with the particular responsibilities of being a parent, fulfilling a promise, or being the president of an organization or corporation. In ancient China the egalitarianism of the Mohist school of philosophy was in tension with the Confucian emphasis on the particular responsibilities of family and political service.

The Song Dynasty Neo-Confucian philosopher Zhangzai (Chang Tsai) wrote in his famous *Western Inscription*, "Heaven is my father and Earth is my mother. . . . All people are my brothers and sisters, and all things are my companions"[4] There is a universality and generality to this viewpoint, which is in sharp contrast to the Confucian emphasis on duties to one's superior and to one's parents, husband, and older brother. But the *Western Inscription* goes on to talk about specific models of exemplary human behavior, citing six legendary or historical figures and how they specifically fulfilled their responsibilities.

This interplay between general and specific is part of the moral life and both must be considered. It will not do to treat all living beings as worthy of respect unless you treat very specific creatures so. Emerson's generalities about Nature need to be brought down to earth with Thoreau's concern for a very specific pond.

The third conjectural implication of this view is that human distinctiveness needs to be joined with a sense of parity between species. We humans are definitely superior to the other animals in some ways. But then, other animals are superior to us in their own ways. I can do long division and work out proofs in symbolic logic, which makes me superior to any animal or plant that I know. But, when I gloat about this, I hear the singing of the male Northern cardinal in the horse chestnut tree. In a flash of insight I realize that he is far superior to me in his song. So perhaps he is superior to me. Or perhaps rather in different respects each of us is superior to the other. Indeed, rather than talk about superiority, perhaps we should speak of difference.

A fourth possible implication of sensing the sacredness of the Earth and our sibling creatures is that we need to learn selective withdrawal from markets. Markets are mindless and without morals. They are supposed to be. The major value that markets fulfill is efficiency. But efficiency is a short-term value. When markets are run by transnational corporations, moral responsibility is diffused. And markets are not concerned about environmental degradation. The global market is not the Messiah.

Now I am not sure what selective withdrawal means. Thoreau's cabin and the Amish come immediately to mind. Please note that neither Thoreau nor the Amish have been completely withdrawn from the market. Both Thoreau and the Amish bought material for their houses and their tools on the market and both earned cash in the market. I am not sure what withdrawal means for most of us in the 21st century, but I am sure that it calls for serious thought.

The fifth conjectural environmental implication of treating at least some, and perhaps all, of nature as sacred is that there must be a focus on ecojustice. By ecojustice I mean developing fair, equitable, and genuinely sustainable policies for humans with moral consideration for nonhumans. I will not elaborate here my concept of that much-abused word "sustainability." The centrality of ecojustice follows immediately from respect for the sacredness of life and habitat. Respect means care. American environmentalism, with its canon of nature writing centering on Thoreau, John Muir, and Aldo Leopold, has too often focused on valuing the nonhuman world to the neglect of the native peoples who are displaced from the sacred natural areas, although a serious study of Thoreau and Leopold would correct this.

The topic of ecojustice is fraught with dangers that cannot be avoided. One danger is that activists may impose their own narrow view on other folk, a situation in which the environmental warrior proclaims, "I know what is best for you. We'll do it my way." Constant effort must be maintained to work with humility and to ensure democratic processes. There is no simple solution, but we cannot be paralyzed just by recognizing the dangers. One of the great values of the United Nations Earth Charter movement is its attempt to pursue ecojustice democratically.

Another difficulty is that environmental disasters often produce long-term damage as well as immediate destruction. These effects can be described as slow violence.[5] Slow violence can attack future generations. The time scale of slow violence has several consequences. 1) Slow violence is difficult to study empirically. 2) It is difficult to perceive and appreciate slow violence. 3) It is easy for a corporation or nation to evade legal and moral responsibility for these long-term effects.

The long-term temporal scale of environmental destruction makes moral culpability and responsibility difficult to assess and accept. There is a Muslim proverb that whoever finds the pasture gate open is responsible for closing it. There is great validity to that notion. However, long-term and diffuse environmental degradation is a lot more complicated than an open gate. Assuming responsibility for climate change, or Amazon deforestation, or environmental destruction generally is neither easy nor clear. In similar fashion the line between ordinary duty and heroic living is not easy to discern.

BEING RESPONSIBLE

It remains to explore the question: How can you and I think and act responsibly?

My first suggestion is that we should be scientifically informed and empirically cautious. This is not obvious to many people. Let me elaborate. There is a strong anti-scientific bias today, at least in the United States. In part this is due to a weakness in scientific education for many people. In part it is due to the over-reaching of some so-called experts who ride their theories beyond appropriate bounds. In part it is because too often scientists have been seduced by grants or sponsorship into unconsciously biasing their results. Too many consumer products, too much air quality, and too much drinking water and food have been prematurely declared safe. The public is leery of government or industry proclamations. I can understand the concern of many people about measles vaccination. I say I can understand their concern, although I do not share it. Then too, the need for empirical testing has been used as a shield for corporate interests. From the dangers of tobacco to global warming, the first defense of vested interest is to call for more testing.

Having said all of this, having acknowledged the reasons, both valid and invalid, for caution in the use of science, let me be absolutely clear. We need the best science, the best empirical inquiry we can get. I am always struck by the irony of some Daoist practitioners. Some of them, it seems, in searching for the elixir of immortality, actually shortened their lives by consuming mercury in their potions. The first rule in attempting to be wise is to seek the results of the best empirical inquiry.

The second rule in attempting to be wise is to admit our limits. It seems to me that the only way to speak with any integrity about our situation today is to speak with humility, to recognize that one might be wrong. We must often act and make decisions. Any parent or supervisor knows that. But we should always be ready to second-guess ourselves. We see through a dark glass. To be human is to be biased. But that is no excuse to stay mired in our biases.

The first rule of pontificating, of pretending to have wisdom, is to seek the best scientific results. The second rule is to admit our limits and speak with humility. I say this with irony and yet with sincerity.

SUMMARY

In summary, religious naturalism affirms the possibility and desirability of a robust, non-theistic religious or spiritual life. To adopt a religious attitude toward something is to hold it sacred, of great significance, or overriding importance. The Whiteheadean themes of intellectual humility and what I call appreciative discernment are important. I suggest that it is safest to learn from at least two of the world's great wisdom traditions, including those of indigenous peoples; that we should familiarize ourselves with the contested areas within traditions; and that we should place these traditions within a dialogical relationship with each other and with the scientific world view.

We should treat our sibling creatures and their habitats, indeed, the entire universe, as sacred, whatever that will mean in practice. We should contemplate the tension between these generalities and specific concern for particular responsibilities. A sense of human distinctiveness should be combined with a sense of parity between species. The cardinal and I are each superior to the other in certain ways. We need to learn selective withdrawal from the markets. We need a focus on ecojustice. And we should do all of this with humility and with use of the best empirical inquiry and the best science available. As generalities these may seem like truisms. But they will take more than a life-time to explore and implement.

The Yamuna River in India is one of her most sacred rivers—a goddess. Yet it is filled with garbage, dead animals, and odiferous scum. Bathing in it incurs the risk of diarrhea, hepatitis, and cholera. So holding something sacred does not guarantee that it will be treated with ecological sensitivity. Yet Bidisha Mallik, in the 2014 issue of *Environmental Ethics,* maintains that a holistic approach to river restoration that combines scientific, cultural, and religious values could make the difference.

ENDNOTES

1   Alfred North Whitehead, *Dialogues of Alfred North Whitehead,* ed. Lucien Price (New York: Mentor Books, 1956), 277.

2   Hans-Georg Gadamer, *Truth and Method,* trans. Garrett Barden and John Cumming (New York: The Seabury Press, 1975), 250–61; Paul Ricoeur, "Listening to the Parables of Jesus," in *The Philosophy of Paul Ricoeur: An Anthology of His Work,* ed. Charles E. Reagan and David Stewart (Boston: Beacon Press, 1978), 239–45.

3   Owen Flanagan, *The Bodhisattva's Brain: Buddhism Naturalized* (Cambridge, MA: MIT Press, 2013); Sam Harris, *The End of Faith: Religion, Terror, and the Future of Reason* (New York: W. W. Norton & Company, 2004), 204–21; Robert Cummings Neville, *Boston Confucianism: Portable Tradition in the Late-Modern World* (Albany: State University of New York Press, 2000).

4   Wing-tsit Chan, *A Source Book in Chinese Philosophy* (Princeton: Princeton University Press, 1963), 497.

5   See Rob Nixon, *Slow Violence and the Environmentalism of the Poor* (Cambridge, MA: Harvard University Press, 2011).

$\cancel{\text{≈}}$ 14 $\cancel{\text{≈}}$

WISDOM IN ANCIENT AND CONTEMPORARY NATURALISM

Karl E. Peters

ABSTRACT: *How can we think in ways that help transform human beings to minimize suffering and move toward a more ecological civilization? In this essay, I rethink the materialistic, atomistic Epicurean understanding of reality and ethics as presented in Lucretius'* De Rerum Natura (On the Nature of Things) *in relation to some contemporary neuroscience and evolutionary thinking and to the naturalistic theology of Henry Nelson Wieman. Responding to several obstacles to human transformation, I suggest that the way forward to a more ecological civilization can be guided by a general process perspective of "dynamic relational naturalism" to counter the "consumerist worldview" that is based on individualistic, materialistic progress.*

WE ARE APPROACHING environmental and human catastrophe. Because of human population growth and a material, fossil fuel-driven standard of living that has rapidly increased greenhouse gases, we are in the midst of a transformation of our planet as a whole—of air, water, and land, of ecosystems and species habitats. One result will be an increasing rate of species extinction, even though some new species will be created. There will also be an increasing migration of plants, animals, and humans as their existing habitats become arid, due to the loss of food and water and to desert-creating droughts, or flooded, due to rising sea levels. Human migration, in particular, will upset existing social systems, leading to more stress and violence. In the end, there likely will be a substantial reduction of the human population—accompanied by much suffering.

Our task in these essays is a creative one—how can we help transform human beings to minimize suffering and move toward a new and more ecological civilization? We are exploring how we might rethink some aspects of the classical traditions stemming from ancient Greece. My rethinking will couple together a Greek tradition that is often ignored—the materialistic, atomistic Epicurean understanding of reality and ethics—with some contemporary science and the naturalistic theology of Henry Nelson Wieman. In moving toward an ecological civilization, we can be helped by a naturalistic worldview that uses the findings of science and embodies a general process perspective of dynamic relationalism to counter our current consumerist worldview, which is a materialistic and individualistic form of naturalism.

ANCIENT NATURALISM

In January 1417, most likely in the library of the Benedictine Abbey of Fulda, Germany (northeast of Frankfurt), Italian book hunter Poggio Bracciolini made the discovery of a lifetime. It was a manuscript of a book written almost 1500 years earlier—*De Rerum Natura (On the Nature of Things)* by Lucretius.[1] According to Harvard historian Stephen Greenblatt, this poetic, philosophical work was a key factor in enabling the Renaissance and reintroducing an empirically based, naturalistic view of the universe, which contributed to the rise of modern science.

In his own time, around 50 BCE, Lucretius voiced in poetic form the essential teachings of the earlier Greek philosophers Democritus and Epicurus. With Poggio's 15th-century discovery, a second, usually overlooked, wisdom tradition was revived as an alternative to the dominant Western religious tradition stemming from Plato and Aristotle.

Plato, Aristotle, and many of their successors understood the created universe as an embodiment of universal ideal types—Platonic ideas or eternal objects. A significant aspect of causality understood in terms of these universal types are the formal and final causes of creation. Theologians saw these types as residing in the mind of a personal God who created the world.

In contrast, Democritus, Epicurus, and Lucretius saw the ultimate origin of the universe to be atoms in motion. Atoms occasionally swerved from their natural downward paths through empty space (the void) so that they collided with each other. As they collided, they produced conglomerate entities composed of atoms that in turn collided with other atoms and conglomerates of atoms to build the world as we know it. Everything came into being over time by chance collisions of atoms that stuck together and then uncoupled only to become new conglomerates. Other than an infinite variety of the kinds of atoms, which themselves did not change, everything was in process and was relational. Lucretius told this story in a poem and thus a "scientific vision of the world—a vision of atoms randomly moving in an infinite universe—was in its origins imbued with a poet's sense of wonder."[2]

This view of the universe was complemented with an epistemology based on sense experience and with an ethics based on the experiences of pleasure and pain. Rather that supporting extravagant and wasteful attempts to gain ever more pleasure, which only leads to more pain, the goal of life was to avoid pain and to experience a calm, joyous sense of well-being. At the beginning of Book II Lucretius gives us the heart of Epicurean ethics by contrasting a lifestyle of "getting to the top" with one of simplicity:

> . . . nothing is sweeter than to dwell in peace
> high in the well-walled temples of the wise,
> whence looking down we may see other men wavering,

> wandering, seeking a way of life,
> with wit against wit, line against noble line, contending, striving,
> 　　　straining night and day,
> to rise to the top of the heap, High Lord of Things.
> O wretched minds of men, O poor blind hearts! How great the
> 　　　perils, how dark the night of life
> where our brief hour is spent! Oh, not to see
> that nature demands no favor but that pain
> be sundered from the flesh, that in the mind
> be a sense of joy, unmixed with care and fear!
> Now for our physical life, we see that little—
> so little!—is needed to remove our pain.
> For Nature does not ask that vast delights of a more tickling kind
> 　　　be spread before us,
> even if through in the house there are no statues
> of golden boys with flaming lamps in hand
> to furnish light for banquets all night long,
> and there's no silver to glitter nor gold to gleam,
> no lyre to echo from coffered, gilded ceiling.
> Why! Men can lie on soft turf side by side
> under a tall tree's branches near a stream,
> and easily, pleasantly, care for creature needs—
> especially when the sun shines, and the year in season sprinkles
> 　　　the fresh green grass with flowers.[3]

Although this may seem naive, because pain from an accident or disease is hard to avoid, the idea of the joy of living simply can be part of the wisdom of an ecological civilization.

The thinking of Lucretius carries forward from the Renaissance. According to Greenblatt, it is present in Thomas More's *Utopia*, which idealized Epicureanism for an entire society in a Christian context, with an afterlife of rewards and punishments as a primary motivator. One finds it in the thinking of Giordano Bruno, who ridiculed a Christianity in which God numbered the hairs on our heads and controlled every event. Greenberg writes that for Bruno "the whole idea is absurd. There is an order in the universe, but it is one built into the nature of things, into the matter that composes everything, from stars to men to bedbugs. Nature is not an abstract capacity, but a generative mother, bringing forth everything that exists. We have, in other words, entered a Lucretian universe."[4] We might add that Bruno, executed on February 17, 1600, anticipated an evolutionary universe. His Lucretian understanding informed the rise of the modern science worldview.

In 1623, Galileo published *The Assayer*. Like Lucretius, he argued there was no difference between the celestial and terrestrial world, that everything could be understood through reason and observation, that the testimony of the senses trumped religious claims to authority, and that nature was constituted by a limited number of "minims" or atoms that combined in innumerable ways.[5]

Among others informed by Lucretius were Shakespeare, Montaigne, and Lucy Huchinson. Even though Huchinson came to vehemently reject Lucretius's thinking, earlier in her life she translated his work into English. Also influenced were Enlightenment thinkers such as Newton, Dryden, Voltaire, Diderot, and Hume. Finally, Greenblatt traces the impact of Lucretius to Thomas Jefferson, who wrote to someone who asked for his philosophy of life, "I am an Epicurean." Like More, Jefferson transposed Lucretius from a life of withdrawal for a few into the public domain. In the founding document of a new republic we find "a distinctly Lucretian turn. The turn was toward a government whose end was not only to secure the lives and the liberties of its citizens but to serve 'the pursuit of Happiness.' The atoms of Lucretius had left their traces on the Declaration of Independence."[6]

FEATURES OF CONTEMPORARY NATURALISTIC WORLDVIEWS

Henry Nelson Wieman has stated that the world we know is always relative to our human mind.[7] This is another way of saying that our worldviews—which include our understandings of the way things are, how we acquire knowledge, what we value, and how we should behave—are humanly constructed. The worldview of the Greek atomists was a human construction, as was the worldview of Plato and Aristotle. So is Greenblatt's history of the rediscovery of Epicureanism and its history into the modern period. Modern science is a human construction. We cannot get out of what Wieman calls the "egocentric predicament." We may conjecture, sometimes with good reasons, that there is something "out there," that there is more than we can know. Yet, even this "more" is also an idea; it is still relative to our human minds.

This construction of worlds relative to human minds is not done by individuals alone. Individual thinkers always work in a particular context. It is more accurate to think of worldviews as the result of specific, creative phases of cultural evolution in which many individuals are interacting. Constructionist theologian Gordon Kaufman calls the process of construction-in-context "serendipitous creativity."[8] Serendipitous creativity points to a system, the parts of which come together in unpredictable ways to create such things as new life, new truth, and new community. For example, the interactions of our genes, our family environment, our wider society, and our natural world work together to make each of us a unique human being. All these parts working together create something of value, a living human organism.

We also can use the idea of serendipitous creativity to talk about progress in science. If one reads James Watson's book *The Double Helix*, one can see how serendipitous creativity describes a system of discovery in which such things as experimental facts, competing scientists, and human imagination interacted to give rise to the discovery of the structure of **DNA**.[9] No one fact, no one scientist, no one act of thought produced the discovery. Many of these coming together resulted in one of the major scientific discoveries of the 20th century.

Serendipitous creativity is also a way of understanding how human communities are created. No human alone creates such communities. The interactions among humans and between humans and the natural world create communities in ways that cannot be planned or foreseen by any one individual. For example, Kaufman writes that the professional community of "modern science has certainly been a human creation, but no individual or group at the time of its origins in the 17th century had any notion of the complex institutional structures, modes of education and discipline, moral and communal commitments, financial and physical resources, not to say ways of thinking . . . which constitute science today."[10] The same is the case with modern democratic governments. No one person simply thought out and produced the complex political systems we have today. Many individuals contributed to their evolution over time, but no one could have planned or predicted their contemporary manifestations. It is the same with the building of cities. "Any modern city is the product of human planning and intention—every brick was laid by a deliberate human act—but no one simply decided modern London or New York or Tokyo would be a fine thing to build, worked out the plans, and then brought it into being."[11]

The naturalistic consumerist worldview. Also a construction, relative to our minds, is our contemporary cultural consumerist worldview that equates happiness with material well-being, that regards our planet as a resource for our use and enjoyment, and that measures progress materialistically by gross domestic product (**GDP**). This consumerist view of our planetary world and our life in it originated after World War II. Fueled by the war, the American economy experienced a boom. However, after the war ended in 1945, this war economy could not be sustained, even though it continued in part as a "cold war economy." How could the American economy be sustained in peace time? The answer was to find ways to support economic growth through consumerism.

In 1955 marketing consultant Victor Lebow wrote an article in the *Journal of Retailing* about the decline in the amount that retailers were able to mark up their prices, hence lowering their income. This decline was due to growth in three sectors of the economy. The first was the increasing production by manufacturers of a wider variety of household goods along with the development of television by which the dominant producers could advertise to a "captive audience." From the late 1940s to 1960 the percentage of household-owned television sets grew from 5% to 95%. The second sector was the growing number of retail businesses, and the third was the greater freedom of consumers to choose among products or not to choose any. The growth of variety offered by manufacturing and advertising, of retail sellers, and of consumers with more choices contributed to the decline in retailer mark-up. To counter the negative impact of these factors on retail businesses, Lebow suggested the need for the cultural development of a consumerist mentality—a new form of "spirituality." "Our enormously productive economy demands that we make consumption our way of life, that we convert the buying and use of goods into rituals, that we seek our spiritual satisfactions, our ego satisfactions, in consumption. . . . The very meaning and significance of our lives today expressed in consumptive terms." "We need things consumed, burned up, worn out, replaced, and discarded at an ever increasing pace. We need to have people eat, drink, dress, ride, live, with ever more complicated and, therefore, constantly more expensive consumption."[12] Here is a new form of being religious—a naturalistic spirituality centered in material consumption.

Even though Lebow forcefully enunciated a vision and a mission, the consumerist worldview and civilization was not simply created by the mind of one or a few individuals. It historically evolved out of a complex set of interrelated processes arising out of World War II, such as the rapid growth of the postwar population, the baby boomers, the developing competition with the Soviet Union for world domination, material technologies invented during the war that were used in new domestic products, and a democratically inspired sense that being a good citizen included supporting the economy by consuming. Just as modern science and New York City emerged through a complex set of interacting processes, so did the naturalism of consumerism. In consumerism, Jefferson's Lucretian "pursuit of happiness" came to be measured by material well-being.

A naturalistic ecological worldview. In keeping with the goal of this book and the overall "Seizing an Alternative" conference,[13] I suggest that we facilitate construction of a naturalistic, ecological worldview that embodies a process perspective, uses findings of science, offers a social, relational Epicurean ethics, and enables a sense of what is sacred. This approach is needed to counter the current naturalistic, consumerist worldview.

From the perspective of process philosophy, everything is constituted out of relationships, and everything is always becoming. In terms of modern science, everything is evolving in relationship with other evolving processes or events. A Universe Story is being constructed by many scientifically informed people; the entire universe is evolving so that new systems emerge out of older simpler systems— molecules from atoms; bacteria, plants, and animals from molecules; self-conscious humans from the primate lineage of animals.[14] Human beings have emerged as complex, relational, ever-becoming, biological-cultural systems—constituted by atoms from exploding stars, a variety of living forms, histories of symbol systems, and a communal self-consciousness that can construct a Universe Story and our place in it.

Even though we humans are distinct from other life-forms in many ways (as is every form of life), we are created in relationship to other creatures. One example of this is our complex brain. A common, simple physical model of our overall brain is based on Paul MacLean's "Triune Brain" developed in the 1960s.[15] Figure 1 is from Harold Carey.[16] In our brainstem (Reptilian Brain), we share instinctive survival processes common to reptiles—fighting, fleeing, freezing, feeding, etc. In the old mammalian structure of our brains (the Limbic System) we share some emotions with some other mammals, including emotions of pain and pleasure, and of fear. The Epicureans understood these emotions as the basis of human behavior. They also provided the basis for ethics—seek to decrease fear and pain by enjoying the simple pleasures of a more contemplative life with friends.

YOUR THREE BRAINS 2

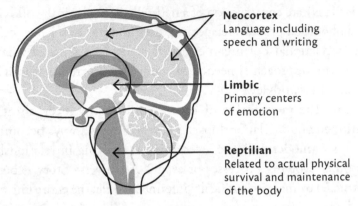

Neocortex
Language including
speech and writing

Limbic
Primary centers
of emotion

Reptilian
Related to actual physical
survival and maintenance
of the body

Figure 14.1

Psychiatrist Randolph Nesse gives us a more detailed understanding of emotions from a behavioral and introspective perspective.[17] In Figure 2, "resources" are in upright font, "emotions" in italics, and "situations" in capitals. Emotions on the right side of the tree are

Figure 14.2

related to the losses of resources—from loss in our physical capacities to the losses of loved ones, families, and status in a community. This results in feelings of pain, sadness, grief, jealousy, anger, guilt, and shame. Those on the left side are related to desires for resources that we don't yet have or fully possess—material, families and friends, and social status. When we acquire them we experience feelings that are positive emotions—physical pleasure, love of partner, familial love, friendship, and self-esteem.

An Epicurean approach to these positive and negative emotions would probably focus on the intensity of desire and hope on the one hand, and on fear and anxiety on the other. These basic emotions are important for surviving and for well-being. However, in excess they can lead to great stress and unhappiness. Better, according to the Epicureans, is a simpler life with the moderation of emotions and a minimization of fear and anxiety, allowing for one to live in "flow" with contentment and joy.

As mammals evolved, a third part of the triune brain became more complex and seems to be most complex in humans—the neocortex. This is a system whose neural pathways are linked to the evolutionarily older parts of the brain. It is the growth of these connections, rather than the growth in size of the neocortex itself, that is probably more significant. These connections make possible the reflection on emotional and instinctual behaviors and their guidance toward future behaviors. Two aspects of the neocortex are significant for our purposes. One is the expansion of what is sometimes called the "social brain network"—a system of areas of the neocortex connected with areas of the limbic system.[18] The second is the growth of the frontal and the prefrontal cortex, parts of which function as an "executive" that can exert control over other parts of the brain and that guides behavior and regulates emotions.

One of many developments in the social brain network is mirror neurons. These are neurons in us that replicate the firing of the same neurons in others when we observe their facial expressions and their behaviors.[19] Mirror neurons in the social brain network are a neurological basis for empathy. According to Daniel Goleman there are three kinds of empathy. Cognitive empathy is thinking like other persons think—taking their perspective, "standing in their shoes." Emotional empathy is the basis for rapport with others—"I feel with you." The third is "empathic concern"—"I sense you need some help and I am spontaneously ready to give it."[20]

Writing that empathy is the basis for compassion, Goleman continues that "different varieties of empathy seem to rely on distinct brain circuitry." Tania Singer holds that key brain areas associated with emotional empathy are the insula and the mirror neurons. "The insula senses signals from our whole body. When we're empathizing with someone, our mirror neurons mimic within us that person's state. The anterior area of the insula reads that pattern and tells us what that state is."[21] Singer has "done Functional Magnetic Resonance Imaging (FMRI) studies of couples, for example, when one partner is getting a brain scan while seeing that the other partner is about to get a shock. At the moment the partner sees this, the part of his or her brain lights up that would do so if he or she were actually getting the shock, rather than just seeing the partner get it"[22]

A second development in the brain evolution of humans is the enlarging of the frontal cortex, and especially the prefrontal cortex that covers the frontal cortex. Overall, the prefrontal cortex includes areas that are responsible for "executive function." "Executive function relates to abilities to differentiate among conflicting thoughts, determine good and bad, better and best, same and different, future consequences of current activities, working toward a defined goal, prediction of outcomes, expectation based on actions, and social 'control' (the ability to suppress urges that, if not suppressed, could lead to socially unacceptable outcomes)."[23] The particular area related to social control by controlling the emotions is an area right above the eye sockets called the orbital frontal cortex—which has neural connections to the limbic system, especially the amygdala. When there are well developed social brain networks and fully developed prefrontal cortices in human individuals, and when these remain intact, it is possible for humans to responsibly control their behavior and guide themselves to be less be self-serving and more cooperative with other humans, the ecosystems in which we live, and planet Earth as a whole.

SOME OBSTACLES TO BECOMING AN ECOLOGICAL CIVILIZATION

Obstacle One. Humans are ambivalent creatures. We have evolved to be both individually self-protective and also to desire relationships with others. However, not all humans are alike. There is individual variability in our brains—in the neural networks that are self-protective and pro-social.

One kind of variability is developmental. From the womb on, the human brain is developing capacities to stand and walk, to learn language, to have sexual feelings, and to control personal behavior. Important is the relatively late completion of the prefrontal cortex—the area of the neocortex that is responsible for foreseeing the consequences of our actions and for regulating our emotions. It is the last section of the brain to undergo myelination, the coating of neurons with insulating fatty tissue (White Matter), which speeds up the transmission of signals through the neurons. Myelination is not completed until the early to mid-twenties. This means that teenagers have poorer foresight of the consequences of their actions and poorer control of emotions than those who are older and whose brains have completed maturation, just as walking and speaking require the maturation of other brain areas. Hence, the so-called "teen brain" more likely engages in risky behavior because it is not fully aware of the consequences, and also because he or she lacks control over a key emotional center in the limbic system, the right amygdala. The right amygdala responds fearfully to threats even before we are cognizant of them. A fully developed prefrontal cortex is capable of overriding this immediate reaction most of the time. But a teenager's underdeveloped prefrontal cortex is not. Teenagers probably would not make good Epicureans.

Other forms of brain variability between individuals derive from gene variation, brain damage, and childrearing. For example, variations in certain genes can contribute to neurochemical brain development that makes some humans more aggressive and un-caring of others. The **MAOA** gene directs the formation of the enzyme monoaminoxidase, which functions to deactivate neurotransmitters such as serotonin in regions of the brain such as the amygdala. One variant of the **MAOA** gene produces a lower level of the enzyme than the other, normal variant. The lower amount is not as effective in deactivating the neurotransmitters, allowing them to build up.[24] As they increase, the individual person becomes more prone to anger, aggression, and violence, especially if they suffered adverse environmental factors while growing up.

A key part of the prefrontal cortex is the orbital frontal cortex, located just above the eyes. This area can vary in structure and function, along with its connection to the amygdala, deep in the limbic part of the brain. The orbital frontal cortex regulates the expression of feelings of fear and fight centered in the right amygdala. As indicated above, it is not fully developed until a human is in his or her mid-twenties, and this late development is a factor in erratic and risky teenage behavior. Also, different degrees of development, or damage because of trauma, can contribute to variability of later adult aggressive, asocial, or criminal behavior. The classic case is that of Phinias Gage. In 1848 Gage, an intelligent, sociable, hard worker, was tamping down some explosive powder to clear away rock from a railway bed when a spark ignited the powder and blew his tamping rod through his left cheek and eye, and up through the left-front part of his brain. He survived. His intelligence was not affected, but his ability to plan for the future, to follow learned social rules, and to decide what actions would best enable his own survival were compromised. Research by Hanna Damasio and her colleagues strongly suggested that these disabled functions were due to "selective damage in the prefrontal cortices of Gage's brain."[25] More recent is a study of men who had antisocial personality disorder (psychopathy or sociopathy). All had committed violent crimes and their behavior was characterized by "irresponsible actions, cheating, impulsiveness and lack of affect or remorse. . . . Images of their brains revealed that the neuronal volume of their prefrontal cortexes was 11–14% lower than in normal men."[26]

The environment in which a child is raised also contributes to neural development. Studies have shown that children raised in a chronically highly stressful environment with poor parental nurturing have difficulty interrelating positively with others. Some may grow up to look out only for themselves and to manipulate others. They show little empathy. Yet they can be charismatically attractive, and sometimes they can be chosen as leaders in business, government, education, and even in religious communities.[27]

Because of genetic and brain variation, as well as upbringing, some people can develop antisocial personality disorder and even become psychopaths or sociopaths. They are people "without conscience and incapable of empathy, guilt, or loyalty to anyone but themselves."[28] Or they might be "almost psychopaths," who measure not quite as high on the Hare psychopathic inventory[29] as do full-blown psychopaths.[30] Estimates vary about how many there are in the wider population, but various researchers suggest that one to four in a hundred people we meet in our daily lives are psychopaths or almost psychopaths. So are 15% of those on Wall Street and 25% of those in prison. The fact that so many leaders in society are primarily oriented only toward their own success, often manipulating and dominating others, is an obstacle to developing a mutually relational ecological society of people concerned for the good of the whole.

A naturalistic alternative to consumerism and the hierarchical structure of domination illustrated by psychopaths and almost psychopaths can be a modern version of Epicureanism. One important component of an ecological civilization, namely, its wisdom, is an ecological life orientation. With an ecological orientation one can understand and evaluate the different kinds of good to which people and communities can aspire. Daniel R. DeNicola suggests that there are three kinds of value or good.[31] The first kind is gained at the expense of others. Either it is in limited supply or acquiring it hinders other people's ability to acquire it. When one person or group competes to attain such a good, the chances of others having it are diminished. Material things are such goods. So are power, money, and status in a community or a nation. These are the goods to which Lucretius is referring when he writes about "seeking a way of life with wit against wit, line against noble line, contending, striving, straining night and day, to rise to the top of the heap." These are the goods of consumerism and of striving for power over others.

A second kind of good is gained without hindering others from also attaining it. Enjoying sunshine and fresh air is available to everyone unless people pursuing material goods pollute the air. Korean Buddhist monk Bup Jung writes:

> I often recall the words of a youngster from a few summers ago, who had come with his father from Seoul to visit the mountains where I dwell. "Papa, the breeze is sweet!" Then, drinking gulps of water drawn from the well in his hand, he exclaimed, "Ah, it's delicious, truly delicious." Recollections of this five-year old's precocious comments echo in my ears to this day.

> Sweet breeze! How direct and poetic an expression, compared to the clichéd descriptions of fresh and clear. Years of drinking water distilled by the fumes of chemicals, must have enhanced the flavor of the mineral water springing from the mountains. . . .

> Who has stolen the "sweet breeze" from our youngsters? Who has adulterated our delicious water? . . . Seduced by excessive materialism, man has forgotten the natural privileges bestowed on him by nature and the environment, and is destroying his benefactor.[32]

There are many simple gifts from nature and human interaction that all can enjoy if we are open to them. We can find pleasure in another person's company and serenity in pleasant natural surroundings. With an Epicurean attitude toward other living things, one can understand the following sonnet by Alan Nordstrom, titled "Mighty Mite":

> This tiny flying insect shares the lamp
> I use at 3 a.m. to read and write,
> and I resist my rash impulse to stamp
> it with my thumb, put out its little light—
> for what? Because he flits and vexes me?
> Because he busily scours the chair arm next
> to me or courts the bulb distractingly?
> What right do I have to crush his little ec-
> stasy by exercising might at whim?
> My magnifying glass brings him to view:
> One wing's askew. Is he all right? So flim-
> sy, delicate, precise, and living, too –
> Yes, there he goes, a-whir again, aloft,
> mighty enough to turn one hard heart soft.[33]

Finally, there is a kind of good that is actually creative. The more people seek it, the more of it there is. Developing our capacities for friendship and love creates opportunities for others to be our friends and to love us in return. Seeking peace among the variety of the world's peoples increases peace for everyone. We might call this kind of good "spiritual" good, because if we seek fulfillment through love and peace, we reduce our dependence on material goods, we use less energy and matter, and we give off less material pollution.

One example of this kind of "spiritual creativity" is what I call "listening love": accepting others—being at peace with them, showing love for them. Buddhist Monk Thich Nhat Hanh writes: "When we are mindful, touching deeply the present moment, we can see and listen deeply, and the fruits are always understanding, acceptance, love, and the desire to relieve suffering and bring joy. When our beautiful child comes up to us and smiles, we are completely there for her." He goes on to say that "the most precious gift we can offer others is our presence. . . . If you love someone but rarely make yourself available to him or her, that is not true love. . . . But when we are mindfully present to those we love, they will bloom like flowers."[34]

One can easily imagine the descriptions of living by Bup Jung, Alan Nordstrom, and Thich Nhat Hanh taking place in the same Epicurean setting described by Lucretius quoted earlier in this chapter.

Obstacle Two. Yet, even the second and third kinds of good can lead us into a trap, the trap of obsessively trying to preserve what has already been created, starting with our own existence. At a basic psychological level, Epicurus and Lucretius saw this as the fear of death. They argued that, if humans were to accept that this life is all there is, they would no longer fear death and would indeed be happier. They could be content with what they already have, with few material goods, but with the joys of experiencing the beauty of the natural world and of friendship.

As presented by Lucretius, the Epicurean life is largely individualistic. One withdraws from society to "dwell in peace high in the well-walled temples of the wise" from which one can observe the hectic, stressful life and imagine being in a lovely natural place with friends. However, one does not attempt to change the conditions of living as More visualized in his Utopia and as Jefferson and others tried to actualize in the "American experiment." Such a shift requires a dynamic-relational understanding such as one finds in process thought. All things are constituted as relational systems; they are internally relational entities—atoms consisting of subatomic particles, molecules being relationships of atoms, organisms being relationships of molecules. Individual humans also are constituted as dynamic systems of relationships. We are what I have called social-ecological selves, continuously dependent on the sun, Earth, atoms, molecules, organisms, and the thinking and behaviors that go back through human centuries.[35] Further, as individual, relational systems, we are parts of larger relational systems—families, hometowns, volunteer organizations, nation states, and worldwide economic and computerized communications networks. We are each a dynamic-relational system within more extensive communal-dynamic relational systems. This gives us the basis of a social-ecological understanding of epicureanism that lifts up DeNicola's second and third kinds of good in simple, interacting, and joyful relationships that minimize material consumption—an epicureanism for an ecological civilization.

One way of developing this kind of thinking is with two basic ideas of Henry Nelson Wieman: his idea of qualitative meaning and his distinction between created and creative good.

Qualitative meaning is a relational concept that includes not just ideas and behaviors but also feelings. The word "meaning" signifies the interconnectedness of things in a dynamic web so that thinking, doing, or feeling one particular event leads to the thinking, doing, and feeling of others. The word "qualitative" refers to "felt quality," an aesthetic appreciation of other aspects of the dynamic webs in which we find ourselves. We not only think and do with others but we also feel with others the various aspects of our world. Wieman distinguishes between instrumentally related systems and systems of intrinsic value. An example of the former is a working machine, such as an automobile, airplane, or computer. In systems of intrinsic value the various parts of a system vivify each other with felt qualities. Dancing, music, and visual works of art are examples of this kind of system—a system of qualitative meaning.[36] So are some everyday events, such as that described in Dietrich Bonhoeffer's letter from Tegel Prison to his parents, dated Sunday July 3, 1943.

> When the bells of the prison chapel start ringing at about six o'clock on a Saturday evening, that is the best time to write home. It is remarkable what power church bells have over human beings, and how deeply they can affect us. So many of our life's experiences gather around them. All discontent, selfishness, and ingratitude melt away, and in a moment we are left with only our pleasant memories hovering around us like gracious spirits. I always think first of those quiet

summer evenings in Friedrichsbrunn, then of all the different parishes that I have worked in, then of all our family occasions, weddings, christenings, and confirmations—tomorrow my godchild is being confirmed!—I really cannot count all the memories that come alive in me, and they inspire peace, thankfulness, and confidence. If only one could help other people more![37]

Yet systems of instrumental and qualitative meaning, of instrumental value and intrinsic value, are only part of the picture. They are systems that have been already created. Because they can have great value, they can trap us into holding on to the status quo when other things are changing all around us. A problem with the Epicurean idea of individual simple and peaceful happiness or of the peaceful harmony of a social system is that these can be static—held onto by people who refuse to change when change is called for. Wieman responds to this trap by arguing that there is a good that is greater than instrumental value and the value of qualitative meaning already realized. It is that which creates such meaning.

Simply put, this is Wieman's distinction between created good and creative good. Created goods are either good in and of themselves (intrinsic good) or because they lead to the realization of other good (instrumentally good). Human beings are created goods in Wieman's terms. Mutually supportive human communities are created goods. Ecosystems are created goods. Even planet Earth is a created good. Those who want to save a species are trying to save a created good. Those who are concerned about the future of humanity are concerned with a created good.

Yet there is something more important than either intrinsic or instrumental good—the creativity that has produced these kinds of good. Creativity is embodied in interactions among humans, between humans and the rest of the natural world, and in the natural world itself. Creative interaction can take place among already created goods, but in a way that allows for the emergence of new good rather than maintaining created goods in their existing forms.[38] Because the creative process is the continuing source of all human good, it is, according to Wieman, the ultimate good—the sacred or God.

Even though one can argue philosophically that creativity is more fundamental than what has been created, there still is the problem of emotional attachment to what has been created for two reasons. First, we already know well that which has been created—spouse, children, home, car, town, business, the current economic system, and so on. Second, our spouse and family, the make of our car, where we live, and the work we do—these have become part of our identity. The thought of radically changing who we are in order to become part of an ecological civilization can generate a sense of loss that manifests itself in grief. This expands the Epicurean idea about the fear of our own physical death. What we also fear is the death of those things that shape who we are—acquiring more material possessions in a consumerist lifestyle, power as the leader of a business that exploits the planet to make a profit for stockholders, a religion that assures us that God will take care of everything, or an already created set of ideas as to what an ecological civilization might be. All these— lifestyle, power, religion, ideas about the future—are created goods. Because they help define who we are in ways that are familiar to and comfortable for us, we fear their loss. We grieve at the thought of their needing to be re-formed in a process of transformation that is leading to a future that cannot now be fully known. We need to be transformed so our identities are not bound up with what has been created; for example, with a particular political, economic, or religious system. Rather we need to find our identity as creatures in "God," in the ongoing creativity that is forever making all things new.

LIVING IN CREATIVITY—LOVE AND WISDOM

One reason why created goods cannot demand our total commitment is that they change. As the Buddha taught, all things are transient. The only thing permanent is change itself. Following Wieman, we can construct a structure to this change. One aspect of the structure involves processes among existing parts of the world that give rise to the new; another involves processes that integrate the new with the old—with both old and new undergoing transformation. In one of his last books, *Religious Inquiry*, Wieman calls this two-aspect process "creative interchange."

One way Wieman characterizes creative interchange is as a dual process of love and wisdom. Wisdom

> is the search for coherence in the development of the individual, in social development and in knowledge. Love is the desire to bring into each of these forms of coherence the innovations relevant to each kind of development. Development means expanding the range and coherence of what can be known, controlled, and valued by the individual in community with others. In this sense wisdom and love are necessary to the development of the individual, necessary to the development of viable social relations, necessary to the development of knowledge, of culture, and of the continuity of history. . . .
>
> The systematic order, insofar as it is attained, is always open-ended. This method of seeking coherence is wisdom; where love seeks to bring into the order thus achieved other ideas, values, persons, cultures, and social developments.[39]

Today a significant question is whether reaching out in love can bring into our current social order the values of nonhumans, ecosystems, and the planet itself, and whether we can then integrate these values into a new coherence (new wisdom) of a planetary ecological era. A new ecological age will be an age in which humans increasingly come to love all things, seeking ever new wisdom of dynamic coherences that mutually contribute to the good of all humans and the rest of the world—an ecological civilization. Humans need to become converted from commitments to created goods for themselves that make up their current way of life to an ultimate commitment to creativity that brings new patterns of personal, social, economic, technological, and political living for the well-being of all.

ENDNOTES

1   Lucretius, *The Nature of Things*, trans. Frank O. Copley, Kindle Edition (New York: W. W. Norton, 2011), 44–40.

2   Steven Greenblatt, *The Swerve: How the World Became Modern* (New York: W. W. Norton), 8.

3   Lucretius, 29.

4   Greenblatt, 237.

5   Greenblatt, 254.

6   Greenblatt, 263.

7   Henry Nelson Wieman, *The Source of Human Good* (Carbondale: Southern Illinois University Press, 1946), 16.

8   Gordon D. Kaufman, *In the Face of Mystery: A Constructive Theology* (Cambridge: Harvard University Press, 1993), 264–80.

9   James Watson, *The Double Helix: A Personal Account of the Discovery of the Structure of DNA* (New York: W. W. Norton, 1981).

10 Gordon D. Kaufman, *Theology for a Nuclear Age* (Philadelphia: Westminster Press, 1985), 40.

11 Kaufman, *Theology for a Nuclear Age* 40–41.

12 Victor Lebow, "Price Competition in 1955," *Journal of Retailing* (1955), 5–11, 45–6.

13 The conference was held June 4–7, 2015 at Pomona College, Claremont, CA. https://www.ctr4process.org/whitehead2015/

14 For a more detailed understanding of the evolution of humans as emergent phenomena, see Ursula Goodenough and Terrence Deacon, "From Biology to Consciousness to Morality," *Zygon: Journal of Religion and Science* 38, no. 4 (2003), 801–19. For a short overview of the evolution of the universe, see Brian Thomas Swimme and Mary Evelyn Tucker, *Journey of the Universe* (New Haven: Yale University Press, 2011).

15 See Paul D. McLean, "Evolution of the Psychencephalon," *Zygon: Journal of Religion and Science* 17, no. 2 (1982), 187–211. DOI: 10.1111/j.1467-9744.1982.tb00478.x. Accessed 5/25/2015. While McLean's structural model is useful to begin understanding the overall brain, it is the growth of neural interconnections between parts of the brain, as well as size, that reveal important evolutionary developments.

16 Harold Carey, "Your Three Brains—Slide 23," in "Accelerated Learning 2.0: How Your Brain and Memory Work" *Slide Share* (August 7, 2008), http://www.slideshare.net/hccarey/accelerated-learning?qid=db552fdb-1dea-4fa0-b4c2-ecbee0efb3a9&v=&b=&from_search=1. Licensed by Creative Commons: Attribution 4.0 International (CC BY 4.0), https://creativecommons.org/licenses/by/4.0/. Accessed 11/9/2016.

17 Randolph M. Nesse, "Natural Selection and the Elusiveness of Happiness," *Philosophical Transactions of the Royal Society* 359 (2004), 1333–47. Permission granted by The Royal Society through RightsLink, The Copyright Clearance Center, License Number 3984831308727. The image itself came from http://www.randolphnesse.com/articles/emotions. Accessed 5/25/2015.

18 William J. Shoemaker, "The Social Brain Network and Human Moral Behavior," *Zygon: Journal of Religion and Science* 47, no. 4 (2012), 806–20. DOI: 10.1111/j.1467-9744.2012.01295.x. Accessed 5/25/2015.

19 Shoemaker, "The Social Brain Network," 811–12.

20 Daniel Goleman, *The Brain and Emotional Intelligence: New Insights* (Florence, MA: More Than Sound, 2011), 75–76.

21 Goleman, *The Brain and Emotional Intelligence*, 76.

22 Goleman, *The Brain and Emotional Intelligence*, 77.

23 *Wikipedia*, "Prefrontal Cortex," https://en.wikipedia.org/wiki/Prefrontal_cortex. Accessed 7/20/2016.

24 Kevin M. Beaver, Matt DeLisi, Michael G. Vaughn, and J. C. Barnes, "Monoamine Oxidase: A Genotype Is Associated with Gang Membership and Weapon Use," *Comprehensive Psychiatry* 51, no. 2 (2010), 130–34. Esse Viding and Uta Frith, "Genes for Susceptibility to Violence Lurk in the Brain," *Proceedings of the National Academy of Sciences* 103, no. 16 (2006), 6085–86.

25 Antonio R. Damasio, *Decartes' Error: Emotion, Reason, and the Human Brain,* (New York: Avon Books, 1994), 33.

26 http://thebrain.mcgill.ca/flash/a/a_05/a_05_cr/a_05_cr_her/a_05_cr_her.html. Accessed 7/20/ 2016.

27 Center for the Developing Child, "Toxic Stress: the Facts," http://developingchild.harvard.edu/topics/science_of_early_childhood/toxic_stress_response/ (2012). Accessed 5/25/2015; Child Welfare Information Gateway, "Understanding the Effects of Maltreatment on Brain Development," www.childwelfare.gov/pubs/issue_briefs/brain_development/ (November 2009). Accessed 5/15/2015; Bruce D. Perry, "Childhood Experience and the Expression of Genetic Potential: What Childhood Neglect Tells Us About Nature and Nurture," *Brain and Mind* 3 (2002), 79–100; and "Examining Child Maltreatment Through a Neurodevelopmental Lens: Clinical Applications of the Neurosequential Model of Therapeutics," *Journal of Loss and Trauma* 14 (2009), 240–55.

28 Paul Babiak and Robert D. Hare, *Snakes in Suits: When Psychopaths Go to Work*, Kindle Edition (San Francisco: HarperCollins, 2009), 19.

29 Robert D. Hare, "Comparison of Procedures for the Assessment of Psychopathy," *Journal of Consulting and Clinical Psychology* 53, no. 1 (1985), 7–16, http://dx.doi.org/10.1037/0022-006X.53.1.7. See also http://vistriai.com/psychopathtest/ to quickly learn about testing for psychopathy. Accessed 5/25/2015.

30 Ronald Schouten and James Silver, *Almost a Psychopath: Do I (or Does Someone I Know) Have a Problem with Manipulation and Lack of Empathy?* (Center City, MN: Hazelden, 2012).

31 Daniel R. DeNicola, "A Typology of Conceptions of the Good," *The Personalist* (1978).

32 Bup Jung, "Man and Nature," in *The Human Encounter with Nature: Destruction and Reconstruction*, Christian Academy, ed. Vol. 5 of *The World Community in Post-Industrial Society* (Seoul: Wooseok, 1989), 92–99 and passim.

33 Alan Nordstrom, "Mighty Mite," poem received in a personal communication.

34 Thich Nhat Hanh, *Living Buddha, Living Christ* (New York:

Riverhead Books), 1995, 14.

35   Karl E. Peters, *Dancing with the Sacred* (Harrisburg, Pennsylvania: Trinity Press International, 2002), 68–73.

36   Wieman, 17–19.

37   Dietrich Bonhoeffer, "To His Parents, 3 July 1943," in *Letters and Papers from Prison*, Enlarged Edition, Eberhard Bethge, ed. (New York: Macmillan, 1978), 73.

38   Karl E. Peters, "Pragmatically Defining the God Concepts of Henry Nelson Wieman and Gordon Kaufman," in *New Essays in Religious Naturalism*, Larry Axel and Creighton Peden, eds. Highlands Institute, Vol. II (Macon, GA: Mercer University Press, 1993), 199–210.

39   Henry Nelson Wieman, *Religious Inquiry* (Boston: Beacon Press, 1966), 124.

CONTRIBUTORS

GEORGE ALLAN is Professor of Philosophy Emeritus at Dickinson College, where he taught for thirty-three years and was also its senior academic officer for two decades. His publications are mainly on topics in social philosophy and philosophy of education, influenced by the metaphysical ideas of process philosophers such as Whitehead and Langer, and of the American pragmatists. His most recent book is *Modes of Learning: Whitehead's Metaphysics and the Stages of Education* (SUNY, 2012).

LAWRENCE CAHOONE is Professor of Philosophy at the College of the Holy Cross. His most recent book is *The Orders of Nature* (SUNY, 2013).

REV. DR. ANNA CASE-WINTERS is an ordained Presbyterian minister and Professor of Theology at McCormick Theological Seminary in Chicago. She is the author of three books: *God's Power: Traditional Understandings and Contemporary Challenges*; *Reconstructing a Christian Theology of Nature: Down to Earth;* and *A*

Theological Commentary on the Book of Matthew. Dr. Case-Winters is currently engaged in research and writing in projects that relate theology to science, to eco-justice issues, and to the church in the world today. Her upcoming book explores the theological/ethical implications of the incarnation. Dr. Case-Winters is a member of the American Academy of Religion and is past president of the American Theological Society, Midwest Division.

DAVID EMORY CONNER studied process philosophy with John Cobb, David Griffin, Charles Milligan, and Harvey Potthoff, who was himself a student of Whitehead's at Harvard. Conner has written several articles focusing on science and religion and on an empirical approach to process theology. He is co-pastor of the Wheat Ridge (Colorado) Congregation of the United Church of Christ.

DONALD A. CROSBY (Ph.D. Columbia University, 1963) is Professor of Philosophy Emeritus at Colorado State University. His latest book is *Nature as Sacred Ground: A Metaphysics for Religious Naturalism* (SUNY, 2015). Forthcoming from the same press in 2017 is another work entitled *The Extraordinary in the Ordinary: Seven Miracles of Everyday Life.* Crosby's main research interests are in the areas of religious naturalism, metaphysics, and American philosophy.

PETE A.Y. GUNTER was founding chairperson of the philosophy department at the University of North Texas. He played a major role in turning the department into a program in philosophy and environmental ethics. A process philosopher, he created and continues to add to the international Bergson bibliography (online, *Presses Universitaires de France*). Gunter is the author of *Bergson and the Evolution of Physics* (1969) and *Bergson and Modern Thought* (1987). He has also written on the relevance of Alfred North Whitehead's philosophy to environmental issues.

J. THOMAS HOWE is Associate Professor of Religious Studies and Director of the Honors Program at Regis University in Denver, Colorado. He is the author of *Faithful to the Earth: Nietzsche and Whitehead on God and the Meaning of Human Life*, "Affirmations after God: Friedrich Nietzsche and Richard Dawkins on Atheism," and other essays on process thought. He studied at Lake Forest College, Yale Divinity School, and Claremont Graduate University.

LEEMON MCHENRY, Ph.D. University of Edinburgh, Scotland, has taught philosophy at Old Dominion University, Davidson College, Central Michigan University, Wittenberg University, and California State University, Northridge, and has held visiting research positions at Johns Hopkins University, UCLA, and the Institute for Advanced Studies in the Humanities, Edinburgh. His most recent book is *The Event Universe: The Revisionary Metaphysics of Alfred North Whitehead* (Edinburgh University Press, 2015).

ROBERT CUMMINGS NEVILLE is Professor of Philosophy, Religion, and Theology at Boston University. He has recently published *The Good Is One, Its Manifestations Many* (SUNY, 2016), *Seasons of the Christian Life* (Cascade/Wipf&Stock, 2016), and *Nurture in Time and Eternity* (Cascade/Wipf&Stock, 2016). He recently completed a large trilogy called *Philosophical Theology: Ultimates, Existence*, and *Religion* (SUNY, 2013, 2014, and 2015).

KARL E. PETERS (Ph.D. Columbia University) is Professor Emeritus of Philosophy and Religion at Rollins College and a former editor and co-editor of *Zygon: Journal of Religion and Science*. His publications include *Dancing with the Sacred: Evolution, Ecology, and* God; *Spiritual Transformations: Science, Religion, and Human Becoming*; and over thirty-five essays on religion in the context of science and evolutionary thought.

PATRICK SHADE teaches philosophy and interdisciplinary courses at Rhodes College, with special attention given to ethical and educational issues. His research interests center largely on hope, having developed a pragmatic theory in *Habits of Hope* (Vanderbilt, 2001), which stresses the role of habits such as persistence, resourcefulness, and courage. He is currently exploring how hope functions in the pursuit of transgressive goods, i.e., goods that transgress the norms of a given status quo. He believes philosophical discourse should draw on resources in other disciplines, such as literature and the sciences.

ERIC STEINHART grew up on a farm in Pennsylvania. He received the B.S. degree in Computer Science from the Pennsylvania State University, after which he worked as a software designer. Many of his algorithms have been patented. He earned an M.A. in Philosophy from Boston College and was awarded a Ph.D. in Philosophy from SUNY at Stony Brook. He has taught at Dartmouth College and William Paterson University. His books and articles have concerned Nietzsche, metaphor, mathematics, life after death, and new and non-traditional theologies. He has been interested in using new computational concepts to solve old philosophical problems. He is especially interested in new and emerging religions. He loves New England and the American West, and enjoys all types of hiking and biking, chess, and photography.

JEROME A. STONE is the author of *A Minimalist Vision of Transcendence: A Naturalist Philosophy of Religion*; *Religious Naturalism Today: The Rebirth of a Forgotten Alternative*; and *Sacred Nature: The Environmental Potential of Religious Naturalism* (forthcoming) and co-editor of *The Chicago School of Theology—Pioneers in Religious Inquiry*. He is Professor Emeritus in the Department of Philosophy at William Rainey Harper College, where his classes included Environmental Ethics and non-Western Philosophy; he also was on the adjunct faculty of Meadville Lombard Theological School. Stone was a United Church of Christ pastor for 18 years and is currently community minister involved in adult education at the Unitarian Church of Evanston. His Ph.D. is in philosophical theology from the University of Chicago.

DEMIAN WHEELER is Assistant Professor of Philosophical Theology and Religious Studies at United Theological Seminary of the Twin Cities. Previously, he taught at Union Theological Seminary and Marymount Manhattan College , both in New York City. Wheeler received his Ph.D. from Union Theological Seminary, where he specialized in American liberal theology. His research and scholarship focus on the Chicago School of American liberal theology and the streams of theological and philosophical thought that flow into and out of it: pragmatic historicism, religious naturalism, empirical theology, and process philosophy. His first book, *Religion within the Limits of History Alone: Pragmatic Historicism and the Future of Theology,* is forthcoming from State University of New York Press.

9 781940 447407